THE PELICAN GUIDE TO

Sacramento and the Gold Country

American River Parkway (courtesy Wildside Photography/David K. Rosen)

THE PELICAN GUIDE TO
Sacramento and the Gold Country

Faren Maree Bachelis

Pelican Publishing Company
Gretna 1987

For Maree Bache Poss

Library of Congress Cataloging-in-Publication Data

Bachelis, Faren Maree.
  The Pelican guide to Sacramento and the gold
country.

  Bibliography: p.
  Includes index.
    1. Sacramento (Calif.)—Description—Guide-books.
2. Sacramento Region (Calif.)—Description and
travel—Guide-books. 3. Gold mines and mining—
California—Sacramento Region—Guide-books.
4. Historic sites—California—Sacramento Region—
Guide-books. 5. California—Gold discoveries.
I. Title.
F869.S12B24 1987   917.94'540453   86-12209
ISBN 0-88289-497-8

Photographs by Faren Bachelis
unless otherwise indicated

Maps by Scott M. Olson

Manufactured in the United States of America
Published by Pelican Publishing Company, Inc.
1101 Monroe Street, Gretna, Louisiana 70053

Contents

List of Maps

Acknowledgments

This book is the result of the assistance of hundreds of people who answered questions, made helpful suggestions, and read portions of the manuscript. Special thanks go to Stephen G. Helmich, historian with the Sacramento History Center; Bob Elrod, long-time Sacramento resident; Carol Peters, Golden Chain Council of the Mother Lode; and Sonsie Carbonara Conroy, editor, indexer, and friend. Also of tremendous assistance were the reference librarians at the California State Library and the Sacramento Public Library. Directors, officers, and employees of historical societies, chambers of commerce, state and county parks, and city and county offices were of immeasurable assistance. Most of all, I'd like to thank my husband (and best friend) Larry Bauman for ideas, editing, encouragement, and loving support, without which this book would never have come into being.

I would particularly like to thank the following people for their assistance: Brenda Boswell, publications director, California Department of Parks and Recreation; Betty Boyd; Liz Brenner, Sacramento City Department of Community Services; Bill Center, American River Recreation Association; Jack Chatfield, California Department of Parks and Recreation; Dan D'Agostini; Janis Edwards; Linda Fairchild, Sierra Nevada Recreation Corporation; Barry Garland, California State Railroad Museum, California Department of Parks and Recreation; Charlene Glaze, City of Isleton; Victoria Goff; Bill

Gunter, Sacramento Traditional Jazz Society; Alison Harvey and Dave Loera; Laurie Hensley, Old Sacramento Visitors Center; Marilyn Isenberg; Nancy Kaiser, Sacramento County Department of Parks and Recreation; Connie King; Patricia J. Kramer, Sacramento City College; Bill Lemen; Ming's Printing and Copying; Tom and Sally Myers; John Palmer, Palmer Photographic; Nadine Penick, Rio Vista Chamber of Commerce; John and Maree Poss; Paul Ratcliffe, Sierra Shutterbug; David K. Rosen, Wildside Photography; Lynn Russell, Sierra Foothills Winery Association; Susan Shaver, Assembly Chief Clerk's Office; Bruce Shaw; Susan Swayne, Sacramento Collection, Sacramento Public Library; Susan Valdes, California Almond Growers Exchange; Jim Vestal, *Sacramento Union;* Kevin Wolff, Friends of the River; and Richard Yanes.

THE PELICAN GUIDE TO

Sacramento
and the
Gold Country

Pony Express Monument

Introduction

Sacramento is rapidly becoming the historic capital of the West. Even the most cursory look at its rich and colorful history reads like an abbreviated account of the expansion and settlement of the West, perhaps the most exciting and romantic period in American history. Woven throughout Sacramento's history are tales of trappers and mountain men, Indians and Spanish explorers, pioneers crossing the dusty prairies in search of a new life, and goldseekers chasing dreams of fabulous riches.

Sacramento's history is inextricably linked to the gold country, a region of oak-dotted rolling hills and pine-clad slopes on the western flanks of the formidable Sierra Nevada. As it was more than a century ago, Sacramento is still the gateway to the heart of the gold country, traversed today by Highway 49, also known as the Golden Chain Highway, which stretches some 267 miles from Mariposa in the south to Sierraville in the north. The first gold nuggets from Coloma were examined in Sacramento, which became the primary staging area for the greatest gold rush in human history. Sacramento was the port of destination for riverboats churning their way up the Sacramento River, the western terminus of the Pony Express and the telegraph, and the birthplace of the transcontinental railroad.

Perhaps more than any other California city, Sacramento has a keen sense of its own history, which has been preserved and maintained in its many historical attractions. These include historic Old Sacramento, the world's largest railroad museum, the new Sacramento History Center, and the restored capitol. The commitment to historic preservation is reflected throughout the region, from the charmingly restored Victorian houses in downtown Sacramento to the numerous structures and sites throughout the county registered as California historical landmarks or listed on the National Register of Historic Places.

As much as Sacramento's identity is rooted in the past, it's also planted firmly in the present. Much of its modern identity stems from its role as the capital of the most populous state in the union, with an annual budget equalling that of a small nation. The Sacramento metropolitan area is growing three times as fast as other comparable U.S. metropolitan areas. This growth is helping to transform the city's image from that of a sleepy agricultural and government town to that of a sophisticated region where visual and performing arts are coming of age, specialty restaurants and shops are appearing all over town, and shoppers can find just about anything they might need. Sacramento is becoming a major tourist destination as well. Millions come here every year, drawn not only by the historical attractions but by major events such as the international Dixieland Jazz Festival, the Sacramento Water Festival, and the California International Marathon.

A Thumbnail Sketch of the Land and Its People

Encompassing 997 square miles, Sacramento County occupies the southern portion of the Sacramento Valley, a rich agricultural area bounded on the west by the coast ranges and on the east by the Sierra Nevada and stretching some 175 miles from the Mokelumne River in the south to Redding in the north. It's part of California's Great Central Valley, a level plain comprising some forty-three thousand square miles that was once the bed of a great inland sea. The southern portion of the Great Central Valley is occupied by the San Joaquin Valley, stretching from San Joaquin County in the north to the Tehachapi Mountains beyond Bakersfield in the south.

The first known human residents of the Sacramento Valley were the Maidu Indians, who lived along the banks of the Sacramento and American rivers as far back as two thousand years ago. Theirs was largely a peaceful existence, in tune with the land and the seasons. They spent much of their time fishing in the bountiful waters, hunting wildlife, and searching for nuts, roots, and fruit. The first whites to explore the Sacramento area were trappers and explorers, the most famous of whom was Jedediah Smith, who visited the area in the early 1800s. Although they were familiar with the region, the Spanish concentrated their efforts searching for suitable mission sites along the coast.

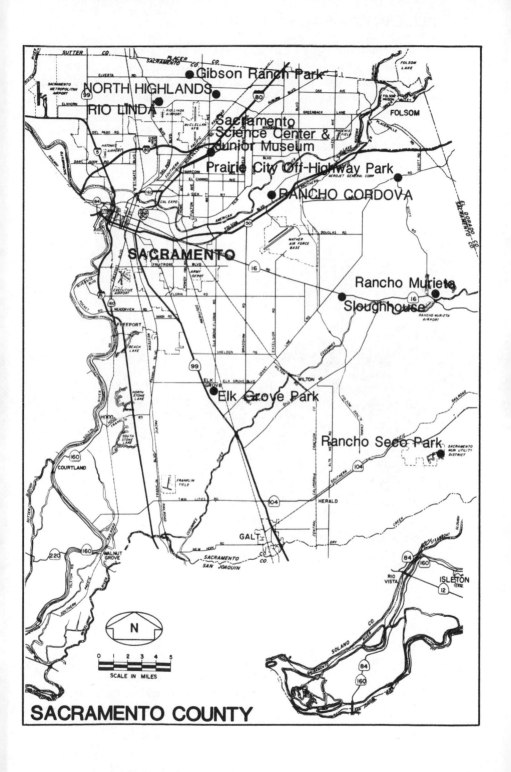

SACRAMENTO COUNTY

The first white settlement in Sacramento was founded in 1839 by John Augustus Sutter, a German-Swiss immigrant. After being given a forty-eight-thousand-acre Mexican land grant, Sutter established the colony of New Helvetia that grew and prospered as an agricultural and trade center. Sutter had grandiose plans for expanding his little inland empire, but they were thwarted with the discovery of gold at Coloma in 1848. His workers abandoned the agricultural fields for the gold fields, squatters took over his land, creditors hounded him, and money-hungry business partners succeeded in taking what was left. Captain Sutter's son, John Sutter, Jr., is credited with founding the city of Sacramento (named for the river the Spanish called the Rio de Sacramento), which became the prime trading center for the gold miners.

Captain John Augustus Sutter, 1855 (courtesy Eleanor McClatchy Collection, City of Sacramento, Museum and History Division)

During this period the land's vast agricultural potential began to be realized. For the next 100 years or so, agriculture and its related industries dominated Sacramento's economy, and the bulk of the area's population lived within the city. It might have remained so, and Sacramento might have remained a quiet farm and government town, were it not for the second great population influx that took place in the late 1940s and early 1950s. During World War II, the government activated Sacramento's two air bases, Mather

Field and McClellan Air Force Base. Then, in the 1950s, two major aerospace companies—Aerojet-General and McDonnell Douglas—opened facilities in the Rancho Cordova area. This generated a great deal of growth, especially in the suburbs, which added to the population and the economic base.

The bulk of Sacramento County's 905,500 people live in the urban area, which occupies the northern part of the county. The southern region is dominated by open, rolling farmland and grazing pasture. Agriculture does not play the major role it once did in Sacramento's economy, but more than two-thirds of the land outside the urban area is agricultural. Within the county are four incorporated cities: Sacramento, Folsom, Isleton, and Galt. Among several communities considering incorporation are Rancho Cordova, Orangevale, and Citrus Heights.

John A. Sutter, Jr. (courtesy Sacramento City Library Collection, City of Sacramento, Museum and History Division)

At this point we should establish what is meant geographically by the terms *Sacramento* and *Sacramento area,* which you'll find are used interchangeably. The central city, also referred to as downtown, is where the city started. It's packaged all neat and tidy—a rectangle bounded by the American and Sacramento rivers on the north and west and the Business 80 freeway on the south and east. The next category is the actual city limits, which spread out primarily to the north and south of downtown. Roughly 322,500 people live within the city limits, which include communities such as Del Paso Heights,

Greenhaven, and North Sacramento (an incorporated city from 1924 until 1964, when it was annexed to the city of Sacramento). Next you have the suburbs, located outside the city limits mostly in the northeast and east. The suburbs have been growing rapidly and steadily since the postwar years and include communities such as Carmichael, Rancho Cordova, Orangevale, Rio Linda, and North Highlands. The suburbs have also been growing in South Sacramento, more commonly referred to as the south area, which is being eyed as the next major growth area. West Sacramento, incidentally, isn't part of Sacramento at all; it's a separate city in Yolo County just across the Sacramento River from downtown.

The largest category is the Sacramento metropolitan area (a term used primarily by demographers). This region includes Sacramento, Yolo, and Placer counties. The statistic that ranks the Sacramento area as the seventh fastest-growing metropolitan area in the country refers to these three counties. This region's population has already passed the one million mark and is expected to hit a 10.2 percent annual growth rate by 1987. For the purposes of this book, the term *Sacramento* refers to the land in and around the city, and *Sacramento area* refers to the city and its suburbs.

Sacramento has long had the image of a government town; today one out of three workers in the county works for the government, and the three largest non-manufacturing employers are the state, federal, and county governments, in that order. But in recent years, the government has been growing more slowly, and there are fewer government jobs. As a result, Sacramento is changing its image and diversifying its economic base, encouraging growth in other areas. Two rapidly growing industries are retail trade (restaurants, stores, automobile dealerships) and services (health, entertainment, hotels). Together these industries employ more workers than government does. Manufacturing (high-tech, food processing, aerospace, construction) is also growing, with food processing at the top of the list because of the area's almond and tomato industries. Sacramento is on its way to becoming a major center of high-tech industry, with the bulk of high-tech growth in Folsom and the U.S. 50 Corridor (east of Watt Avenue).

Since the 1970s, tourism has also been having a growing financial impact on the community. Visitors are drawn to the area not only for its numerous attractions, but also for its agreeable climate conducive to year-round recreation. Sacramento's climate is characterized by warm, dry summers and mild, moderately moist winters. Average annual rainfall is seventeen inches. The region experiences four distinct seasons, but without the rough edges. Fall is ushered in by a dramatic display of fall color, with daytime temperatures around seventy-five degrees and crisp nights. The rainy season generally lasts from November through March. During the winter months, the average high temperature is in the low fifties, with dense valley fog appearing in December and January. Known locally as "tule fog," it usually burns off by midmorning but can linger for several days. By April, spring is in full bloom, with daytime temperatures in the sixties. In June the temperature rises to the eighties and hovers around the mid-nineties for the rest of the summer. There is an average of eleven days of temperatures above one hundred. Fortunately, the humidity at this time of year is low (usually in the teens), and the area is usually cooled off at night by delta breezes—sea breezes that come up through the Carquinez Strait and act as a natural air conditioner for the southern Sacramento Valley.

How to Use This Book

This book is designed to help you make the most of your stay in Sacramento and the gold country, whether it will last a day, a weekend, or longer. The material has been organized geographically in a handy and logical manner, with Part I covering Sacramento County and Part II covering the gold country along Highway 49 from Mariposa to Nevada City. The appendix at the back provides easy reference to Sacramento restaurants, lodging, entertainment, transportation, recreation, services, and shopping.

Maps have been provided to help you get your bearings, but it's a good idea to get detailed maps if you want to do some serious exploring. The best maps are those provided free to California State Automobile Association members. These include *Sacramento Valley Region, Metropolitan Sacramento, Yosemite,* and *Lake Tahoe Region.* The *Thomas Brothers Street Atlas for Sacramento County* is also useful. Recommendations for maps for specific geographical areas are included throughout the book.

Hours and admission prices for most of the places specifically mentioned in this book have been omitted for the simple reason that they seem to change every other day. It would be frustrating to plan an entire day's outing around visiting a particular spot only to arrive and find it closed, or find that the "free" admission was now $7.89 per person. It's always a good idea to write or phone ahead anyway, and complete addresses and phone numbers have been provided for this purpose. Where no area code is given, the area code is 916. The area codes are included with phone numbers for places outside this region.

One last note: although attempts have been made to cram as many interesting and useful bits of information as possible into these pages, it's obviously impossible to include everything that was ever known about a place and everything you would want to see there. The idea is to give you the highlights—enough to pique your interest and get you started. You'll surely come across your own discoveries during your explorations. Also, listings for restaurants, shops, and lodgings do not imply endorsements for these establishments; they are only intended to be representative samplings of what's available.

A stately Victorian dwarfed by a modern office building

Part I
SACRAMENTO COUNTY

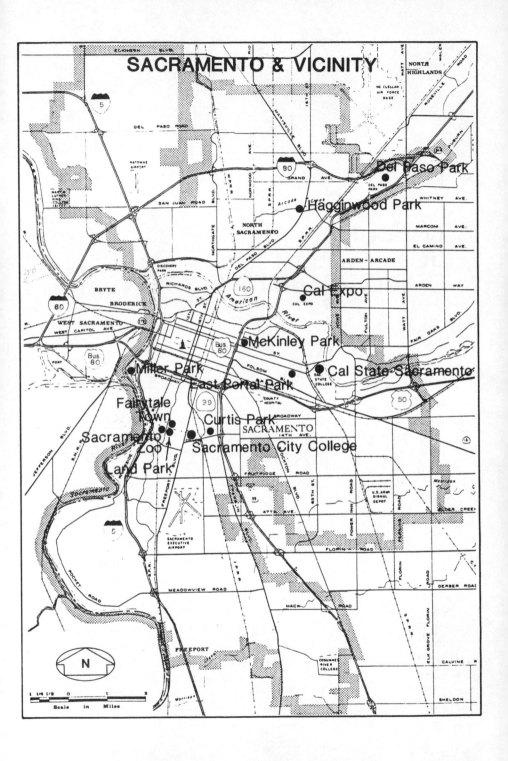

1

Sacramento:
City of Contrast

Sacramento is a city of many faces. It's a city of wedding-cake Victorian homes and mirror-image tract crackerboxes, fast-food emporiums and candlelit bistros. There are environmentally controlled malls where the Muzak puts you in a buying mood, but there are also old-fashioned corner drug stores where you can set a spell and sip a strawberry soda. In a modern office building, a government worker feeds data into a purring computer, while a few blocks away at Sutter's Fort a modern-day pioneer woman feeds hand-carded wool into a spinning wheel. At sunset a fisherman lazily floats down a serene river, while above, where the freeway spans the water, rush-hour commuters make a mad dash for the suburbs. And surrounding all of this are miles and miles of fertile farmland, where the air is sweet with the scent of dark earth and things growing.

Sacramento is a city of contrast and contradiction. It's the capital of the most populous state in the union and has a metropolitan population of more than a million, so you would expect to find a bustling metropolis cast in cement, steel, and glass. But you won't find it. For Sacramento projects a small-town charm and persona characteristic of its neighbors in California's Great Central Valley. However, the small-town feeling gets lost somewhat as you wander out of the heart of the city and into the suburbs, where the main

13

thoroughfares are indistinguishable from each other amid the shopping centers, taco stands, banks, and gas stations. Sacramento hasn't been immune to urban sprawl, and the growth pattern has been helter-skelter. The city never really grew outward from the downtown area like many other cities; instead, tiny communities sprang up here and there over the years, and later developments just sort of filled in the blank spots in between.

Trees and Camellias

One of the first things you'll notice upon entering the city, especially toward downtown, are the trees. The city's streets and parks alone contain some 250,000 of them—flowering, deciduous, fruit, and palm. Sacramento's trees have elicited comparisons with other cities known for their trees, not the least of which are Paris and Washington, D.C. The predominant trees are English and American elms planted mostly by homesick easterners. Another reason for the importation of trees was that much of the native valley oak had long since been stripped from the landscape for firewood and building and to clear land for agriculture. The valley oak, also called the California white oak, is the largest oak in North America, reaching heights of 100 to 150 feet. It grows only in California and can live three hundred to five hundred years. There's also a good sprinkling of sycamore, Modesto and Arizona ash, birch, and English walnut, among others. The citrus trees date from the late 19th century, when an attempt was made to raise oranges commercially (hence the communities of Orangevale and Citrus Heights). Zealous realtors used the lure of fresh oranges to entice potential buyers.

Besides the aesthetic pleasures, the trees provide a saving grace for the city during the summer when temperatures hover in the high nineties. Their branches and leaves provide a lush, verdant canopy for streets and homes that otherwise would be baking in the sun. Because of the age of many of the trees and certain environmental factors, a lot of them have become susceptible to various diseases and insect infestations. As a result, a long-term program is in effect to replace many of the city's older trees.

Although it might appropriately be called the City of Trees, Sacramento is officially known as Camellia City. Between the months of January and March, you don't have to look hard to see why. Nearly every yard and park has camellia bushes, with blossoms ranging in color from pure white and pale pink to the deepest crimson. There are more than a million bushes, some of them tree-sized. The city's first camellias were introduced in 1852 by Boston nurseryman James Warren, who opened the New England Seed Store on J Street near the Embarcadero. Every year in early March, the Camellia Festival celebrates the city's floral heritage with parades, a camellia show displaying thousands of blooms, bicycle races, a grand ball, a marathon race, a regatta, and numerous other events, many of which are free.

Plenty to Do and See

Sacramento is often described in terms of its proximity to Lake Tahoe, the gold country, the wine country, and San Francisco as though there weren't much to do or see in the city itself. Of course, there are the obvious attractions: the state capitol (which recently underwent a six-year, $70 million restoration), Old Sacramento, the Railroad Museum, the Crocker Art Museum, Sutter's Fort, and the Governor's Mansion. Sacramento is now also a major-league city, having recently become the home of the National Basketball Association's Sacramento Kings, formerly of Kansas City. There are plenty of other things to do and see as well; some just take a bit of creativity and searching to find. You'll discover art galleries to explore, historic buildings to admire, elegant Victorians, many lovely parks, rivers, the American River Parkway, and mysterious cemeteries with century-old headstones. You can prowl through musty antique shops and used-book stores piled high with books, sip cappuccino or wine at a European-style cafe, discover a great little restaurant tucked away on a side street, and catch a play, ballet, or concert.

There's also apt to be an event or celebration of some kind nearly every weekend of the year. One source of information on these events as well as general visitor information is the Sacramento Convention and Visitors Bureau, 1311 I Street, 442-5542. If they don't have the information, they can probably tell you who does. The Visitors Bureau publishes a handy brochure listing major attractions, restaurants, accommodations, and information on transportation and tours. The Sacramento Metropolitan Chamber of Commerce can provide information relating to the business community, including an annual business handbook entitled *Sacramento on the Go.* It's at 917 Seventh Street, 443-3771. The Sacramento Area Commerce and Trade Organization (SACTO) works to bring commercial and industrial business (primarily high-tech) to the Sacramento area. SACTO generates several publications that can be helpful for job-seekers, including an annual manufacturers' and processors' guide and a statistical abstract. For information, contact SACTO at 300 Capitol Mall, 441-2144.

Before taking a closer look at the city, let's first examine how Sacramento evolved into what it is today.

The Pioneer Spirit

When Captain John Sutter founded his remote outpost near the confluence of the American and Sacramento rivers in 1839, his dream was to create an empire over which he would rule as an absolute but benevolent monarch. Unwittingly, he played a key role in his own undoing and never realized his dream. Although history may view Sutter as a failure in one sense, he left a legacy that remains with the people of Sacramento to this day. For it was Sutter's pioneer spirit that set the tone for all who would follow in building a thriving city out of the wilderness. It was that spirit of perseverance and determination that carried Sacramentans through fire, flood, and disease, always ready to rebuild and start anew. Sacramento's pioneers had little patience with tragedy.

Early Sacramento may have been a rough-and-tumble Gold Rush town, but through sheer determination, a cultural, religious and educational life was established for its burgeoning population, smoothing the rough edges. When it came to civic and political matters, it was hard to match the enthusiasm of Sacramentans. They played a key role in securing California's statehood. Along with several other Sacramentans, John Sutter attended the first constitutional convention in 1849 at Monterey. Voters ratified the resulting document, and Peter Burnett, another Sacramentan, was elected the state's first governor. California officially became a state a year later, on September 9, 1850. For the next four years, Sacramentans lobbied vigorously to make their city the state's capital. The capital had been located in five different cities, including Monterey and San Jose, and a permanent site had to be chosen. Once again, the spirit of perseverance paid off: on February 25, 1854, the law designating Sacramento the state capital was signed by Governor John Bigler, also a Sacramentan. The first capitol building in Sacramento was the county courthouse at Seventh and I streets, which was destroyed by fire in 1854. A new courthouse was rebuilt at that site and used by the state until the present capitol building was completed in 1869. The land for the new capitol, bounded by L, N, Tenth, and Twelfth streets, was given to the state by the city in 1860. Twelve years later, six additional blocks were acquired to create Capitol Park.

Probably very few, if any, capital cities can claim that they were organizing for statehood and cityhood at the same time. But Sacramento can. Sacramento began as a municipality in July 1849 when the first city council was elected, with A. M. Winn its first president and ex-officio mayor. The voters quickly defeated the first city charter, which would have imposed controls on gambling—Sacramento was a gambling town. The offending sections were removed, and the charter was passed in October 1849. The following February, California's first state legislature authorized the incorporation of the city of Sacramento, and two months later Hardin Bigelow was elected the city's first mayor.

With incorporation and statehood out of the way, Sacramentans next turned their attention to making their city the home of the California State Fair, the first of which had been held in San Francisco in 1854. Agriculture formed the basis of the state's economy by this time, and Sacramento County was already firmly established as a prime agricultural region. After a good amount of wheeling and dealing, including donating land and a facility, the people of Sacramento got what they wanted; in 1861 Sacramento was made the permanent home of the state fair. This was a real coup for Sacramentans, for it served to reinforce their city's position as the state's political and economic center. The state fair was held at several downtown locations (including an elegant pavilion at Fifteenth and N streets in Capitol Park) until 1905, when it moved to a site at Stockton Boulevard and Broadway.

In the years between 1848 and 1877, Sacramento was one of the nation's best-known cities, due in large part to the Gold Rush, which brought thousands of new residents to the area. As the rush for gold waned, another kind of riches sustained the city and propelled it securely into the 20th century. The Sacramento Valley had been found to be one of the most fertile agricultural areas in the world, and Sacramento became the center of the valley's trade. By the 1890s, agriculture in Sacramento County was in full swing, with twenty thousand acres of fruit orchards, ten thousand acres of vineyards, seventy-five thousand acres of vegetables, and two thousand acres of hops. Much of these goods was used in Sacramento, but a significant amount was sold to eastern and foreign markets. Hay, grain, stock, and dairy farming supplemented these products.

From its humble beginnings as a tent city at the Embarcadero, the city had been growing steadily and evenly to the east. By 1860 the central city was well established within the boundaries marked by the Sacramento and American rivers and Thirty-First and Y streets. Up until the late 1880s, transportation within the four-and-a-half-square-mile city was provided by horse-drawn carriages, streetcars, and freight wagons. Mule wagons were used to haul agricultural goods. Every neighborhood had its corner grocery, offering most every kind of good and service needed; the proprietors usually lived upstairs. The debut of the electric railway in 1887 heralded the beginning of an expanding pattern of growth that continues today. For the first time, outlying areas could be considered for residential development. The streetcar helped to create Sacramento's first suburbs and commuters.

The Growth of the Suburbs

One of the first of these suburbs was a popular residential area called Oak Park, founded in 1889. It included a portion of land to the east and south of the central city. Several streetcar lines ran to Oak Park, which also was the site of a large amusement park called Joyland. Built in the late 1800s, the popular park was located near what is now McClatchy Park and boasted a wooden roller coaster, a penny arcade, a theater, a skating rink, and a ballpark. In

1910 Oak Park became the city's first annexation. Streetcars remained in use until they were phased out during the late 1940s.

Another factor contributing to Sacramento's growth was the automobile, which allowed for even more development in outlying areas during the early 1900s. The already-established fruit colonies of Fair Oaks, Citrus Heights, and Orangevale (where there were once orange groves as far as the eye could see) were beginning to grow. In 1910 development began in the area north of the American River, which for years had been the forty-four-thousand-acre Rancho del Paso land grant. Owned by James Ben Ali Haggin, a businessman and thoroughbred horse rancher, the land grant stretched from Rio Linda south to the American River and from Northgate Boulevard east to Carmichael. The rancho was sold in 1910 to a development company whose national advertising described the area as another Garden of Eden that would provide "all the best varieties of deciduous and citrus fruits." The land was then subdivided into farms and homesites. From this land sprang the communities of Rio Linda and North Sacramento, which was incorporated in 1925 and annexed to Sacramento in 1964 (the city's last annexation). The city bought a portion of the land grant for what later became Del Paso Park and Haggin Oaks Golf Course.

The city has several attractive neighborhoods that grew around parks during the early decades of the century. The Curtis Park neighborhood was developed on the site of the Louisiana Race Track, built in 1855. With its entrance at Twelfth Avenue and Franklin Boulevard, the popular track was the site of horse races, horse and cattle exhibitions, and stock shows. A farmer named Curtis later bought the property, and by 1892 the track was a prime piece of real estate valued at $250,000. The McKinley Park neighborhood grew up around what was once called East Park. During the early 1920s, William Land Park and the golf course were developed by the city, which had purchased the land that was formerly a cattle ranch. Residential development subsequently took place between Broadway and Sutterville; the area around the park became an elegant neighborhood.

Large-scale suburban development and expansion in Sacramento didn't occur until after World War II. Most of this growth took place around the two air bases activated during the war, Mather Field (now Mather Air Force Base) in the east and McClellan Air Force Base in the northeast. After the war, the bases continued to have military importance because of the developing cold war and later the space race, which attracted aerospace firms such as Aerojet and McDonnell Douglas to Sacramento. As a result, the 1950s saw the population in the unincorporated areas outside the city overtake and surpass the city's population. During this decade the Sacramento area population nearly doubled. By 1960, 60 percent of the population of metropolitan Sacramento (318,633) lived in the unincorporated areas.

Regional shopping centers were built to serve the burgeoning suburban population. The state's first suburban shopping center, Town and Country Village, was built in 1945, and others followed. Old highways were improved and new ones built to accommodate the new generation of commuters. The effect of the flight to suburbia on the downtown business area was disastrous. What had been a vital and thriving business district for more than a century became an anemic shell of its former self, its lifeblood drawn away to relocate in malls and shopping centers near the freeways. Since the 1960s, redevelopment efforts have begun to pump new life into downtown, and the prognosis is good.

Getting Around

Whether by bicycle, foot, car, or bus, Sacramento is a fairly easy place to get around. The city is traversed by freeways that lead to most of the outlying areas. Downtown is the easiest, as it's laid out in a grid pattern with east-west streets lettered (A, B, C) and north-south streets numbered (First, Second, Third). Thus if you know the street address of your destination, you can easily pinpoint what block it's on. At first, the one-way streets might be a bit confusing, but once you know which street goes which way, you shouldn't have any problem. Also, when driving, don't take off immediately when a red light turns green. For some reason, a lot of downtown drivers tend to run red lights. Parking is rarely a problem unless you're near the capitol on a weekday. You'll find rush-hour congestion typical of most larger cities, but it's bearable and nothing like the car-choked streets of L.A. You should carry a city map with you for anything outside downtown, as it can get a bit tricky finding your way at first. The California State Automobile Association publishes a good one. One way to get your bearings if you're new to Sacramento is to take a commercial bus tour of the city. Several companies offer tours, some even including dinner at popular restaurants. This way you can relax, leave the maps at home, and let someone else do the driving.

If the idea of letting someone else drive is appealing, try Sacramento Regional Transit. With nearly two hundred buses, it provides regular bus service throughout the metropolitan area and into Roseville. The service is particularly good downtown. Persons in wheelchairs can ride on certain routes that are served by buses with mechanical lifts. The best source of information on transportation in Sacramento is the bus schedule booklet, inserted in newspapers several times a year or available free from RT headquarters, which will also mail you a copy (see appendix for complete address). It includes schedules, fares, information on connecting service, and various tips on bus travel. Individual route schedules are also available at RT headquarters, 1400 29th Street, or by calling 321-BUSS. From time to time, when funding is available, RT operates open-air trams that run along the K Street Mall.

At a projected cost of $165 million, Sacramento's proposed light-rail system operated by Regional Transit will link downtown with northern and eastern suburbs via 18.3 miles of track. Running every fifteen minutes, modern electric trolleys will serve all the major employment areas downtown, including the five-block stretch of the K Street Mall. A park and ride system is being developed, and bus routes will be shifted to make connections.

Because it's mostly flat, Sacramento is an ideal place for bicycling, with a number of commuter and scenic routes. In addition to several trails limited to bicycles only (including the thirty-three-mile trail through the American River Parkway), both the city and county have extensive networks of street bike lanes. Commuter and scenic bike route maps and information are available from the city's Traffic Engineering Division at 915 I Street (see appendix for complete address), 449-5307.

Arts, Culture and Entertainment

In addition to an intense pioneer spirit, early Sacramentans had a fervent appreciation of the arts. It was in Sacramento that California's first theater (the Eagle in 1849) and the West's first public art museum (the Crocker in 1871) were built. This love affair with the arts has persisted to this day in Sacramento, where the performing and visual arts continue to thrive. Throughout the year there are numerous events and programs from which to choose, including ballet, opera, theater, classical music, jazz, rock and roll, art exhibits, films, and poetry readings. The following is just a sampling of what the city has to offer in the way of arts and entertainment. More detailed listings, including addresses and phone numbers, appear in the appendix.

Run jointly by the city and county, the Sacramento Metropolitan Arts Commission at 800 Tenth Street provides a number of programs and services to help foster and develop support of the arts. One of the commission's best services is the Discover Sacramento Hotline (449-5566), a computerized information center that provides taped information twenty-four hours a day on things going on in Sacramento, from plays and sporting events to festivals and special recreational outings. The only catch is, you need a Touch-Tone phone to punch in the three-digit codes for the events. (If you have a rotary-dial phone, call the Arts Commission at 449-5558 to find out what's going on.) You can obtain a *Discover Sacramento Directory,* which lists event sponsors and directions on how to use the hotline service, at the Arts Commission office and at libraries and hotels. The Arts Commission also publishes a directory listing Sacramento artists and cultural groups. Other good sources are the entertainment sections of the *Sacramento Bee* and the *Sacramento Union,* as well as the *Suttertown News* and the monthly arts publication *On the Wing.*

The Sacramento Community Center's 2,450-seat theater is the city's major performing arts center, site of performances by the Sacramento Symphony, the Sacramento Ballet Company, and the Sacramento Opera Association. The Sacramento Symphony presents some two hundred performances a year at the Community Center, some of which feature distinguished guest artists such as Itzhak Perlman and Andre Watts. In the fall and spring the Symphony presents affordable Kinder Koncerts for children. From fall to spring the Sacramento Ballet Company presents classical and story ballets chosen from its diverse repertory, which includes *Giselle, The Nutcracker,* and *Coppelia.* The Sacramento Opera Association offers performances year-round. Past productions have included *La Bohème, The Magic Flute,* and *Carmen.* The Community Center also hosts many other performing arts programs and lectures by prominent speakers. There is also an exhibit hall and activities building at the Center, which is located at Fourteenth and L. For a recorded listing of upcoming events, call 449-5324.

At this writing there are some nineteen theatrical groups in Sacramento, offering an eclectic mix that ranges from Shakespeare to improv. And although some say Sacramento is not a theater town, the city does offer a variety of theaters and groups from which to choose.

Located at Fourteenth and H streets, the Sacramento Theater Company (446-7501), formerly the Eleanor McClatchy Performing Arts Center, is the city's largest theater company. STC's Mainstage Theater season runs from September through May with six productions. Across the courtyard is the more intimate Stage Two Theater, with four productions running from October through April. STC's Music Circus offers a summer stock season of theater-in-the-round under the air-conditioned oldest musical tent outside the East. The season runs from July to September and has featured star headliners in musicals such as *Annie, Grease,* and *They're Playing Our Song.* The Music Circus is located at Fifteenth and H streets, 441-3163.

Dinner theater is also available in Sacramento. Garbeau's Dinner Theater (985-6361) is located in a new 300-seat theater on the second floor of the Nimbus Winery at Highway 50 and Hazel Avenue. In addition to serving up fine productions Wednesday through Sunday, Garbeau's offers a choice of fourteen dinner entrees. Lunch is also served.

Sacramento has a wealth of visual art to enjoy with the fine Crocker Art Museum, several galleries at the area's colleges and universities, and scores of private galleries (around twenty in Sacramento alone). A representative sampling includes the Artists' Collaborative Gallery (1007 Second Street,

444-3764); Artists Contemporary Gallery (542 Downtown Plaza, 446-3694); Djurovich Gallery (727½ J Street, 446-3806); Himovitz/Salomon Gallery (1020 Tenth Street, 448-8723); Matrix Gallery (2424 Castro Way, 456-8337); and I Street Gallery (1725 I Street, 447-7014). The Jerome Evans Gallery (1826 Capitol Avenue, 448-3759) publishes a guide to local art galleries and museums.

Poetry is also alive and well in Sacramento, thanks largely to the efforts of the Poet Tree, an organization dedicated to supporting and promoting poetry in the community. The Poet Tree sponsors readings by local and visiting poets, publishes the monthly *Poet News* newspaper, and twice a year publishes *Quercus,* an anthology of work by local poets. The group works closely with the Sacramento Writers and Artists Coop, which sponsors poetry readings at cafes and art galleries around town and publishes poetry and fiction. The Poet Tree is located at 2791 Twenty-fourth Street, 739-1885.

The nightlife scene in Sacramento isn't as diverse as some might wish, although things seem to be opening up somewhat. One problem is that clubs are scattered throughout the region instead of being concentrated in just one area. Once again, creativity and planning are called for—things won't just jump out at you like they do in L.A. or San Francisco. Here's just a sampling of what's around. For Tahitian floor shows it's the Zombie Hut on Freeport; try Laughs Unlimited in Old Sacramento for good comedy; rock out at the El Dorado Saloon on Fair Oaks Boulevard; hear jazz nightly at On Broadway, Broadway and Nineteenth; enjoy high-tech disco at Confetti on Arden Way; and sample folk music at the Fox & Goose, Tenth and R.

If your tastes run toward esoteric, revival, and foreign films, you'll love the Tower Theater. Located at Sixteenth and Broadway (443-1982), it's a venerable old theater that's been divided into three theaters that show revival films, current foreign films, and new releases that may be critically acclaimed but don't always draw large crowds. They even sell fresh coffee, herb tea, and popcorn with real butter. Prices are a bit lower here than at mainstream theaters, and discount passes are available. (Trivia buffs will be interested to learn that the Tower Records store chain started in 1941 from a small table in the former Tower Drug Store next door.) The area around Sixteenth and Broadway is becoming a nightlife "in spot," with the Tower, dessert shops, book and record stores, restaurants, and nightclubs all within several blocks of each other.

Ethnic Festivals

Sacramento has always had a tradition of ethnic and cultural diversity. It started with the Gold Rush, when would-be miners from all over the world flocked to the area, and continues today with the arrival of relatively new waves of immigrants who bring with them a rich cultural heritage. Unlike the melting pot days of old when immigrants shed their ethnic and cultural identities in order to be assimilated, today many groups are devoted to preserving their heritage.

The Sacramento History Center recently completed an ethnic communities survey that identified at least 100 ethnic and cultural groups in the area, including Russians, Arabs, Croatians, Chinese, Germans, Vietnamese, Guatemalans, French, and Finns. The results of this survey are now on display at the Sacramento History Center's Community Gallery, with exhibits of artifacts, photos, and a film.

The most recent tide of immigration began in the 1970s as a result of the war in Southeast Asia. The Sacramento area's Indochinese community, which includes some sixteen thousand Vietnamese, Cambodians, and Laotians in Sacramento County alone, is one of the nation's largest. Most of Sacramento's Indochinese are clustered in several neighborhoods, including downtown (especially Southside), the Stockton Boulevard/Fruitridge Road

Dancers at the Cinco de Mayo festival

area, and parts of Del Paso Heights/North Highlands and Rancho Cordova.

Although most of the ethnic neighborhoods have dispersed, there are still a few areas with concentrations of ethnic and cultural groups. The city has been the fortunate beneficiary of much of this cultural heritage in the form of festivals, architecture, religious institutions, clubs and associations, and a variety of unique and different perspectives. The Greek Orthodox Church at Alhambra and F sponsors a Greek Food Festival every September, featuring delicious homemade Greek food, music, dance, and cultural exhibits. An estimated fifty thousand Italian-Americans live in the Sacramento area, with a large population in the vicinity of St. Mary's Church at Fifty-eighth and M streets. East Portal Park, in the same area, is the site of two courts where bocce, a popular Italian game similar to English lawn bowling, is played. Temple B'Nai Israel, the oldest synagogue west of the Mississippi River, is the site of a popular annual Legislative Seder attended by lawmakers and lobbyists of all faiths. Alkali Flat is the home of a portion of the city's Mexican-American and Chicano community, which sponsors the Cinco de Mayo festival in May and the Mexican Independence Day celebration in September.

The Buddhist Church of Sacramento (with the second largest membership in America) sponsors an annual bazaar every August. The bazaar attracts upwards of twenty-five thousand people to sample homemade Japanese noodles, chicken teriyaki, tempura, and sushi. Of an estimated two thousand Pakistanis living in the Sacramento Valley, about five hundred live in Sacramento. In 1947 Sacramento's Pakistanis built the Muslim Mosque at Fourth and V streets, the first mosque built west of the Mississippi River. A minaret (prayer tower) was recently built on the mosque site.

Croatians first immigrated from the Dalmatian Coast in Croatia (now part of Yugoslavia) during the Gold Rush. Today an estimated ten thousand Croatians live in the Sacramento metropolitan area. The Croatian-American Cultural Center on Auburn Boulevard is the site of the annual Croatian Festival, featuring traditional food, drink, and dance. St. Elizabeth's Portuguese National Church at Twelfth and S streets is the oldest Portuguese national church west of New England. It serves a portion of Sacramento's large Portuguese community, many of whom live in the Pocket area (Greenhaven and Freeport). For more than 100 years, the Portuguese Spring Festival of the Holy Spirit has been held, complete with colorful parades and large feasts.

One good place to get a feel for the city's ethnic diversity is the Farmer's Market held on Sunday mornings at Sixth and W streets. There's a real cosmopolitan atmosphere because of the many different immigrant groups that frequent the outdoor market.

Shopping

Sacramento is a shopper's paradise if you don't mind driving. Gone are the good old days when you could get everything you needed on one trip downtown. The bright side of this, however, is that you can find just about any kind of product or service, often at a discount, because there are so many shopping centers and stores from which to choose. There are eleven large shopping centers and malls in the Sacramento area, three of them inside the city limits. These are the Arden Fair Mall on Arden Way east of Business 80, Lake Crest Shopping Center on Florin Road west of I-5, and Downtown Plaza at the western end of the K Street Mall.

"Off-price" stores and shopping centers are a growing phenomenon. Many large discount stores such as Marshalls and Ross that sell a variety of goods well below retail prices are locating together in shopping centers, so you can do all your discount shopping in one location.

A good source of information on discount shopping in Sacramento is Victoria Goff's handy booklet *Bargain Hunting in Sacramento.* You'll find everything listed alphabetically from appliances to weight control. With this helpful guide, you can expect to save 20 to 70 percent on everyday needs and many luxury items. Goff's low-priced booklet is available at local bookstores or by writing D & R Publishing, P.O. Box 781, West Sacramento, CA 95691.

Antiques stores are plentiful—about fifty in the city alone. Two areas with concentrations of antique shops are Old Sacramento and the two blocks of Fifty-seventh Street between H and J. The latter region has been dubbed "Antique Row" and consists of two complexes across the street from each other. The Gravy Boat Complex has ten antique shops offering such merchandise as oak furniture, jukeboxes, antique plumbing accessories, and Victorian clothing. Across the street is the Sacramento Antique Centre, a collection of shops with a fine selection of antiques and collectibles.

Sacramento lies in one of the most fertile valleys in the world, so it's no surprise that consumers here often get the pick of many crops. You even have the choice of going to the farmer or having the farmer come to you. There are three certified growers' markets in Sacramento. The only one that is open year-round is the Sacramento Certified Farmers' Market at Eighth and W (under the freeway), held every Sunday from 8 A.M. to noon, rain or shine. It's a large, colorful market where you can find organically grown and raised fruits, vegetables, eggs, honey, nuts, dried fruits, and fish, along with large varieties of ethnic produce. The other two locations are Florin Mall and Country Club Centre. For more information, call the California Department of Food and Agriculture, 445-5294. The department publishes a free

Farmer-to-Consumer Directory that lists Sacramento County farmers who let visitors come to their farms and pick fruits and vegetables. Within a short drive of the city are a number of farms where you can save money by picking your own cherries, pumpkins, pears, peaches, apples, figs, tomatoes, olives, and much more. The Cooperative Agricultural Extension Service also publishes a directory of farmers' markets and produce stands in the Sacramento area. For a free copy of *Sacramento Farm Trails,* send a self-addressed, stamped legal-size envelope to Sacramento Farm Trails, 4145 Branch Center Road, Sacramento, CA 95827.

A flea market is another place where you can find good buys on produce, although produce is not the main attraction. The three flea markets in the area are on Folsom Boulevard, in Roseville, and in Galt. All are open year-round. Auction City and Flea Market is at 8521 Folsom near the eastern edge of the city (383-0880). It's open weekends from 7 A.M. to 6 P.M. Sellers pay a fee; buyers don't. Denio's Roseville Farmers Market and Auction is at 98 Atkinson Street in Roseville (782-2704). Same days and hours as Auction City; sellers pay a fee, buyers free. Lots of good buys here, though a bit commercialized. The Galt Flea Market is at 1050 C Street in Galt (209/745-2437). Open Wednesdays only, 7 A.M. to 3 P.M.; free admission for buyers. If you know how to shop at a flea market, you can save lots of money on everything from furniture, tools, and antiques to jewelry, collectibles, and appliances. The trick is to get there early for the best selection or late for the best buys. And don't be afraid to haggle—that's half the fun, and it can save you money.

Parks and Recreation

In addition to being called the Camellia City and the City of Trees, Sacramento could be called the City of Parks. The city is dotted with more than ninety parks covering nearly two thousand acres. John Sutter, Jr., probably had something to do with the city's acknowledgment of the importance of parks. In 1848 he set aside ten blocks of land, two and a half acres each, as parks. Eight of these parks remain today, all in the central city. The city's parks range from patches of grass and trees to large community recreation centers with clubhouses, pools, barbecue pits, and picnic tables. The Sacramento Department of Community Services also oversees thirty-nine lighted tennis courts, five municipal golf courses, ten community centers, thirteen municipal swimming pools, fifty ball fields, and many other special facilities. Several major parks lie within the city, including the state-run Capitol Park and William Land Park, the city's second largest park (see next section). McKinley Park at Alhambra Boulevard and H Street has been a city park since 1902. Facilities in this lush, thirty-six-acre park include a clubhouse, teen center, garden-arts center (with free art and garden shows), swimming pool, tennis courts, baseball diamonds, basketball court, horseshoe pits, an elaborate jungle gym for big and little kids, a recreation center for the disabled, and a rose garden with 190 species of roses in full bloom in June. The rose garden is a popular spot for weddings. Bring your old bread so the kids can feed the ducks in the duck pond.

The nine-acre East Portal Park at Fifty-first and M streets has playgrounds, picnic areas, baseball diamonds, and bocce courts. Hagginwood Park at Arcade and Marysville boulevards is a fourteen-acre park featuring a senior center, clubhouse, horseshoe pits, wading pool, playground, picnic areas, and baseball fields.

The city's largest park is Del Paso Park at Auburn Boulevard and Fulton Avenue. The 948-acre park includes the Haggin Oaks Golf Course, with one eighteen-hole and two nine-hole golf courses. There's a pro shop (481-4506), clubhouse, food concessions, and a driving range. (The city also operates a golf course on Freeport Boulevard just south of Executive Airport. The Bing Maloney Golf Course, 428-9401, is an eighteen-hole course with a pro shop, spacious clubhouse, food concessions, driving range, and lockers.) Del Paso Park also has a four-field softball complex, baseball diamond, nature areas, picnic facilities, and riding/hiking trails. Adjacent to Del Paso Park is the Sacramento Horseman's Association, 3200 Longview Drive (489-4101). The association sponsors numerous equestrian events, including horse shows, at its two arenas and has a large clubhouse and facilities for boarding horses. No horses are available for rent, but you can bring your own horse to ride on equestrian trails along Arcade Creek, a natural habitat area that also offers superb birdwatching.

Located at Broadway and the Sacramento River, Miller Park is the home of the 285-slip Sacramento Boat Harbor (449-5712). This fifty-seven-acre park has free boat launching facilities, picnic areas and barbecues, a softball diamond, soccer fields, and a snack bar. A major expansion project is in the works at the harbor.

Information on city parks and recreation programs can be obtained from the Sacramento Department of Community Services (449-5200). Its *Facility Guide* contains lots of useful information on parks, recreation, the zoo (see next section), Crocker Art Museum, golf courses, metropolitan arts activities, and the Sacramento History Center. Community Services also publishes recreation guides three times a year that are available free at libraries and other city facilities. These resources are the best way to learn about the myriad activities and programs sponsored year-round by the city. Here are a few of the recreational activities offered: sports, aquatics, after-school programs, performing and visual arts, a costume and talent bank, teen programs, and a variety of classes. There are special summer programs for children and seven centers and a number of sports programs for seniors. Other good sources of information on recreation are the *Sacramento Union* and the *Sacramento Bee*.

The Sacramento County Department of Parks and Recreation (366-2061) oversees twenty-five parks on more than eight thousand acres of county parklands. Major county parks include Ancil Hoffman Park, C. M. Goethe Park, Discovery Park, Elk Grove Park, Gibson Ranch, and Prairie City (described individually in later chapters). The county parks department publishes a colorful brochure, including details on county parks and their facilities as well as a map showing park locations.

WILLIAM LAND PARK
AND THE SACRAMENTO ZOO

William Land Park is Sacramento's second largest park, spread over 161 acres just south of downtown on South Land Park Drive between Thirteenth Avenue and Sutterville Road. Originally a cattle ranch, the land was purchased in 1922 with funds bequeathed to the city by William Land, who had owned two large downtown hotels. More than three thousand trees of about fifty varieties grow in this perennially verdant park. Attractions include the Sacramento Zoo, a children's theme park, and amusement and pony rides. The park features a fishing pond with a large population of friendly ducks that the children can feed, flower gardens planted in seasonal flowers, plenty of picnic tables and barbecues, an amphitheater, and many acres of grassy spots on which to plunk down a blanket and have a picnic. Recreational facilities include a children's wading pool and play area, clubhouse, archery range, baseball diamond, basketball court, soccer field, four softball fields, and a nine-hole golf course. Encompassing seventy-five acres, William Land Golf Course is the city's oldest municipal golf course. Facilities at the par-34 course include a small pro shop, a food concession, restrooms, and plenty of parking. Reservations are recommended; call 455-5014.

Land Park also has a two-mile walking and jogging path with fitness stations at regular intervals that include balance and hand-walk beams, sit-up and push-up stands, and a body-curl bar. Free maps of the path are available from the community services department, 449-5200.

On warm spring weekends and throughout the summer, the park bustles with golfers, picnickers, sports enthusiasts, joggers, and sun worshippers. A couple of spots offer a secluded respite from the crowds. Adjacent to the amphitheater and across from Fairytale Town is a lovely little rock garden planted in succulents and a variety of annuals and perennials. A little stream meanders through the garden, and you can relax on a bench next to it for some serious contemplation. For a romantic picnic, try the grassy area behind the Charles Swanston statue near the west end of the zoo by Fifteenth Avenue. It's a pleasant garden area with granite pathways bordered by colorful flowers and quaint benches shaded by wisteria-laden trellises.

Considered one of the best small zoos in the country, the Sacramento Zoo is one of the city's best sources of inexpensive, year-round entertainment. Established in 1927 and occupying twenty acres in Land Park, the zoo offers 150 exhibits of 167 animal species, with a total of about 500 animals. The beautiful parklike setting, including large grassy areas, trees, flowers, and botanical gardens, is conducive to leisurely strolling. Most of the exhibits have been carefully designed to create more natural environments for zoo inhabitants, 60 percent of which are endangered species from throughout the world. You'll find ring-tailed lemurs, Patagonian conures, African cheetahs, a Nile hippopotamus, bears, flamingoes, Siberian tigers, giraffes, elephants, and more. The reptile house has a particularly complete collection.

A sloth bear at the Sacramento Zoo

The Sacramento Zoo and Sacramento Zoological Society sponsor a number of programs to help improve the zoo and increase community involvement. Through the "Adopt-an-Animal" program, you can choose an animal from among the zoo's holdings and pay an "adoption" fee, which goes toward improving the animals' habitat at the zoo. (No, you don't get to take the animal home with you!) Every spring a "Photo Days" weekend is held, during which photographers are admitted for a reduced fee. Special activities are arranged, such as feedings of the giraffes, cheetahs, and great apes and "arctic ice floes" for the polar bears. Photographers are then encouraged to submit their photos for the zoo's annual calendar. A number of summer classes for children are also offered, including a Zoo Overnight Camp where children explore the zoo at night by flashlight. Guides lead general zoo tours year-round.

The zoo's facilities include concession stands, picnic tables (bring a picnic lunch), a gift booth, stroller rentals, and wheelchair ramps (restrooms are not wheelchair accessible). The zoo is open year-round. And remember, please don't feed the animals; it's not good for them. For information call the zoo at 449-5885.

FAIRYTALE TOWN

Just across the street from the zoo is Fairytale Town, a three-acre theme park for children. Kids love playing in and on the twenty-six miniature sets depicting scenes from children's stories and nursery rhymes such as "The Three Little Pigs," "Cinderella," and "The Old Lady Who Lived in a Shoe." They can climb the rigging of a pirate ship and visit King Arthur's Castle and Sherwood Forest. There's also a petting zoo where they can get to know baby farm animals such as lambs, pigs, and goats. On weekend afternoons, puppet shows, dance acts, and skits are performed in a children's theater. The Sacramento Community Services Department sponsors a number of summer events and workshops for children at Fairytale Town, including parades, contests, day camps, and classes in drama, crafts, and puppetry. King Arthur's Castle and Sherwood Forest are available for birthday parties and group gatherings. For information call 449-5233.

Nearby is a small children's amusement park with concession-operated rides and pony rides. The park and pony rides are operated on weekends in the winter (weather permitting) and daily during the summer.

Cal Expo

Home of the California State Fair, Waterworld USA, and the Golden State Raceway, Cal Expo is a seven-hundred-acre fairground offering events year-round. Located five miles from downtown, the facility is just off Business 80 at 1600 Exposition Boulevard. Throughout the year there are numerous events such as rodeos, motocross and horse racing, livestock auctions, cat and dog shows, car shows, and trade shows. During the summer, harness racing is held at the Golden State Raceway.

The main attraction is the California State Fair, which has been held in Sacramento since 1861 and at Cal Expo since 1968. Held every year during

The California State Fair

the last week of August and the first week of September, the fair features big-name entertainment, agriculture exhibits, art shows, a carnival with midway rides and games, and pony rides and petting zoos for children. Special events include a State Fair Rodeo, a Wild West show, and pari-mutuel horse racing. A mile-long monorail takes sightseers around the grounds, which include a recently constructed 10,000-seat amphitheater. For information on the state fair and other events, call Cal Expo at 924-2000. Cal Expo has been having financial troubles in recent years and its future as the home of the state fair is uncertain.

During the summer months, kids and adults can cool their heels at Waterworld USA, a fourteen-acre aquatic park at Cal Expo that boasts the world's largest water slide. Waterworld USA has a total of six water slides that offer something for thrill-seekers of all ages; you ride down the slides on special mats at speeds of 10 to 40 m.p.h. Other attractions include skeeter, bumper, and paddle boats, pools, picnic areas, games, an electronic arcade, food, entertainment, and lockers (be sure to bring a bathing suit). For information call 924-0555.

California State University, Sacramento

Located at the eastern edge of the city about three and a half miles from downtown, California State University, Sacramento, is the seventh largest of nineteen campuses in the California State University system. Sac State, as it is called by the locals, was established in 1947 and shared facilities with Sacramento City College until 1953, when it moved to its present location at 6000 J Street. The three-hundred-acre, tree-covered campus is nestled on the banks of the American River, which is spanned by a footbridge resembling a miniature Golden Gate. Built in 1967, the Guy West Bridge is a twin-tower suspension bridge named for the university's founding president.

Sac State is basically a commuter college, with only about 5 percent of its twenty-two thousand students living on campus. The majority of the students (65 percent) are residents of Sacramento County. Bachelor's and master's degrees are offered in more than fifty fields, with computer science and electronic engineering the largest and most popular programs. The university sponsors many events year-round that are open to the public, including lectures, films, concerts, exhibits, and plays. From October to April, the University Theatre offers full-scale theatrical productions. Serious plays in a more intimate setting are offered during the same period at the Playwright's Theatre. The Robert Else Gallery and the Witt Gallery offer changing exhibitions of contemporary and student art, respectively.

Campus tours are given by student tour guides, and you may sit in on a class lecture if you wish. For tour information, call 278-6523. For general information on Sac State, call 278-6011.

Other Sacramento Schools and Colleges

Besides Sac State, several postsecondary schools and colleges are located within the city and county of Sacramento, including three community colleges, three law schools, eight top-notch performing arts schools, numerous trade and technical schools, and even a nannie college. Nearby in Yolo County is the University of California at Davis.

Established in 1916, Sacramento City College is the city's oldest college. It's located at 3835 Freeport Boulevard, just across from William Land Park. Serving the central portion of the city, the sixty-acre campus has a mix of old and new tile-roofed brick buildings in a pleasant setting of expansive lawns, large trees, and a variety of flowering shrubs. A two-year college, Sacramento City College has sixteen thousand students who can choose from nearly one thousand courses and more than forty-five majors in which associate degrees and certificates of achievement are offered. There's also a full program of community education classes, most of which have low fees and are short-term, on both day and evening schedules.

In addition to academic programs, the school offers a variety of services and programs for the community, many of which are free or low-cost. Inexpensive dental and hair care services are offered through the college's dental clinic and school of cosmetology. The Gregory Kondos Art Gallery features changing exhibits of contemporary regional art. The Sacramento City Actor's Theater performs five plays during the school year at the school's Art

Court Theatre, with Shakespeare and classical performances during the summer. And the music department offers concerts and recitals during the year. Hughes Stadium is the site of collegiate sporting events and other year-round events such as the Sacramento Blues Festival in September and the annual Pig Bowl in January (Sacramento City Police vs. County Sheriffs). The Sacramento City College Observatory offers inexpensive guided tours of its facilities, which include a powerful telescope and star charts. Located on the roof of the Rodda Hall South Building, the observatory is open by reservation only. For tour reservations and general information on Sacramento City College, call 449-7443.

Sacramento's two other community colleges are American River College, serving the north area (near I-80 and Madison, 484-8100), and Cosumnes River College, serving the south area (near Highway 99 and Mack Road, 686-7451).

California's first nannie college opened its doors in 1983 in Sacramento. The California Nannie College offers a 12-week course to train professionals in the art of caring for children. Classes include child-rearing, child development, creative play, nutrition, and health and safety. Experience at local day-care centers is included. (To clear up any confusion that may arise over terminology, a nannie is involved solely in child care, whereas a governess tutors and can administer formal education.) In Great Britain, a bastion of nanniedom, there are more than 150 nannie colleges turning out some two thousand nannies a year. More information on the California Nannie College, which also helps graduates find jobs, is available at 484-0163.

Founded in 1976, the Learning Exchange is an independent organization providing short-term courses for adults in a wide and eclectic variety of subjects. The class catalog is published six times a year, offering an average of 150 classes in subject areas ranging from arts and crafts, computers, and personal growth to singles, fashion, and sports. It's sort of a "university without walls" concept; classes are held at teachers' homes, in churches, and at other Sacramento locations. Free catalogues are available at many restaurants, bookstores, and other public places or from the Learning Exchange at 2384 Fair Oaks Boulevard, 972-9242.

UNIVERSITY OF CALIFORNIA, DAVIS

The University of California, Davis (UCD), is located in the city of Davis about fifteen miles west of Sacramento on I-80. With nineteen thousand students, the university has one of the largest and most comprehensive agricultural programs in the nation. In addition to its other colleges, UCD has graduate professional schools in administration, law, medicine, and veterinary medicine (the only veterinary medicine school in the state). UCD is also the site of the California Primate Research Center. The UCD School of

Medicine operates the University of California, Davis, Medical Center in Sacramento. UC Davis Extension offers a variety of short-term classes throughout the year, many of which are available in Sacramento. Call 752-0880 to get on the mailing list for the *Venture* extension catalogue, published four times a year.

The campus offers an extensive program of community and cultural events open to the public. UCD is known for its fine art galleries, and performances by well-known entertainers are offered, as well as lectures by prominent speakers.

A favorite locale for a spring stroll is the UCD arboretum, stretching for nearly two miles along Putah Creek. More than 1,600 varieties of flowers, shrubs, and trees are on display, all of which require little irrigation or maintenance. Admission to the arboretum is free, and it's open year-round. Parking is available at Lot 47 on La Rue Road across from the arboretum headquarters, where you can purchase self-guided tour pamphlets. Free guided tours are available every weekend.

UCD's cure for spring fever is the annual Picnic Day sponsored by the Associated Students. Held in April, the outdoor festival attracts close to seventy-five thousand people who enjoy parades, floats, exhibits, water shows, a horse show, skydiving exhibitions, and concerts. (The dachshund race is not to be missed.) Another popular UCD event is the Whole Earth Festival in early May. It's like a mini–Renaissance fair with music, arts and crafts, food, and entertainment. Admission is free to both events. For more information on UCD programs and events, call 752-1011.

Surrounded by farmland planted in tomatoes, barley, and fruit orchards, the city of Davis (pop. 40,000) is known primarily as a college town. Davis has achieved international recognition for its dedication to the practical application of solar energy and ecological principles. It's a friendly, progressive city of tree-lined streets and bicycle lanes (Davis boasts one bicycle for nearly every resident). The Palms Public Playhouse and the Blue Mango are popular spots for entertainment and dining.

2

Old Sacramento:
Yesterday and Today

It is a warm summer evening at the Embarcadero. A gentle delta breeze rustles the moored schooners' riggings against massive wooden masts. The golden light of the setting sun's waning rays bathes the wooden and brick buildings, casting long shadows along the rutted roads and planked sidewalks. A stagecoach arrives in a swirl of dust and pounding hooves, and in the distance a riverboat's whistle pierces the air. As the gas streetlights are lit and twilight settles upon the riverfront, the sounds of a honky-tonk piano, clinking glasses, and laughter drift from a nearby saloon.

The place is Old Sacramento, and this scenario was likely repeated many times during its heyday from 1850 to the 1870s. This is the site of the birth of Sacramento and some of the most important and colorful events in the history of California and America. Old Sacramento was the main riverboat landing for Sutter's Fort, the gateway to the gold country, the birthplace of the transcontinental railway, and the western terminus of the Pony Express and of telegraph and stagecoach lines. Here you'll find the site where ground was broken for the West's first railway, the pioneer chambers of the California Supreme Court, the Wells Fargo offices, and the early offices of the oldest continually published newspaper in the West, the *Sacramento Union*.

Historically, the original city of Sacramento extended far beyond the present boundaries of Old Sacramento, which was the heart of the commer-

35

Lithograph depicting Sacramento in 1849 (courtesy California State Library Collection, City of Sacramento, Museum and History Division)

cial business district. By the late 1850s the city had grown eastward from the Sacramento River to Thirty-first Street (Alhambra Boulevard) and was bounded on the north by the American River and on the south by Y Street (Broadway). The ravages of time, progress, and redevelopment took their toll on the old city, but a portion of it has been preserved as a historical restoration project. The term *Old Sacramento* is a modern one used to refer to this project. In the old days it was simply called Sacramento or Sacramento City.

The area that is known today as Old Sacramento is bounded by I-5 and downtown Sacramento on the east, the Sacramento River on the west, Capitol Mall on the south and the I Street Bridge on the north. This twenty-eight-acre area boasts more buildings and sites dating back to the Gold Rush than any other city on the Pacific Coast. Within its ten blocks are more than sixty authentic structures that have been restored to the 1850–1870 period, and the restoration continues. Old Sacramento has been designated a national historic landmark and has been referred to as "the Williamsburg of the West."

Old Sacramento wasn't always such a picture-postcard scene. As was the case with many 19th-century cities, Old Sacramento after its glory days became an industrial area dominated by train yards, warehouses, cheap

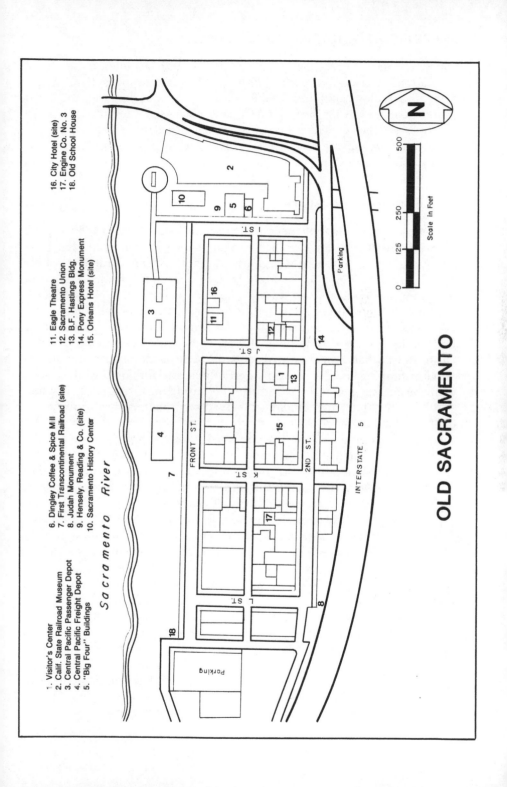

1. Visitor's Center
2. Calif. State Railroad Museum
3. Central Pacific Passenger Depot
4. Central Pacific Freight Depot
5. "Big Four" Buildings

6. Dingley Coffee & Spice Mll
7. First Transcontinental Railroad (site)
8. Judah Monument
9. Hensely. Reading & Co. (site)
10. Sacramento History Center

11. Eagle Theatre
12. Sacramento Union
13. B.F. Hastings Bldg.
14. Pony Express Monument
15. Orleans Hotel (site)

16. City Hotel (site)
17. Engine Co. No. 3
18. Old School House

Sacramento River

FRONT ST.

INTERSTATE 5

2ND ST.

Parking

Scale in Feet

0   125   250   500

OLD SACRAMENTO

hotels, and bars. As recently as the mid-1950s, Old Sacramento was one of the nation's worst slums—a red-light district that supported transients, crime, tuberculosis, and fires. In the late 1960s it came close to being razed entirely to make way for the new I-5 freeway. Thanks to the efforts of a group of people who recognized the historical importance of the area, however, Old Sacramento was spared and has been restored to provide a glimpse into Sacramento's past.

The Founding of a City

The first permanent settlement in the area was established in 1839 by John Augustus Sutter. The enterprising German-Swiss immigrant had been given a forty-eight-thousand-acre Mexican land grant near the confluence of the American and Sacramento rivers. He built a fort on high ground a couple of miles east of the Sacramento River and called his settlement New Helvetia. The pioneer outpost became a haven for weary travelers and a center for trade. Hoping to attract settlers, Sutter planned a town two miles south of the Embarcadero on the Sacramento River, to be called Sutterville. He had created the Embarcadero (the area now called Old Sacramento) primarily as a port for shipping because of the dangerous potential for flooding in the area. Many businesses had begun to locate either inside the fort or close to it, and as ruler of his little kingdom, Sutter seemed secure in his absolute power— until that fateful day in 1848.

Sutter had contracted James W. Marshall, a thirty-seven-year-old carpenter, to build a sawmill about fifty miles east of New Helvetia on the American River in the Sierra foothills. On January 24, 1848, while inspecting the mill's water channel, Marshall discovered gold, thus precipitating one of the most exciting events in history: the California Gold Rush.

Sam Brannan, a Mormon pioneer businessman who would later become California's first millionaire, had left San Francisco a couple of years earlier to establish a store outside Sutter's Fort. He had been eyeing the Embarcadero as an ideal spot to set up shop, because it was closer to the shipping action. After the discovery of gold, he moved his business to the Embarcadero. Brannan, a born promoter, decided to help spread the word of the gold strike. The legend holds that he went to San Francisco and, with a bottle of gold dust in one hand and his beaver hat in the other, stood in the streets waving his arms wildly and shouting, "Gold, gold, gold from the American River!"

Things went from bad to worse for Sutter. Some shaky investments were plaguing him, and he was forced to sell some of his holdings. Sutter's son, John Jr., had arrived in New Helvetia earlier, and Sutter had turned his business dealings over to him, thinking he had an ally in his son. However, the younger Sutter teamed up with Brannan in his efforts to develop the Embarcadero as a trade center instead of Sutterville. Sutter Jr. and Brannan hired Captain William Warren to survey the Embarcadero in the winter of 1848, and they named it Sacramento City.

To pay off his father's debts, John Sutter, Jr., auctioned off business lots at the Embarcadero in January 1849. The lots sold fast at $500 each, and by June they were going for $5,000. At the time there were only a couple of log cabins at the Embarcadero and fewer than 150 people living in the Sutter's Fort area. But as a torrent of humanity began to pour into the area, the Embarcadero became the primary supply center for the miners, and Sacramento City was on its way. Sutterville was quickly forgotten as all attention focused on the new city. The rush for gold would cause Captain Sutter to see his crops trampled, his cattle stolen, his fort abandoned, and his dreams of an empire dashed to bits.

BOOMTOWN ON THE RIVER

As the Gold Rush gained momentum, merchants at Sutter's Fort found it more convenient to load their mine-bound goods at the Embarcadero. Because the debarkation point for the miners was the waterfront, that's where they moved their businesses. By June 1848 there were thirty buildings at the Embarcadero used for stores and warehouses, along with more than one hundred houses. Construction was ramshackle and makeshift; the builders often used wood and canvas taken from ships moored nearby. By October Sacramento's population numbered more than two thousand.

Hensley & Reading Co. built what is believed to be Sacramento's first business structure and moored its storeship on the nearby riverbank. After Sam Brannan moved to the Embarcadero, he, too, moored his storeship on the banks of the Sacramento. These and many other hulls took the place of warehouses in the days when storage space and building materials were at a premium; ships also served for a time as a post office and the city jail. By the end of 1849, Sacramento had become a real waterfront city, with well-defined streets and many buildings such as saloons, stores, one of California's first hotels, and the state's first theater, the Eagle. In just ten short years, Sacramento had been transformed from wilderness to city.

As the gateway to the mines, Sacramento became the terminus of the greatest migration the world had seen since the Crusades of the 13th century. As the center of banking and express between the diggings and San Francisco, it became the major supply and commercial center for the miners, supplying provisions from the rapidly growing and prospering town at highly inflated prices.

Bret Harte captured much of the color and flavor of the '49ers in his stories "The Outcasts of Poker Flat" and "The Luck of Roaring Camp." An authentic pioneer song reflects the spirit of the times:

> Oh, California, that's the land for me!
> I'm bound for the Sacramento
> With a washbowl on my knee.

Sacramento was a boomtown, with sales in the thousands of dollars daily and all the trappings. Gambling halls were plentiful, especially along J Street, the gambling center, where games like monte, faro, and fantan were played. Sacramento's first sheriff, in fact, was a professional gambler. Saloons flourished, along with assay offices, banks, hotels, and the ever-important provision stores.

Everything was outrageously overpriced, but who cared? Gold was so plentiful that for a time the miners didn't even bother to hide their booty; they left it lying around in bags and on tabletops. Lumber sold for $1 a board foot, milk for $1 a quart, and bread for 50 cents a loaf. Store clerks made $500 a month (when they could be kept away from the diggings, that is). For lack of better lodgings, hundreds of goldseekers were forced to camp and sleep in the open. But no one seemed to mind much—not when suffering from "gold fever."

FIRE, FLOOD, AND DISEASE

If 1849 represented the best of all times for Sacramento, then 1850 was the worst. Sutter had chosen his site for Sutterville wisely—high ground safe from flooding. Sacramento, however, couldn't have been in a worse location, and with January's heavy rains came the overflowing of the Sacramento and American rivers. For a mile beyond the Embarcadero, the city was under several feet of water, with heavy losses of life and property. After the waters receded, the first levees were constructed.

Soon after the flood, on April 4, 1850, the city had its first serious fire. At least eight buildings were destroyed. The city was highly susceptible to fire, since most of the buildings were made of wood and much of the light at that time was provided by oil lamps and torches. But the worst was yet to come. On October 18, 1850, the steamship *Oregon* arrived in San Francisco. It was a joyous occasion, for the ship was carrying the news that California had been admitted to the Union. On board, however, was a passenger with cholera who continued his trip by riverboat to Sacramento. The disease spread swiftly and widely, with as many as sixty deaths a day. In panic, four-fifths of the population of Sacramento fled, and by November, when the epidemic ended, more than six hundred people had been buried in long trenches at the Sacramento City Cemetery.

There was no stopping the burgeoning city, however, and in spite of these disasters it continued to grow. By 1852 the population had grown to more than twelve thousand. In the year between April 1852 and April 1853, 410 ships arrived at the Embarcadero, delivering 165,000 tons of freight. The area was covered with tents and sheds, piles of lumber, covered wagons, and an auction ring between the river and Front Street buildings. Business was growing by leaps and bounds.

Then came the disastrous fire of November 2, 1852. Heavy north winds fanned the inferno, which started in a millinery shop. Most of the buildings from the waterfront to Eighth Street were destroyed, and seven-eighths of the city was left in ruins. At that time, Sacramento had five hundred business buildings and two thousand residents. With few exceptions, all of the pioneer business structures were destroyed, with damages totaling nearly $6 million. The city rebuilt, however, and this time new city ordinances required all commercial buildings to be built with fireproof materials.

Until 1853, little attention had been paid to Sacramento's sidewalks and streets. Much of the time they were muddy mires that were difficult to navigate. One poetic observer expressed his thoughts on a sign nailed to the side of a building:

> *This road is not passable*
> *Not even jackassable;*
> *When that you travel,*
> *Pray take your own gravel.*

That year the streets were graded and planked with Oregon fir and California pine three and a half inches thick, and in 1854 a new ordinance required that wood, stone, or brick be used to construct streets and sidewalks.

The city was again hit by major flooding in March 1852, and the people decided it was time to do something to remedy the problem once and for all. A proposal was made to raise the city above the river's flood level with fill dirt. When the project was begun in 1853, J Street was raised about four feet above its original level. At that time it was also first proposed that the level of the streets be raised up to six feet and the buildings raised on screw jacks, the spaces to be filled in with brick and lumber. Although the plan met with a degree of approval, it wasn't until after the disastrous flood of 1862 that the idea was totally accepted. Thousands of tons of dirt were transported by wagon, and by 1873 Sacramento's entire business district (including parts of I, J, K, and L streets and connecting cross streets) was raised eight feet. The bed of the American River was also straightened and moved further north of the city. Higher levees were built around the urban center. As a result, the city was finally relatively safe from inundation.

During the street-raising era, many streets were surfaced with gravel or river cobble. During the 1880s and 1890s, the streets were paved with cobblestones quarried near Folsom and transported to Sacramento on the Sacramento Valley Railroad. The cobblestones can still be seen along Front Street and in the alleys between Front and Second streets. Evidence of how far the city was raised can by seen at the centers of alleys in the middle of blocks and in the underground spaces under Old Sacramento's sidewalks, especially at the corner of Second and I (in the patio of Fulton's Prime Rib) and in the lower level of the Stanford Brothers Warehouse at Front and L streets.

PROGRESS TAKES ITS TOLL

The birth of the Central Pacific Railroad in the 1860s had a major impact on Sacramento. All materials needed in the construction of the railroad were shipped around Cape Horn to Sacramento, which became a staging area for the railroad. The railroad was among the city's leading employers, and maintenance and repair facilities sprang up to the north. The scene along the Embarcadero had grown much more complex, with railroad tracks, trains, depots, sheds, docks, and horsedrawn streetcars as well as piers and ships. During this time Sacramento was developing as an important agricultural trade center, yet remaining a center for commercial business. The city continued to grow and prosper and by 1870 had a population of 24,640.

The area maintained its commercial importance into the 20th century, but as more sophisticated forms of communication and transportation came into use, the importance of the river declined, and the city grew away from the waterfront. Commerce began moving east, and there was a gradual decline in the area west of Third Street. Warehouses, skid-row rooming houses and hotels, second-hand stores, and saloons characterized Old Sacramento well into the mid-1960s. Many of the original buildings from the 1850 to 1870 period were crumbling, and there was talk of tearing down the entire area when I-5 was being planned.

The efforts of historians and the Sacramento Redevelopment Agency saved the historic area from an unceremonious death, and painstaking care has been taken to return the city to its original look and feel. The project is an ongoing one, with more and more buildings being restored, relocated, or rebuilt. Restoration guidelines require that the exteriors of the buildings be historically accurate and that authentic materials, including the original brick, be used wherever possible. Wavy wooden plank sidewalks have been restored, and the streets have been paved with cobblestones. Romantic streetlights designed to look like 1860s gas lamps were added to provide another touch of authenticity. The end result is a visual and historical delight. Eventually more than one hundred restored and reconstructed buildings will grace Old Sacramento.

Future plans include a massive $13 million riverfront conversion project that will convert four and a half acres along the riverfront into a replica of the 1855–1870 period. The waterfront will feature two historical recreations: an 1870s wharf reflecting the railroad and river commerce that spurred Sacramento's growth and an 1840s landing area at the place where Gold Rush settlers founded the city. The plan calls for replicas of Gold Rush–era ships to be built and moored on the waterfront. The *Delta King,* a majestic paddlewheeler that steamed its way up the Sacramento River between Sacramento and San Francisco in the 1920s and 1930s, has been restored and is now moored at the wharf. The five-story "king of paddlewheelers" features restaurants, shops, a convention center, a dinner theater, and cabins and suites on its upper decks.

Just south of the Old Sacramento wharf between the Tower and Pioneer bridges is the site of a planned $40 million riverfront development anchored by a hotel and water museum. Called the Docks, the eleven-acre project located on the east bank of the river will also include a modern marina with up to one hundred berths, as well as waterfront shops, restaurants, and other attractions.

A Walk into the Past

Because Old Sacramento is such a perfect blending of the old and new, there are at least two ways you can enjoy your visit. One is from the historical point of view, immersing yourself in the district's colorful history and retracing the steps of the famous, the not-so-famous, and the infamous. The other way is just to wander around, taking in the sights, doing a little shopping, and enjoying a meal or snack at one of many eateries.

After you park your car in the roomy garage under I-5, you should first make your way to the Visitors Center (1 on the map, 443-7815) at 130 J Street, which also houses a post office. The staff there will help you with any questions you have, and you'll find a good selection of brochures and books on Old Sacramento. For history buffs, a good book is Robert Miller's *Guide to Old Sacramento.* (Cars will eventually be banned from the streets here, but until they are, make sure you look before crossing the street.)

History comes alive in Old Sacramento. It's pretty hard to walk more than a few steps in any direction and not come face to face with a building or site that figured in Sacramento's early history (there are fourteen state historical landmarks here). A portion of the area is designated a state historic park. Run and maintained by the state, the park includes the California State Railroad Museum, the Central Pacific Passenger Depot, the "Big Four" Buildings, the Eagle Theatre, and the B. F. Hastings Building.

With more than sixty authentic buildings remaining, it's difficult to choose just a few of the noteworthy. What follows is a look at some of the more outstanding buildings and sites. Entries have been loosely organized into a walking tour, with each entry numbered to correspond with the map. Of course, you may start at any point or create your own order. A little romanticism and a lot of imagination will help at parking lots or vacant lots where buildings once stood or important events occurred. Because Old Sacramento is constantly being developed, it is quite possible you will find some new additions or changes.

Walking tours are available on Saturdays and Sundays at 10:30 A.M. and 1:30 P.M. beginning at the Central Pacific Passenger Depot at Front and J streets. The hour-long, free tours are conducted by costumed guides who will tell the history of fires, floods, the Gold Rush, and the railroad. For tour information call 323-9278.

C. P. Huntington *locomotive, California State Railroad Museum*

California State Railroad Museum (2)

The California State Railroad Museum is part of the Railroad Museum complex that includes the Central Pacific Passenger Depot and Freight Depot and the "Big Four" Buildings, all part of Old Sacramento Historic Park, which is operated by the California Department of Parks and Recreation.

Opened in May 1981 at a cost of $14 million, the museum houses one of the world's largest collections of railroad relics in its 100,000 square feet of exhibit space and is regarded as the finest interpretive rail museum in the country. The five-acre site houses twenty-two restored locomotives and cars and forty interpretive exhibits. In the first two years of operation, more than one million people visited the museum. This is probably the closest you'll ever come to experiencing the sights and sounds of more than one hundred years of railroad history. Brochures for self-guided tours are available, and the museum is fully wheelchair accessible.

There are two 145-seat theaters where you first see a seven-minute slide show and then an impressive twelve-minute film about the history of Western railroading. Next you'll take a step back into history as you enter a gigantic diorama, the largest of its kind in the world. Titled "The Sierra Scene," it authentically recreates an 1865 railroad camp at Donner Summit high in the Sierra in the dead of winter. The ten-thousand-square-foot, full-scale diorama depicts the most grueling and difficult task that faced the builders of the transcontinental railroad: fighting the bitter cold, snow, and ice to chisel a track through solid granite. The centerpiece is Sacramento's first locomotive, the *Governor Stanford* (Central Pacific No. 1), a forty-ton, woodburning steam locomotive built in 1862 in Philadelphia, then disassembled and shipped to San Francisco.

You leave the exhibit through a tunnel with simulated snow-covered granite to enter the Great Hall, the museum's main exhibit area. Everywhere are vintage locomotives and passenger and freight cars in realistic settings. Among the most popular are the delightfully whimsical *C. P. Huntington* (Southern Pacific No. 1), built in 1863 and Southern Pacific's first locomotive; and Cab-Ahead No. 4294, the last steam engine purchased by Southern Pacific and the last of its kind in the world. Many of the cars and locomotives on display are completely functional and could be put into use today.

Don't expect to be just an observer as you go through the museum. Inside the *St. Hyacinthe,* a Canadian National Railways Pullman sleeper built in 1929, you experience the sounds and motion of a moving train. The car sways, the lights dim, the wheels clack, and lights flash by the windows simulating a passing train.

Every September, the museum hosts the U.S. National Handcar Races. Teams from throughout the country compete on tracks adjacent to the museum. Museum hours are 10–5 daily (445-7373).

CENTRAL PACIFIC PASSENGER DEPOT (3)

The Central Pacific Passenger Depot served as the western terminus of the first transcontinental railroad. Built in 1867, the station was a revolving door for thousands of travelers on their way east and west. The reconstruction of the depot is built on the same site as the original, and sitting in a waiting room replete with sights and sounds designed to simulate the feeling of 1876, it's easy to imagine yourself being carried more than one hundred years back in time.

Exhibits include three 1870s vintage locomotives, two 19th-century passenger coaches, and a 1908 Northwestern Pacific 4-6-0 engine. The station tracks are connected to the Railroad Museum with a turntable so rolling stock exhibits may be changed. On summer weekends a steam train takes riders on a short trip to Land Park (a longer route is planned). Passengers may board the excursion trains nearby from the passenger platform at the reconstructed Central Pacific Freight Depot (4).

"Big Four" Buildings (5)

The "Big Four" Buildings are two separate buildings: the Stanford Brothers Building on the left and the Huntington and Hopkins Hardware Store in the center. To the right is the Dingley Coffee and Spice Mill (6). The first two were originally located at 220–224 K Street, under the present-day I-5 freeway. They were demolished to make way for the freeway in 1966 but were reconstructed in 1969 on the present site using the original brick. The exteriors have been restored to their 1867–1869 appearance.

The Stanford Building was built in 1852 and served as a wholesale merchandise store for grocer Leland Stanford. Collis P. Huntington built his hardware store after the 1852 fire; it provided the miners' needs, from shovels and blasting powder to pitch and rubber hoses. The "Big Four" who gave these buildings their name were Leland Stanford, Mark Hopkins, Collis P. Huntington, and Charles Crocker, founders of the Central Pacific Railroad.

The Huntington and Hopkins Hardware Store is now operated as a museum exhibiting a history of hardware technology. The California Railroad Museum Library and Art Gallery with its extensive non-circulating book and archival collections is located upstairs, along with the "Big Four" boardroom where the idea of the transcontinental railroad was first proposed. The collection emphasizes the railroads of California, Nevada, and the West. Materials include reference works, monographs, and periodicals. The hardware store is open daily 10–5, and the research library is open Tuesday through Saturday 1–5; both are free (445-7373).

The Dingley Coffee and Spice Mill was built in 1852 by Nathaniel Dingley, whose original mill on Front Street was destroyed by the fire of 1852. His trade extended throughout Northern California and Nevada. Restored by the state in 1969, the building now houses Milepost 1, the Railroad Museum's gift shop and bookstore operated by the Pacific Coast Chapter of the Railway and Locomotive Historical Society. Railroad fans will delight in the vast collection of railroad books, models, and other assorted items.

BIRTH OF THE
TRANSCONTINENTAL RAILROAD

Although the "Big Four" reaped the accolades and profit for the idea (they all became millionaires), it was dreamer, lobbyist, and visionary Theodore Dehone Judah who really deserves the credit for the transcontinental railroad. Judah was a brilliant young Connecticut-born civil engineer who came west to plan and build the West's first railroad. Completed in 1855 at a cost of $1 million, the Sacramento Valley Railroad stretched twenty-two miles from Sacramento to Negro Bar (Folsom) and removed a full day from the trip from Sacramento to the mines.

At the time it was built, the railroad line was considered necessary only to ship mine-bound goods. But Judah had much grander plans. His real dream was to build a railroad that would cross the continent, and he was the first to survey the Sierra Nevada for a suitable route. After initial attempts at locating financial support met with opposition and ridicule, Judah finally found his way to the "Big Four," who were the first to take him seriously. These four businessmen backed Judah and on June 28, 1861, founded the Central Pacific Railroad Company. Leland Stanford, thirty-six, became president; his thirty-nine-year-old partner, Collis Huntington, was vice president; and Mark Hopkins, forty-seven, became their treasurer. The three were later joined by Charles Crocker, a thirty-eight-year-old dry–goods store owner. Judah was to be the railroad's chief engineer.

Judah traveled again to Washington and was instrumental in the passage of the Pacific Railroad Act, signed by President Lincoln on July 1, 1862. The bill provided a government land subsidy to the builders of the railroad, consisting of 1,280,000 acres of public lands for each one hundred miles of completed track. On January 8, 1863, ground was broken by Leland Stanford, by then governor of California, at the foot of Front and K streets (7).

Soon afterward, a dispute arose over the route of the proposed railroad, and Judah was squeezed out of his decision-making role in the company. In October 1863 he traveled to New York to find new backers to buy out the other partners, but he contracted yellow fever while crossing the Isthmus of Panama. He died a week after his arrival in New York at the age of 38, never to see his dream come to fruition. The only public recognition of his efforts is a monument of California granite with bronze elements that was erected originally at Fourth and I. Commissioned by the employees of the Southern Pacific Railroad Company, successor to the Central Pacific, it now stands at Second and L streets (8).

Six years after his death, Judah's dream was realized on a lonely plateau at Promontory, Utah. On May 10, 1869, Governor Leland Stanford drove in the final golden spike in a ceremony completing the railroad. The historic moment is depicted in Thomas Hill's painting, *Driving of the Last Spike,* once housed in Sacramento's capitol and now on display at the Railroad Museum. The East and the West were now linked by rail, and the golden promise of the West was accessible to all.

HENSLEY, READING & CO. (9)

Directly to the west of the "Big Four" Complex is what is believed to be the site of the first frame structure in the city of Sacramento. Samuel Hensley and Pierson Reading came to California by wagon train in 1843 and were hired by Captain John Sutter when they arrived in Sacramento. They operated a trading post inside Fort Sutter but were lured to the Embarcadero by the mining trade. They built their two-story store in 1849, selling supplies to the miners. They also moored their storeship, a 250-ton Peruvian bark, to the riverbank. The store was one of only two structures built before August 1849 that remained standing after the fire of 1852.

Sacramento History Center (10)

The Sacramento History Center is housed in an exact replica of Sacramento's first city hall and water works, which stood on this site from 1854 to 1912. A reservoir on the roof of the original building provided the city's first water system, one of the first municipal water systems on the West Coast. Most of the city's government was located here, with offices for the mayor, marshall, assessor, collector, and surveyor, as well as the council chambers, jury room, and city jail, which was the scene of several executions by hanging.

The Sacramento History Center, which opened in 1985, is the only regional history museum, archive, and visitor center in the Sacramento metropolitan area. The historical exterior of the two-story, $5 million center belies its high-tech interior. In an ultramodern environment of gleaming chrome, stainless steel, black slate floors, mirrored ceilings, and glossy white walls, the newest technological advances have been used to create a showplace for the Sacramento Valley's past, present, and future.

Within 19,500 square feet of exhibit space, some two thousand artifacts and documents are displayed in four galleries or theme exhibition areas. Sacramento's story is told using such media as video, authentic audio, participatory activities, and a computerized retrieval system. By touching the screens of video monitors located in the galleries, visitors can retrieve historical information and programming from the center's 600,000-photograph library, hundreds of thousands of feet of TV news film, or hundreds of newspapers.

Four "Sacramento Valley Story" galleries tell the story of Sacramento's social, cultural, and material history. The Topomorphology Gallery has four major exhibits showing how humans have manipulated and altered their environment. A highlight is the large gold specimen collection gathered in the gold country by the Bank of America.

The Community Gallery, the largest in terms of floor space, illustrates the growth and development of the Sacramento Valley region, the communities that were formed, and the people who created them. The focus of this exhibit is the ethnic history of the people who have lived here. Visitors can scan thousands of photos on video discs, and if they want more information they can tap into the center's data bank.

The largest gallery in terms of volume, the Agricultural Technology Gallery, showcases agricultural inventions and innovations in the Sacramento Valley. Included are displays of agricultural machinery (much of it functioning) such as tractors, harvesters, milking machines, and a portion of a cannery complete with moving cans. The Eleanor McClatchy Gallery contains rotating exhibitions complementing the other galleries. It features the collection of Eleanor McClatchy, newspaper heiress and arts patron, including early California and Gold Rush newspapers, as well as printing and theater memorabilia. Located within the gallery is a reading room where visitors and scholars can research the archival collections of the center and use the video/computer programs in depth.

The Sacramento History Center/Museum and History Division is administered by the city of Sacramento's Department of Community Services in conjunction with the private, nonprofit History Center Inc. It serves as a repository for the city and county's historic artifacts and archives. Much of the material has been catalogued and indexed for public use. Other resources and services include records for genealogists, a non-circulating library and manuscript collection, historical photos that may be copied, and historic structure authentication.

The Sacramento History Center is open daily from 10–5. Self-guided tour brochures are available, and the center is fully wheelchair accessible. For more information call the center at 447-2057.

Eagle Theatre (11)

Until the fall of 1849, about the only entertainment available to the '49ers was to be found in the gambling halls and saloons. Probably few complained, but some had to believe that there was more to life than beer and burlesque. A little culture, it was thought, would help smooth the rough edges of the rough-and-tumble town.

And so the Eagle Theatre, California's first permanent theater, opened its doors on October 18, 1849, on Front Street at J. Although it was constructed only of wood and canvas with a sheet-iron roof and a dirt floor, the 35-by-60-foot building cost about $75,000, due in part to the inflated costs of labor and materials in the boomtown. Carpenters earned $50 a day while working on the Eagle, as did the fellow who painted the curtain and backdrop.

The opening performance was *The Spectre of the Forest,* with Mrs. Elizabeth Ray of New Zealand's Royal Theatre as leading lady. Among the audience at that performance was Bayard Taylor, author of *El Dorado,* an early description of the Gold Rush days. Taylor wrote:

> Spectators were dressed in heavy overcoats and felt hats, with boots reaching to the knees. . . . The drop curtain, which is down at present, exhibits a glaring landscape, with dark brown trees in the foreground and lilac-colored mountains against a yellow sky.

Despite the less-than-opulent surroundings, the Eagle packed 'em in three times a week during the ten-week season. The theater held about four hundred people, who paid $5 for box seats and $3 for pit seats (usually in gold dust). Like so many other buildings close to the river, however, the Eagle was plagued by flooding. On January 4, 1850, just three short months after opening, the Eagle met its demise during its final performance when the Sacramento River overflowed its banks, flooding the entire Embarcadero. The flooding that night didn't faze the rowdy miners, who remained perched on a railing around the orchestra pit, gleefully shoving each other into the muddy water until the final curtain rang down.

The Eagle Theatre, now a state historical landmark, was reconstructed at its original location in 1975 by the state and the Junior League of Sacramento. Free tours are available Tuesday through Saturday, 10–5 (446-6761). During summer weekends, the Eagle holds melodramas, revues, and plays. *Sacramento Illustrated,* a slick multi-media presentation offered at the theater, makes a fine introduction to Sacramento's history. More than a dozen computer-programmed projectors flash from one to fifteen images on the screen, and separately tracked quadraphonic speakers in each corner of the theater place the audience in the middle of the action as horses and trains travel across the theater screen. Call the Eagle for more information.

Sacramento Union (12)

During its early days, Sacramento was known as the graveyard of newspapers because so many started and later failed. Between 1848 and 1874, some eighty-seven papers, magazines, and other publications were published, but only two survived: the *Sacramento Union* and the *Sacramento Bee.* The oldest continuously published daily newspaper in California, the *Union* got its start on March 19, 1851, as the result of a strike. Two rival newspapers were involved in a rate war and reduced the printers' pay to cut expenses. The printers responded by going on strike and starting their own paper. The original brick building burned down in 1852 and was replaced by a new two-story brick structure in 1853. The reconstructed building now houses the Union Restaurant.

The *Union*'s first editor was Dr. J. F. Morse, a Sacramento historian and physician who saved many lives during the 1850 cholera epidemic. Among the more illustrious writers and journalists who have worked for the *Union* are Bret Harte, Mark Twain, and contemporary columnist Herb Caen, a Sacramento native, who now writes for the *San Francisco Chronicle*. It was the *Union* that commissioned Twain's five-month visit to the Sandwich Islands (Hawaii) in 1866, where he wrote a series of columns on his experiences and impressions.

B. F. Hastings Building (13)

Possibly no other structure in Old Sacramento embodies the spirit of the city's early days more than the B. F. Hastings Building. More historic and courageous enterprises took place here than in any other building in the city. This was the western terminus of the famed Pony Express and the first permanent home of the California Supreme Court. It housed the Sacramento office of Wells Fargo, the Alta California State Telegraph offices, and the office where Theodore Judah planned the western route of the transcontinental railroad.

The building was built in 1852 by Wesley Merritt after his first building on the site, a grocery store, burned down during the 1852 conflagration. Before the new building was completed, Merritt went bankrupt, and it was sold at a sheriff's sale to Benjamin F. Hastings, a pioneer banker who completed it and opened his bank in the corner section in April 1853. Part of the ground floor was leased to clothing merchants, and in early 1854 Wells Fargo and Company moved into a ground-floor space.

The restored building is now operated as a museum as part of Old Sacramento State Historic Park. The Communication Museum exhibits include telegraph sets, antique insulators, and photographs illustrating the era of the telegraph. The Wells Fargo Bank office serves as both a museum and a bank. Upstairs, the old Supreme Court chambers are open to the public, having been restored with authentic furnishings. The museum is open Tuesday through Sunday, 10–5, and admission is free.

THE PONY EXPRESS

The night of April 4, 1860, was cold and rainy. Sam Hamilton mounted his white mustang in front of the B. F. Hastings Building. It was 2:45 A.M., and few people had turned out to bid him farewell on his journey. Hamilton settled into the saddle, spurred his horse, and galloped down J Street out of Sacramento. He rode along the American River and the route of the present

Highway 50 on his sixty-mile run to Sportsman's Hall Station high in the Sierra, where he was met by the next rider. Simultaneously, 1,960 miles away in St. Joseph, Missouri, another rider started on his way west. Thus began the legend of the heroic riders of the Pony Express.

The concept of a pony express was not unique. There had been many in California before transcontinental rail service was established, but none could come close to filling the need facing the organizers of the Pony Express: to carry the mail across the country in only ten days. The operation required two hundred relay stations, five hundred horses, and eighty riders. The horses, primarily mustangs and Mississippi Valley thoroughbreds, were chosen as carefully as the riders, with speed and endurance the most important criteria. The route of the Pony Express roughly followed the overland wagon route, which was dangerous and uncertain.

Riders rode about seventy-five to one hundred miles a day, changing horses at relay stations ten to fifteen miles apart. After the riders arrived in Sacramento, they were put aboard a riverboat for the final leg to San Francisco. About three months after the inauguration of the Pony Express, riders made the twenty-two-mile run between Sacramento and Folsom on the Sacramento Valley Railroad.

It is hard to believe, but the Pony Express lasted just eighteen months. Its demise was signalled by the completion of the transcontinental telegraph line in October 1861. During its short existence, the riders of the Pony Express made 300 trips covering a total distance of 600,000 miles and delivering 34,000 pieces of mail. The Pony Express Monument (14) at Second and J streets commemorates these courageous riders. The bronze statue was created by well-known American sculptor Thomas Holland.

A commemorative ride over the entire 1,960-mile route from St. Joseph to Sacramento was made in 1980. Such rides are now made annually to mark the anniversary of the Pony Express, with descendents of some of the original founders and riders participating. The Pony Express is even revived from time to time when landslides in the Sierra foothills cut off residents' mail service.

Orleans Hotel (15)

The Orleans Hotel was Sacramento's most elegant hotel during the early Gold Rush years. The prefabricated building was built late in 1849 from lumber cut and numbered at eastern mills and shipped around the Horn from New Orleans. Until the middle of 1849, Sacramento's hotels were little more than tents or rough shacks lining the riverbank.

By mid-1849 more recognizable hotels began to appear. The City Hotel (16) on Front Street was Sacramento's first authentic hotel and one of the first in California. But it was no match for the splendid Orleans, one of the largest structures in the city during 1849–1850. During its heyday in the 1850s, the Orleans served as a center of community activity and an unofficial center of California politics, frequented by influential politicians and celebrities. Because of its importance, it was the first structure to be rebuilt after the disastrous fire of 1852. The new Orleans was much larger, rebuilt of brick in only twenty days and six hours; several wings were added later. The rebuilt hotel was even more luxurious and featured three hundred soft beds, elegant parlors, a dining room and bar, a billiard room, and a courtyard with fountains.

Notable guests of the Orleans included newspaperman Horace Greeley and Lola Montez, the notorious and glamorous star of the stage, who stayed for two weeks in July 1853. The California Republican Party was born at a mass meeting held in front of the Orleans on April 19, 1856. The hotel was also the headquarters for the California Stage Company, whose Concord stagecoaches left daily for Marysville, Placerville, and other gold country destinations.

The Orleans began to decline in the 1880s as the city's commercial center moved east to Seventh Street. The building was taken over by a paint company that later became Fuller Paints. The hotel was gutted by fire in 1923 and later razed.

Sacramento Engine Company No. 3 (17)

California's first volunteer fire department, Pioneer Mutual Hook and Ladder No. 1, was organized in Sacramento on March 20, 1850. Volunteer firefighters continued to protect the city until 1872, when Sacramento switched to a professional fire department. The city's early fire department was more than a firefighting group; it also served as a social and political center. Each company had about sixty-five members and its own nickname and motto. The lower floor of the engine house was used for the fire equipment, with the upper floor serving as a reading room and social hall. At first the companies had only hand-operated pumpers with leather hoses held together with rivets.

Engine Company No. 3 was formed on March 27, 1851, and occupied this two-story brick building built in 1853. The company's nickname was the Tigers and its motto was "Always Ready." Its first engine was purchased from the Brooklyn, New York, Fire Department for $1,000. The firehouse remained active until 1919 and is the oldest remaining firehouse in Sacramento. It was the first building to be restored in Old Sacramento and now houses the Firehouse Restaurant.

Old Sacramento Schoolhouse (18)

The Old Sacramento Schoolhouse at Front and L streets is a replica of a one-room schoolhouse as it would have appeared in the Sacramento area during the late 1800s. It is furnished with antiques and reproductions of the era, including desks, a potbellied stove, slates, and McGuffey readers. The schoolhouse is open daily. Student groups can make tour arrangements by calling the Third District PTA, which operates the schoolhouse, at 452-0374.

Old Sacramento Today

The theme of the redevelopment of Old Sacramento has been "Preservation for Use," and it's evident on every block. More than 250 specialty shops, restaurants, saloons, and other businesses make up this splendid 19th-century section of the city. There is a plethora of interesting shops and, unlike many other tourist-oriented shopping areas, much of the merchandise is unique and of high quality. The following is just a sampling of places to browse, have a snack, or spend a little or a lot of money.

The Old Town Gallery, 112 K Street, offers art glass as well as pottery, handcrafted jewelry, and wood sculpture. Across the street at 119 K, the Lady Adams Company, located in the oldest building in Old Sacramento (a state historical landmark), offers a unique collection of music boxes, with more than one thousand to choose from.

Next door at 113 K Street is Evangeline, a popular New Wave gift shop. The store offers a gold mine of goodies for hard-core browsers, with everything from rainbow wigs and Styrofoam granite boulders to buttons, T-shirts, art deco lamps, and piano ashtrays. The Gallery of the American West, on the other side of the Lady Adams Store, has a fine collection of western art and handcrafted American Indian jewelry, including Hopi kachina dolls, Taos Indian moccasins, Navajo rugs, pottery, and baskets.

Heading to Front Street, Kite City at 1201 Front Street has 250 kinds of kites from around the world. For example, you'll find boat kites, plane kites, and a thirty-foot dragon kite. Down the next block is The Emigrants, 1109 Front, specializing in Scandinavian needlework and painted canvases, needlework accessories, and traditional Scandinavian gifts, candles, and holders.

What 19th-century Western town would be complete without a candy store? Old Sacramento offers many to choose from, but for a special treat, take your sweet tooth to Sacramento Sweets, 906 Second Street, where you can sample from a wide array of chocolates and brittles such as cashew brittle, peanut-coconut brittle, mixed-nut glaze, and exotic macadamia-almond-coconut brittle. See the candy being made right in the window and leave your calorie counter at home. Or you might try Almond Plaza down the block at 131 J Street, with its fabulous assortment of almond delights. For a great homemade ice cream cone, try Calico Confections at 1017 Second Street. The shop's shelves are lined with apothecary jars filled with old-fashioned "penny" candies and the specialty is Vic's homemade ice cream, made locally. Next door is Gaylord's Mercantile, an old-fashioned country store stocked with a colorful array of gift items, posters, and general merchandise with an Old Sacramento flavor.

If you want to eat something a bit more substantial than candy and you're not the claustrophobic type, try Fanny Ann's Saloon next door, where you can grab a quick burger or sandwich and a beer. Just about every square inch of its three floors is covered with the oddest assortment of kitsch, junk, memorabilia, and other curiosities, including a full-sized fire engine carriage hanging from the ceiling over the bar. Other quick and cheap eating spots include Dairy Queen at 131 K and Wendy's Hamburgers at 200 K.

Dixieland Jazz, Scottish style

DIXIELAND JAZZ FESTIVAL

Each Memorial Day weekend, Old Sacramento resonates with the toe-tapping sounds of Dixieland jazz. Billed as the largest jazz festival of any type anywhere in the world, Sacramento's Dixieland Jubilee is the ultimate in traditional jazz, attracting upwards of 100,000 devotees to hear more than one hundred bands. Since 1974, the Sacramento Traditional Jazz Society has been putting on this annual extravaganza, which has outgrown its original

Old Sacramento site. During the four-day festival, continuous music can be heard night and day at nearly fifty sites throughout the downtown Sacramento area, from intimate cabarets to outdoor parks to hotel banquet halls. Much of it can be heard for free.

The Jubilee attracts bands from all over the world, including Eastern Bloc nations. Countries represented at past festivals have included Australia, Canada, Finland, Sweden, Denmark, Scotland, England, France, Italy, East Germany, West Germany, Poland, and Hungary. If ever there were an international language, it's got to be music—and one of its dialects is Dixieland.

The festival kicks off with a spirited parade on Friday morning down the K Street Mall to Old Sacramento. Plenty of food and drink is available, but some prices are a bit inflated during the festival, so you might want to pack a picnic lunch to enjoy on one of the many grassy spots in Old Sacramento. If you want to get the most for your money, buy an all-events badge, which will get you into as many events as you could possibly want to go to. Ticket prices for individual events vary with the day and performance. For ticket information, write to Sacramento Dixieland Jubilee, 2787 Del Monte Street, West Sacramento, CA 95691, or call 372-5277. Take note: no cars are allowed in Old Sacramento during this event, but low-fare shuttle buses (free to anyone with a Jubilee badge) are available, and parking outside the festival area is plentiful, especially if you don't mind walking a bit.

While we're on the subject of festivals, Old Sacramento also hosts a rousing Fourth of July celebration—except that it's held on the Third of July (maybe to avoid competition with other events or just to be different). There's an old-fashioned parade, games, costume contests, and fireworks.

3

Downtown Sacramento

Downtown Sacramento just doesn't fit the mold. Although it's the heart of a good-sized city of about 312,000, downtown forces you to throw off any preconceived notions about what an urban area's downtown should look like. Characterized by trees, Victorians, impressive historical architecture, parks, distinct neighborhoods, and an overall relaxed pace, Sacramento's downtown has its own unique identity with the look and feel of a friendly small town—a downright pleasant place to live, work, and visit.

Also known as the central city or "old city," downtown is bounded on the north by the American River, the south by Broadway, the east by Alhambra Boulevard, and the west by the Sacramento River. Because the layout follows a grid pattern with numbered and lettered streets, it's a snap finding your way around. It's also flat, making it ideally suited for walking and bicycling.

The central business district is located in the same area it has occupied for more than a century, north of the capitol along J and K streets. The city and county government centers are in this vicinity, referred to by locals as downtown. The region east of Capitol Park is known as midtown, the heart of which is J, K, and L streets with their variety of specialty shops, businesses, and restaurants. Many state buildings are clustered around the west end of the capitol, although they're also scattered around the central city because of overcrowding.

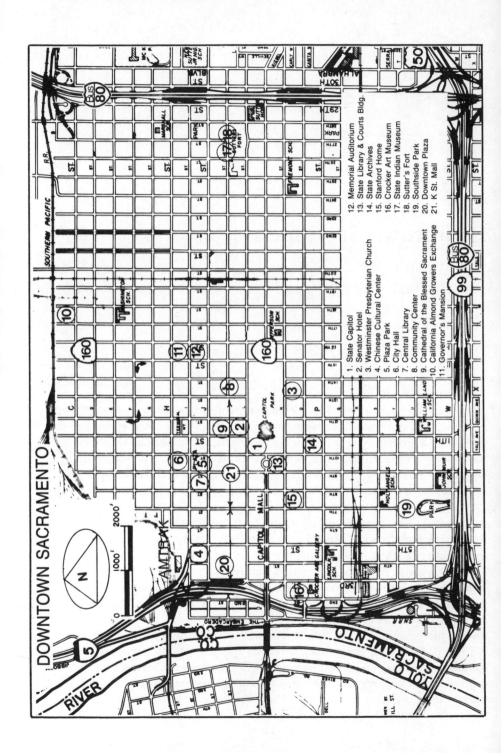

DOWNTOWN SACRAMENTO

1. State Capitol
2. Senator Hotel
3. Westminster Presbyterian Church
4. Chinese Cultural Center
5. Plaza Park
6. City Hall
7. Central Library
8. Community Center
9. Cathedral of the Blessed Sacrament
10. California Almond Growers Exchange
11. Governor's Mansion
12. Memorial Auditorium
13. State Library & Courts Bldg.
14. State Archives
15. Stanford Home
16. Crocker Art Museum
17. State Indian Museum
18. Sutter's Fort
19. Southside Park
20. Downtown Plaza
21. K St. Mall

Downtown Sacramento, looking east (courtesy Sacramento Union/ Steve Yeater)

On weekdays, downtown streets are alive with government workers and visitors, but they are practically deserted at night and on the weekends. With a few exceptions, including Downtown Plaza, most businesses are closed on weekends, so if you need anything you'll have to hit the suburban malls. Efforts are being made to restore downtown to a "24-hour city" where new and renovated hotels, residences, and businesses would bring new life to the sagging business district. Although there are a large number of transients downtown, especially around the Greyhound station and along J and K streets, you should have no problems exploring the area in the daytime. At night, however, it's best to avoid solitary walking in this region, especially along the K Street Mall.

The downtown redevelopment program, which began in earnest during the 1960s, has led to many old structures being razed or renovated and new ones built in what was formerly known as the West End, stretching from the central business district and the capitol to the Sacramento River. Some of the projects resulting from the redevelopment effort include the K Street Mall, Old Sacramento, the Convention Center, Downtown Plaza, the Chinese Cultural Center, and improvements along Capitol Mall, which was formerly lined with seedy bars, flophouses, gas stations, and empty lots. The Sacramento Old City Association is a citizens' group that has been actively working to restore and preserve historic and architecturally notable structures as well as the remaining residential neighborhoods. The long-term goal of this group is to continue programs for preservation and restoration of downtown along with programs to revitalize the area as an attractive place to work, live, shop, and attend cultural events by day and by night.

The end result of this downtown revival is a visual delight—a balanced harmony between the past and the present, the old and the new. Somehow it all manages to fit together, and it works. Most of Sacramento's historical sites are located within a mile of the capitol, making it an easy area to tour. If you're just visiting, try to take at least a couple of days to see everything here.

State Capitol

Set majestically amid a lush forty-acre park in the heart of downtown, its golden dome providing a landmark for visitors and residents, California's state capitol is a prime example of the blending of the old and new. It is here, in the oldest state capitol building still in use west of the Mississippi, that the largest state government in the nation conducts its business. With the completion in 1982 of a six-year, $70 million restoration project, the building has

California State Capitol

become a living museum and a major tourist attraction, drawing a million visitors every year.

Construction of the capitol began in 1860 after the legislature had been housed in several other locations. The project dragged on for fourteen years, interrupted by floods, politics, lack of funds, and the Civil War. The problems were enough to cause the first capitol architect, Reuben Clark, to suffer a mental breakdown; he wound up in a Stockton mental institution. Finally, in 1869, the new capitol opened its doors. It was officially declared complete in 1874, at a total cost of $2.5 million.

The present building is really two structures: the original capitol, known as the old capitol, and the east annex, added in 1952. Nearly all of the historic features are located in the 170,000-square-foot old capitol, which we will refer to here as simply "the capitol."

The best place for a first-time look at the capitol is from the west side on Capitol Mall. The imposing four-story structure of Roman Corinthian design and modeled roughly after the nation's Capitol is surmounted by a copper-clad dome on which sits a cupola with a gold-plated roof. Its crowning ornament, at 220 feet above street level, is a thirty-inch ball that was originally plated with $300 worth (in 1860s dollars) of melted gold coins donated by Sacramentans. During the recent restoration, new gold leaf was used to cover the ball and the state seal above the original doors on the second floor of the west portico. The progress of construction on the transcontinental railroad is reflected in the exterior of the first story. The dark granite at the base was quarried at Folsom. By 1864, the Central Pacific Railroad had reached Rocklin, enabling the lighter granite quarried there to be shipped to Sacramento. The exterior walls of the remaining three floors are thirty inches thick; they were made from brick set in lime mortar and covered with plaster.

Although no major structural changes were made over the years, the capitol underwent frequent remodeling, obscuring much of its 19th-century elegance. Offices were cut in half by mezzanines, fluorescent lights replaced chandeliers, false ceilings and flimsy partitions appeared, and hand-carved walnut stairways disappeared to make room for much-needed office space. During the 1950s, Hollywood setmakers were brought in to redesign the legislative chambers. The resulting "improvements"—red velvet drapes, fake marble columns—prompted at least one lawmaker to liken the legislature to a Victorian bordello.

Despite the aesthetic considerations, the real impetus for the restoration came in 1972 when a study showed that the capitol might collapse during an earthquake. In 1975, after initial proposals to scrap the old building and build a new one were abandoned, it was decided to restore the original building. What followed was the most expensive and thorough restoration project ever undertaken on a single building in this country. An entirely new, reinforced concrete structure with walls eight to ten feet thick was built inside the shell of the old capitol, using steel reinforcing to bind the two together to make a building-within-a-building. It is said that the restored building will withstand an 8.5 magnitude earthquake.

After the exterior and interior walls, floors, and stairwells were in place, attention was focused on the interior restoration. Aided by plans, photographs, and other historical artifacts, master craftspersons and artisans revived the near-lost arts of mosaic tiling, ceiling molding, painting and gilding, and hand-carving wooden stair rails and posts. Delicate laser-beam cleaning brought out original colors. Elaborate fresco designs on ceilings and walls were faithfully recreated using plaster in pastry tubes. Lighting fixtures were accurately reproduced based on old photographs, and some 600,000 tiles in intricate mosaic patterns were mapped, removed, restored, and replaced. Many original artifacts were found and restored to their historic locations. Other interior elements were carefully reconstructed based on microscopic analysis of historic photographs. The end result of this massive project was the restoration of the grandeur of the 1900–1910 period to the capitol, including the senate and assembly chambers and the old ground-floor offices of the governor, secretary of state, treasurer, and attorney general.

A self-guided tour brochure is available from the tour office in the basement, room B-27. You can also pick up information here on the various free daily tours offered on the hour, including a legislative process tour and a restored capitol tour. Foreign language and sign language tours are available. For more information or for group tour reservations, call the tour office at 324-0333. Wheelchair access to the capitol is provided, including ramps at the east entrances.

FIRST FLOOR

The first floor is the best place to begin your capitol tour, as it is the location of the seven restored historical offices.

The best place to view the restored dome of the 120-foot-high rotunda is from the second floor, but the first floor contains the centerpiece of the rotunda, the Carrara marble statue entitled *Columbus' Last Appeal to Queen Isabella*. Completed in 1871 in Florence, Italy, it depicts Columbus pleading with Queen Isabella to finance his voyage to the New World. The statue has remained in this location since 1883.

Floor designs called the Eureka Murals appear at the north and south entrances and corridors on the first floor. Consisting of 320 tiles, each design incorporates symbols from the state seal. The recreation of the elegant ornamental stairs was based on two photographs and some original remnants. The posts, rails, and balusters are fashioned from hand-carved Honduran mahogany, and the light fixtures are copies of the original gaslights. In early 1906 plans were drawn for removing the grand staircases and adding a fourth floor. During the remodeling San Francisco suffered an earthquake and fire and the capitol became the center for relief efforts.

The historical museum rooms of the offices of the governor, secretary of state, treasurer, and attorney general have been restored to their 1906 appearance. More than two years of research using old photographs and records helped restorers recreate the interiors that earlier occupants knew. Many of the original furnishings and artifacts were located and combined with antiques of the period. To visit these offices is to take a step back in time.

The Governor's Office is a three-room suite authentically recreating the 1906 office of Gov. George C. Pardee. The last governor to use these offices was Earl Warren in 1952. The State Archives Exhibit Room has historical documents on display from the state archives. Its decor is based on actual designs of an earlier era. The decorative plaster ceilings were recreated using original techniques. The Secretary of State's Office is a recreation of one of the two offices of Secretary of State C. F. Curry in 1902. The 1906-era State Treasurer's Office represents the office of State Treasurer Truman Reeves. At that time the state didn't keep its money in a bank. Instead, the money—about $7 million in gold and silver coins—was kept in the walk-in vault. The vault has been restored at one-third its former size. The brightly decorated seven-ton safe beside the vault was returned to the capitol from Sutter's Fort and at one time probably stood inside the vault. The stark room next door represents the Treasurer's Office in 1933. The huge vault in this office, with its eleven-ton door, held the state's securities and other assets and was in use from 1929 until restoration began in 1976.

Featuring old periodicals, artifacts, and an original Audubon album, the State Library Exhibit Room reproduces a 1900–1910 reading room in the California State Library. Reference material for the public on the restoration is stored here. The 1906 Attorney General's Office reflects the design prevalent during the time of Attorney General Ulysses S. Webb, who divided his time between this office and another in San Francisco.

SECOND FLOOR

From the rotunda of the second floor you'll get the best view of the magnificent molding and painting of the inner dome. Restored to look as it did in the late 1800s, it is an exquisite blending of pastel shades of blue, pink, and beige, decorative elements of plaster and cast iron, and decorative panels and murals. For the gold decoration a brass alloy was used to simulate gold leaf.

The offices of the speaker of the assembly are to the north of the rotunda; the offices of the senate president pro tempore are to the south. The 1906 marble mosaic floor was first photographed, then removed in sections and cleaned and polished during the restoration. Later the 600,000 individual tiles were replaced to match the original pattern. On the second floor landing, looking west toward Capitol Mall, are glass-paned double doors of black walnut. At one time this was supposed to be the entrance to the building, but the outside stairs were never installed because the builders ran out of funds. The doors were left in place, leading nowhere.

THIRD FLOOR

On the third floor you can view the eighty-member assembly and forty-member senate in session from January to July from the galleries of each chamber. Incorporating Roman Corinthian, Renaissance Revival, and Victorian design elements, the chambers have been restored to their original opulence. From the verdant hues of the assembly chambers to the roseate blush of the senate, these elegant rooms are a testament to the blending of tradition and technology. For in these chambers, a 20th-century government is run in turn-of-the-century surroundings.

Green is the dominant color of the assembly chambers, with red dominating the senate's color scheme. These colors recall the British parliament; the House of Lords chose red decor and the House of Commons used green. In the senate chambers, the portrait of Pres. George Washington is a copy painted by Jane Stuart, daughter of Gilbert Stuart, who painted the well-known original. The painting was saved from the county courthouse fire of 1854 when Gov. John Bigler pleaded with harried firefighters to save it. "There is the portrait of the father of your country," he shouted. "Will you permit it to be destroyed?" A portrait of Pres. Abraham Lincoln hangs in the assembly chambers. Just below the portraits are the Latin mottoes of each house, restored in the only gold leaf used inside the capitol. The assembly motto translates to "It is the duty of the legislators to pass just laws"; the Senate motto is "It is the duty of a senator to protect the liberty of the people."

Modern accoutrements include facilities for TV cameras, sophisticated sound systems, and an electronic voting system in the assembly (the senate votes by roll call). When the legislature is in session, only members, staff, and persons with special permission are admitted to the chamber floor. If you've never watched a session, you should plan on doing so; it can be fascinating and often confusing. Legislators and staff members walk around, hold conferences, read documents, and at times appear oblivious to whomever has the floor. But somehow the work gets done, and the machinery of state government grinds on. Which brings to mind the saying attributed to Count Otto von Bismarck: "People who have respect for law and sausages should watch neither being made."

The controversial portrait of former Gov. Jerry Brown hangs midway across the third floor, at the head of the two grand staircases coming up from the floor below. The colorful, expressionistic, non-traditional portrait contrasts sharply with the other somber portraits of former governors so much so that legislative leaders decided to hang it in this remote location by itself after a great deal of controversy.

BASEMENT

A small theater, tour office, museum exhibit room, gift shop, the Legislative Bill Room, and a restaurant are located on this floor. At the entrance to the gift shop you can see the original brick walls and foundation through a window. The turn-of-the-century cafeteria, open to the public, has a surprisingly pleasant ambience, considering it's tucked away in a basement. The prices are reasonable and there's a great salad bar. The Legislative Bill Room has copies of pending legislation, daily files, histories, journals, and other publications on state government. The publications are available free or for a small fee. Be sure to ask for a copy of *California's Legislature,* published by the state assembly, which explains the legislative process. Children can get numerous educational publications, including reproductions of California's great seal and state flag and a legislative flow chart—a great help to adults as well who are trying to figure out how the system works. Many publications are also available from legislative offices. Californians should plan on visiting their legislators while at the capitol.

EAST ANNEX

Completed in 1952, the six-floor east annex is not historical but is still worth a visit. Most of the legislative offices are located here, as well as legislative hearing rooms and the modern governor's office. On the first floor, Californians can look for their county among the black marble–accented glass showcases with displays for each of the fifty-eight counties.

This section on the capitol wouldn't be complete without at least a mention of several of the more well-known legislative hangouts. This includes saloons and restaurants where much of the real work of the legislature probably takes place. When the legislature is in session, you're practically guaranteed to see political types in any of these restaurant/bar combos: Frank Fat's, 806 L Street, a legendary political hangout known as the state's "unofficial capitol"; Brannan's Bar and Grill, 1117 Eleventh Street, a classy, crowded in-spot; or Posey's Cottage, 1100 O Street, another popular restaurant and bar. Popular legislative bars include David's Brass Rail, 1125 Twelfth Street (favored by Gov. Jerry Brown, who reportedly spent his last evening in office here with Linda Ronstadt), and the Torch Club, 1612 L Street.

Capitol Park

With more than forty thousand trees, shrubs and flowers, forty-acre Capitol Park boasts one of the finest plant life collections in the nation. More than eight hundred varieties of plant life are found in this verdant park, representing every climate and continent in the world from subtropical to subarctic, from the mountains of India to the tropics of Brazil. Seasonal displays of color are provided by blossoming fruit trees, shrubs, and annuals such as pansies, camellias, irises, and roses. Every spring as many as five thousand bulbs from Holland bloom. Along with standard fruit trees, numerous exotic fruit trees produce fruits like Chilean wine dates, kumquats, carob, pawpaws, hackberries, and pistachio nuts.

Two blocks wide and six blocks long, stretching from L to N streets and Ninth to Fifteenth streets, the park is a popular lunch spot for state workers. Several hot dog vendors circle the park daily with pushcarts, or you can get lunch to go from a nearby eatery and enjoy a picnic on the grass. You may feel pressured to share part of your lunch with some of the two-hundred-plus grey and red tree squirrels populating the park. Imported originally from Fresno and Golden Gate Park in 1923, they're used to being hand-fed—but be careful of their sharp claws when they take the food. The best thing to feed them is hard-shelled nuts.

Weather permitting, free hourly tours of the park are offered daily from the capitol tour office, room B-27. Or you can pick up a self-guided tour pamphlet suggesting three walking tours from the park office at Thirteenth and L streets (restrooms are also located here). Serious tree lovers may want to get a copy of *Capitol Park Trees* for detailed information on the park's trees. More information about the park is available from the Building and Grounds Division of the General Services Department at 445-2511.

Development of Capitol Park began in 1869, around the time that the capitol was first occupied. The grounds were graded and the soil enriched with rich silts from the Sacramento River bed. Original plantings in 1870–71 included eight hundred trees and flowering shrubs from all parts of the world. Many of the larger trees surrounding the capitol are part of the original planting, including the coast redwoods (California's state tree) and the deodar cedars. These seventy-five-foot-high cedars that line the west side of the capitol were dug up in the Himalayas in 1870, shipped around the Horn to San Francisco, and transported up the Sacramento River via riverboat. Near the southeast corner of Twelfth and L is a thirty-foot redwood called the Orbit Tree. It was grown from a seed that circled the moon in 1970 aboard Apollo 13.

A large variety of native California plants and trees are located in the California section (bordered by Fourteenth, Fifteenth, Capitol, and N streets), including white oaks, blackberry elders, manzanitas, Digger pines, white spruces, and golden poppies, California's state flower. The agricultural pavilion of the state fair was located at this site until the fair moved to Stockton Boulevard in 1905. This is also the location of a cactus garden representing the California desert. In 1914 school children from every county in the state sent many of the cactus for this section to Gov. Hiram Johnson. Across the mall to the north is a rose garden containing more than eight hundred roses, including experimental plants that have not yet been made available to the public. They're usually in full bloom by May. A two-story, Italian villa–style mansion built in 1870 for Gov. Newton Booth once stood in this section. It was converted into the first state printing office after the legislature failed to provide funds to complete it and Governor Booth refused to move in. The printing office was razed in 1923 and the site planted in acacias, eucalyptus, and California live oaks.

A plot near Twelfth and L streets is known as Memorial Grove and contains trees that were transplanted as saplings from Civil War battlefields. The grove was donated in 1897 by the Ladies of the Grand Army of the Republic in California and Nevada as a tribute to Union veterans. Nearby in a shady area is a picturesque trout pond and a reproduction of the Liberty Bell cast in France and the bell from the U.S.S. *California*. To the north is a bronze statue of Father Junipero Serra, the 18th-century Franciscan friar who led the movement to establish California's missions, and a large state map showing the missions' locations. Near the statue is the Pioneer Camellia Grove, dedicated to California's early settlers. The more than three hundred camellia trees are in full bloom through February and March. The park also has memorials to veterans of the Vietnam War and the California Indians.

SENATOR HOTEL

Overlooking the park at Twelfth and L is the Senator Hotel, the city's social center during its heyday in the 1930s and 1940s and today a plush office complex. The Italian Renaissance building was completed in 1923 at a cost of $2 million and was considered one of the finest hotels on the West Coast; it was *the* place to be seen on Saturday nights. On Mondays an entire column in the *Sacramento Union* was devoted to the goings-on at the Senator. Many came to dine and dance in the elegant Empire Room, where such specialties as Chicken Under Glass were served for $1.75 at tables set with fine china, silver, and linen. Dance music was provided by the big bands of Freddy Martin, Benny Goodman, and Harry James, among others. Mickey Rooney and the Marx Brothers once attended a wedding reception here, and other notable guests have included Charles Lindbergh and Gerald Ford.

The building was condemned as a firetrap in 1979 and closed for repairs. In 1982 a developer purchased the hotel for $2 million and spent another

$5.5 million on its renovation as an office building. The elegantly decorated main floor is used for social events.

WESTMINSTER PRESBYTERIAN CHURCH

On the other side of Capitol Park at Thirteenth and N is the impressive Westminster Presbyterian Church, notable for both its architecture and its serene inner courtyard. The church was established in 1866 at Sixth and K; the existing church was built in 1927 at a cost of $350,000. Its architect, Earl Barnett, also designed the Memorial Auditorium and the Sutter Club. Rising eighty-seven feet above the nave, the shallow, saucer-shaped dome supported on a square base is modeled after the Byzantine design of St. Sophia Cathedral in Istanbul. With its Byzantine dome, half domes, arches, atrium, Venetian bell tower, and other rich ornamentation, the building represents a pleasing blend of Romanesque forms, Mediterranean building materials, and the California mission style.

The main entrance is framed by a massive Byzantine arch decorated with medieval religious symbols and with the church's name engraved in stone over the portal. The interior is dominated by two stained glass rose windows patterned after those in European Gothic cathedrals of the Middle Ages. The church's centerpiece is its impressive Möller pipe organ, rebuilt from a Reuter organ in 1983. In addition to the pipes you can see, which were made in Germany from tin and wood, there are three additional chambers in the church's walls containing pipes, bringing the total number of pipes to 2,929. The rebuilt organ—really six organs with one console—is a delight to see and hear. Note also the fourteen-foot Celtic cross and the stained-glass window featuring St. Patrick killing a dragon.

A little-known feature is the enclosed courtyard surrounded by Byzantine columns and arches, consisting of a balcony, a brick walkway, and a red tiled roof. The serene garden is planted in ferns, camellias, gardenias, red bougainvillea, an olive tree, and a fragrant flower bed. An elaborately decorated fountain is planted with lantana, and there are two concrete benches where you can relax and enjoy the peaceful surroundings.

In the next block at 1400 N Street is a charming older apartment building owned by the state. Its claim to fame is that Gov. Jerry Brown lived here in a top-floor apartment during his administration. Governor Brown moved here in 1974 after shunning the cavernous new Governor's Mansion in Carmichael. After he moved out, top-level political maneuvering and heated debate ensued over who would next occupy the apartment, within easy walking distance of the capitol.

Central Business District

The heart of downtown's central business district stretches from Third to Sixteenth streets and is bisected by two major thoroughfares, J and K streets. Locals refer to this district as "downtown." Here you'll find a mixture of government and office buildings, retail shops, delis, restaurants, residential hotels, galleries, and night spots. Nowhere is the downtown revival more evident than in this area, which for years has had a rundown image. Many old structures built between the turn of the century and the 1920s have been demolished and replaced by new buildings. Some have remained and are undergoing restoration, including the Traveler's Hotel at Fifth and J streets (1914), the Ramona Hotel at Sixth and J (1920s), and the Ruhstaller Building at Ninth and J (1898). All have been converted to office buildings. Plans are being drawn to put in more shops and restaurants to lure people back to downtown after dark, and there are plans to build a high-rise hotel near the Sacramento Community Center.

From the days when it was the main thoroughfare from the Embarcadero to Sutter's Fort, J Street has remained a major east-west route through the city. It leads directly to Sacramento State, where it joins H Street to become Fair Oaks Boulevard. During the Gold Rush, when it was lined with gambling halls and saloons, it became the main route to the interior and points north and east. Ox and mule teams, horses, and foot traffic heading for the northern mines followed J Street to Twelfth Street, where it then turned left to head north across the American River via Lisle's Ferry, which later became Lisle's Bridge and is now the Twelfth Street Bridge.

Chinese Cultural Center

The west end of I Street was the site of Sacramento's Chinese settlement, established around 1850 by Chinese drawn to the area by the Gold Rush and later the railroad. They settled on the south shore of what originally was called Sutter's Lake or Sutter's Slough but later came to be known as China Slough. (A slough, pronounced "slew," is an inlet from a river, a backwater, or a creek in a marsh.) It was an abandoned finger of the Sacramento River running north of I Street from Third to Fifth streets. By the late 1800s, the slough was being used as a waste disposal area by the railroad shops on the north shore and the Chinese on the south shore. The stench was often nearly unbearable, and the slough even caught fire once from the oily debris discharged by the shops. It was filled in by Southern Pacific in 1906; the site is now occupied by the Amtrak station.

The Chinese lived here in wooden houses. Many started grocery stores and laundries; some worked as servants. It was a bustling Chinatown with markets, family associations, bathhouses, restaurants, and theaters. For a couple of years in the early 1860s, a Chinese-language newspaper was published here. During his visit to Sacramento in the early part of this century, Dr. Sun Yat-sen wrote much of the Chinese constitution at the headquarters of the Bing Tong, a Chinese family association, which was located at Fourth and I streets. He was elected the first president of the Chinese republic when he returned to China. Third Street between I and J remained the Chinese Quarter until city redevelopment partially displaced the community in the early 1960s. By this time, however, many of the Chinese had dispersed throughout the city, with many living in Southside from R to W and Third to Sixteenth streets.

Completed in 1973 on the site of the original Chinatown, the Chinese Cultural Center was one of the first products of Sacramento's redevelopment program. Bounded by I, J, Fourth, and Fifth streets, it consists of two blocks of attractive Oriental buildings that successfully blend the architectural lines of East and West. An elaborate wrought-iron entry gate at Fourth and J streets leads down into a sunken inner mall. The Chinese characters above the gateway translate to "Sacramento Chinatown." Landscaped with indigenous Oriental plants and trees, including bamboo, ginkgo, pine, Japanese maple, and juniper, the courtyard is at the original level of the city, eight feet below the current street level.

Today's Chinatown is not really a tourist attraction but rather a cultural, social, business, and educational center for Sacramento's Chinese community. The centerpiece of the courtyard is an eighteen-foot statue of Dr. Sun Yat-sen, placed so that the statesman faces China. The Sun Yat-sen Memorial Hall is the mall's cultural center and is open to visitors. The hall has a reading room with Chinese periodicals and is the site of community events such as lectures and movies. Glass display cases contain Chinese antiques and reproductions from several dynasties, and along the walls are twelve large replicas of Chinese coins.

A flight of steps in the courtyard leads up to the Confucius Temple, built in 1959. The complex includes two residential developments for senior citizens and low-income families, several family associations, shops, a market, and restaurants, including the China Moon Cafe and the LuShan Chinese Buffet.

SOUTHERN PACIFIC DEPOT

Just across I Street from the Chinese Cultural Center are the Southern Pacific yards, shops, and depot. The yards and shops were developed in 1868 to service the Central Pacific Railroad (now the Southern Pacific). Its buildings and tracks today cover an area of thirty city blocks. There have been four terminals; the present immense brick structure was completed in 1923 and now serves as an Amtrak station. When the depot was first built, sixty-four trains went through every day, and the cavernous structure was bustling with activity. At one time, the depot had a restaurant, barbershop, magazine stand, telegraph office, and Travelers Aid station. All of that's gone now, so if you're planning a wait of any kind, it's a good idea to bring your own food and reading material. With only a few trains passing through each day, the travertine marble floors and carved oak benches are now empty most of the time, watched over by an immense mural on the north wall. The fifty-by-fifteen-foot mural, entitled *Breaking Ground at Sacramento Jan. 8, 1863 for the First Transcontinental Railroad,* depicts a crowd scene that includes Theodore Judah and the Big Four. Unless a concerted effort is launched to save this grand old train depot, now slowly going to seed, its days are probably numbered.

City Plaza

Sacramento's city hall overlooks Plaza Park, bounded by I, J, Ninth, and Tenth streets. Built in 1909, the building is the seat of city government. Its clock tower is a pleasing visual landmark—the clock even keeps accurate time. In the old days, Plaza Park was a favorite hitching place for weary travelers. When the surrounding city streets were raised, the plaza level of the park remained unchanged, forming a sunken garden with two ramps for traffic. The park was to have been the location of the first state capitol, but the site was abandoned. During the 1870s and 1880s, circuses were held here, with elephants and horses marching down the ramps. Standing in the park is a statue of Andrew J. Stevens, revered master mechanic with the Central Pacific Railroad, who designed railroad equipment at the shops. The statue was paid for by Central Pacific employees.

Down a block at 828 I is the Sacramento Public Library's Central Branch. The library has long since outgrown the Italian Renaissance structure built in 1919 and has had to keep many of its volumes in storage. The city plans to expand and renovate the existing structure. The Sacramento Public Library has twenty-five branches throughout the city and county offering numerous free services and programs. Every spring the Friends of the Sacramento Library sponsors a huge book sale, with thousands of surplus hardbacks and paperbacks available at great prices. (Watch the papers for the sale date or call the library at 440-5926.)

Nearby at Eleventh and J is another J Street landmark, the fourteen-story Elks Club Building. It was built in 1925 using a "step-back" structural style then popular on the Eastern Seaboard. The building now houses offices.

K Street Mall

In an effort to prevent the continuing downward economic spiral of the central business district, the stretch of K Street between Seventh and Fourteenth streets was turned into a shopping mall in 1969. The $2.1 million K Street Mall featured abstract concrete sculptures, reflecting pools, and fountains designed to serve as a metaphor for California's mountains and waterways. Beset by controversy and financial woes, the mall was doomed from the start and has been blamed for the area's continuing economic problems. Competition from suburban shopping centers and Downtown Plaza increased the mall's financial difficulties. Although the mall is popular on weekdays when workers from nearby state office buildings come here to shop and eat, at night it is inhabited primarily by transients and skateboarders.

But all this will soon be changing. The K Street Mall is undergoing a transformation like many other downtown areas. With the coming of the light-rail transit system, K Street will be transported back to the era of trollies. Parallel street-level tracks with overhead wires will run down the middle of the mall from Seventh to Twelfth streets. It is believed that many of the existing retail stores will be replaced with offices and a mix of entertainment, restaurants, and specialty shops. If funding is available, the colorful K Street trams will continue service from the Sacramento Community Center at Twelfth Street to Old Sacramento during and after the light-rail system construction. The fare is modest, and it's a fun way to get to Old Sacramento without relying on your feet.

Several places on or near the mall offer light meals and take-out, including Pennisi's at 1216 J Street, a Greek deli serving delicious take-out sandwiches, salads, and desserts. Nearby at 816 Twelfth Street is Jim-Denny's Lunch, an authentic Depression-era lunch counter. Housed in a tiny matchbox of a building at the edge of a parking lot, this downtown landmark specializes in no-frills burgers and chili dogs; open weekdays only for breakfast and lunch.

From the early 1850s to the early 1900s, K Street was known as Sacramento's theatrical district. By 1913 ten theaters lined K Street, providing live shows, plays, and movies. Built in 1883, the Clunie Theater at Eighth and K presented such theatrical luminaries as John Drew, Ethel and Lionel Barrymore, Maude Adams, and George M. Cohan until its doors were closed in 1923. One of Sacramento's most popular vaudeville houses was the Empress Theater, built in 1913 at Tenth and K. As the popularity of movies increased, the Empress was replaced by the Hippodrome in 1918. After a major renovation in 1949, it was renamed the Crest and remains today as the last of Sacramento's grand old art deco theaters. Sacramento's first Hippodrome Theater was built in 1854 on K Street between Fourth and Fifth.

Built of brick and seating 1,200, it featured a one-ring circus on its large stage, complete with clowns, acrobats and tightrope walkers. It was later called the National and booked theatrical performances; still later, it was renamed the Metropolitan and became the site of operas and minstrel shows. The structure was destroyed by fire in 1886, and the land is now occupied by the Downtown Plaza shopping mall. During this period, Seventh and K was a major intersection whose landmark was St. Rose of Lima Church, built in 1851. In the 1890s, the church was replaced with a large sandstone post office. The site is now occupied by St. Rose of Lima Park.

CATHEDRAL OF THE BLESSED SACRAMENT

Sacramento's oldest and largest church is the Cathedral of the Blessed Sacrament at Eleventh and K. Completed in 1889 to replace St. Rose of Lima Church, it was modeled after the late Italian Renaissance style of the Church of the Trinity in Paris. The church was built by Patrick Manogue, the first Catholic bishop of Sacramento. For many years, the cathedral marked the east end of the K Street business district. Until 1966 it was the largest Roman Catholic church west of the Mississippi.

The brick structure, covered with a heavy layer of plaster on the Eleventh and K Street façades, is graced with tall spires and an impressive dome rising to a height of 167 feet. The bell tower, surmounted by a twenty-foot golden cross, is 216 feet high and can be seen from miles away. It holds four bells, one of which—the bell that strikes the hour—weighs eight thousand pounds. The others are smaller and strike on the quarter hour. Inside the cathedral are several outstanding works of art. At the east end of the apse is the fine stained-glass *Last Supper* fashioned in Innsbruck, Austria, for the cathedral's dedication. A reproduction of Raphael's *Sistine Madonna* (the original is at the Royal Art Gallery in Dresden) hangs on a wall in the south transept. Rendered in oil, this meticulous copy was a gift of Jane Elizabeth Stanford, wife of California's eighth governor, Leland Stanford. The dome over the transept was closed off in 1932 for structural reasons, but plans are to reopen it for the cathedral's centennial. The church still conducts mass and is always open to visitors, who can arrange tours by calling 444-3070.

DOWNTOWN PLAZA

Downtown Plaza is a shopping center that is a continuation of the K Street Mall between Third and Seventh. Completed in 1974 and graced by fountains, waterways, and concrete sculptures, this pedestrian mall is anchored by three large department stores and features a number of clothing and specialty shops. One of the best things about this shopping center is that most of its large stores are open on Sundays, when most other downtown shops are closed. Weinstock's Department Store serves Sunday brunch in its classy tearoom with delightfully landscaped covered patio.

At the west end of Downtown Plaza is the forty-foot Indo Arch, fashioned in steel by nationally known Sacramento artist Gerald Wahlberg. It was commissioned by the city in 1977 as a symbol of the commitment to public art and was dedicated in 1980. Although the arch caused quite a controversy when installed, it has become a downtown landmark. Facing the arch is Le Terrace restaurant, with outdoor tables shaded by umbrellas where you can relax and do some people-watching. A walkway continues from the Downtown Plaza mall under the freeway to Old Sacramento; colorful murals and enameled copper mosaics decorate the walls of the walkway.

California Almond Growers Exchange

Native to southwestern Asia, the first almonds were brought to California by the Franciscan padres who established California's Spanish missions. Almonds are now the state's largest tree crop and its number one food export. Some 400,000 acres are planted in almonds from Bakersfield to Red Bluff, producing about 60 percent of the world's almond supply. Headquartered at Seventeenth and C streets, the California Almond Growers Exchange is the world's largest almond processing plant, covering thirty-three city blocks and processing more than 1.5 million pounds of almonds daily. The Almond Growers Exchange is a grower-owned cooperative with 5,500 members who supply markets in the U.S. and eighty-eight foreign countries.

The new International Visitors Center and Almond Plaza at 1701 C Street features free tours and tastings six days a week. It is housed in a 200,000-square-foot building that once served as a Del Monte cannery. Built in 1925, the brick building was once one of the largest canneries in the world, processing many varieties of fruits and vegetables. The historic structure was recently added to the National Register of Historic Places.

The lobby of the visitors center includes a map of the world showing where almonds are produced and consumed and how they are used. In a 230-seat theater, a thirty-minute movie tells how almonds are grown, processed, and sold. The visitors center also offers recipes and demonstrations on cooking with almonds, exhibits of almond industry relics, and a photo mural telling the exchange's history. Tour guides take you to the processing plant, where you can see almonds being packaged. The adjacent gift shop offers samples of fourteen types of nuts, four kinds of almond butters, and thirteen varieties of candies. The store sells almond products and also takes orders for shipped gift packs. The visitors center is open Monday through Saturday and tours are given on weekdays. For more information call 446-8409.

Governor's Mansion

Seeming strangely out of place, the Governor's Mansion sits gracefully on the corner of Sixteenth and H streets, one of downtown's busier intersections. A charming Victorian gothic with ornate trim, the city's most well-known Victorian has for more than a century endured the onslaught of encroaching civilization. When the three-story, twenty-three-room house was built in 1877 at a cost of $75,000, the grounds occupied half a city block. The land was semi-rural; only one other building existed on the block. Today the elaborate wrought-iron fence along the sidewalk is all that separates this 19th-century anachronism from 20th-century commercial buildings, neon lights, and the din of rush-hour traffic.

The house was designed by architect Nathaniel Goodell for Albert Gallatin, president of the Huntington & Hopkins Hardware Company, who lived here with his family until 1887. The house was then purchased by Joseph Steffens, a dry goods merchant who was the father of Lincoln Steffens. Lincoln was twenty-one at the time and a student at the University of Cali-

Governor's Mansion

fornia; he would later become a well-known author and muckraking journalist. Joseph Steffens remained here until the mansion was purchased by the state.

In 1903 the house became the first official governor's residence. Before then, California's governors lived in hotels or private residences. The purchase price was $32,500, unfurnished. A small wing was added, and $56,000 was spent to refurbish and decorate. George Pardee became the first governor to reside here, and for the next sixty-four years it served as the home of thirteen California governors. The home was declared unsafe for occupancy by the state fire marshall in 1941, but governors continued to live here until Gov. Ronald Reagan moved out after only a few months in 1967. Funds are being raised to fireproof the mansion, which is now a state historical landmark operated and maintained by the state parks department. Tours are conducted daily 10–5; tickets are available at the carriage house, where you can see a brief slide show on the history of the mansion (445-4209).

In the early days, as today, the mansion was an impressive sight, with its tall mansard roof surmounted by the two-story cupola, deeply hooded dormer windows, gingerbread scrollwork, decorative shingles, bay windows, and porches. The grounds were originally landscaped with ornamental trees and shrubs and included a gazebo (where the swimming pool is now) and a carriage house. The carriage house, which began as a barn and later became a garage, is almost a miniature replica of the mansion and is one of the few remaining Victorian carriage houses in Sacramento.

The basement occupies the ground floor of the mansion and contains servants' quarters, a small wine cellar, a laundry fed by a laundry chute, and storage rooms. Public tours begin one flight up on the main floor. The present furnishings of the spacious mansion reflect the tastes of the thirteen governors who have occupied it, ranging from Victorian elegance to fifties nondescript. The first floor, with fourteen-foot ceilings, contains a library-music room, parlor, sitting room, dining room, kitchen, and pantry.

As you tour the house, there are a number of special features you'll want to look for. For example, every piece of hardware is cast of ornamental bronze (Gallatin got the hardware at cost from Huntington & Hopkins). All of the hardware on the seventy-five massive, nine-foot doors is original. The mirrors over the first-floor coal-burning fireplaces, hand-carved from Italian marble, were made in France and Belgium with frames specially designed for each room. The mirrors in the center of the hearth were called petticoat mirrors. They were provided so ladies could discreetly check whether their petticoats were showing.

The formal parlor in the front of the house was used for teas and special occasions. Four official weddings took place in the mansion, the last of which was held in this room in 1955. Wearing a white lace and chiffon gown, twenty-one-year-old Carolyn Knight, daughter of Gov. Goodwin Knight, married law student Charles Weedman, Jr. The gown was recently discovered in a musty closet in Hollywood and has been placed on display. Weddings are still held at the mansion, which is available for rent for events such as this. The state parks department will even rent a horsedrawn carriage to carry the newlyweds to the wedding reception. The second parlor was for more casual gatherings and includes a TV used by the Knights and the Browns in the '50s. The music room, which was once a library, has a 1902 Steinway baby grand that was purchased by Mrs. George Pardee, who had brought half a freight car full of furnishings from the family home in Oakland.

Gallatin had an ingenious device installed whereby he could summon a servant by pressing a buzzer in any room. A corresponding number in a glass box in the kitchen would drop into view so the servant knew which room to go to. Teddy Roosevelt used to sit on the marble table in the kitchen and argue politics with the cook. In the china cabinet you can see the china service for seventy-two with gold leaf trim. The kitchen and pantry were destroyed in 1917 by a dynamite explosion in an unsuccessful assassination attempt on Governor Stephens.

The bedrooms are located on the second floor. Each of the rooms radiates from a central hallway where there's a wonderful musty smell of dark wood, rich tapestries, plush carpet, and the original wallpaper. John F. Kennedy and Eleanor Roosevelt have stayed overnight in this house, and you can see the room with the single beds where Nancy and Ronald Reagan slept. The master bathroom's claw-foot tub has bright red paint on each of the claws—a detail added by Gov. Pat Brown's young daughter Kathy. On the third floor was an elegant ballroom and game room that in the 1940s was divided into two bedrooms and an office by the Warrens, who had six children. An observatory was located above the third floor.

History has repeated itself; California's governors are once again without an official residence. A sprawling ranch house was built in Carmichael in 1975 for Governor Reagan, but his term of office expired before the house was completed. Gov. Jerry Brown refused to live in it. Gov. George Deukmejian wanted to, but the legislature didn't want him to. Then he decided he didn't want to live there—whereupon the legislature said he could. He bought another home, and the debate continues over such issues as whether the governor should live downtown or in the suburbs.

Memorial Auditorium

A block down from the Governor's Mansion is the Memorial Auditorium, covering the entire block bounded by Fifteenth, Sixteenth, I, and J streets. The immense brick and stone structure, built in 1926 of Byzantine design at a cost of $750,000, was built as Sacramento's tribute to the veterans of World

War I and is listed in the National Register of Historic Places. It stands on the grounds of one of the ten parks donated to the city by John Sutter, Jr. The site was formerly occupied by the Mary J. Watson Grammar School, an elegant Victorian structure.

Over the years the building has served as a civic center and hosted opera, theater, conventions, sporting events, and concerts. During World War II it was used as a temporary detention facility for Sacramento's Japanese population until more permanent concentration camps could be built. On March 30, 1942, all persons of Japanese ancestry, including native-born Americans and long-time legal residents of Sacramento, were ordered to surrender themselves for detention. For this reason, the Memorial Auditorium has been designated a state historical landmark. (A permanent ceramic mural memorial to the internment of Japanese-Americans is located at the County Administration Center, 700 H Street, just inside the south entrance on the west wall.)

Library and Courts Building

Across the street from the state capitol is perhaps the city's most-over-looked spot of splendor. The Library and Courts Building at the west end of Capitol Park at Ninth and Capitol Mall is a jewel box filled with massive pillars of Italian black marble, Grecian statues and lamps, colorful murals of crusaders and Californians, and walls of carved eucalyptus.

The Library and Courts Building is one of two neoclassically styled government buildings called the Capitol Extension Group that were recently added to the National Register of Historic Places. The other building, known as State Office Building No. 1, faces the Library and Courts Building across the fountain plaza. Completed in 1929, the buildings appear to be made of gray granite but actually are made mostly of terra cotta fashioned to look like granite. The buildings feature stone pediments containing figures up to twelve feet tall that tell an allegorical history of California and four Grecian-style statues beside the broad steps.

The California State Library and state supreme court are housed in the Library and Courts Building, open weekdays 8–5. As you enter the building, you pass through two vestibules, the second of which is a memorial to veterans of World War I and features large black marble columns topped with bronze Greek temple lamps. The blue and gold ceiling is encircled by a mural depicting warriors throughout the ages. The state supreme court is head-quartered in San Francisco and meets here just twice a year, in March and November. This is the only time you can see the supreme court chambers, located in a ground-floor room with eucalyptus panels and draped in purple velvet. To find out when the next session will be held, call 322-5957. Monthly sessions of the 3rd District Court of Appeal, also held in this building, are open to the public. Call 445-4677 for information.

The state library, created by the legislature in 1850, was first located at Second and J in Old Sacramento and later in the capitol. The library rooms are on the third floor, accessible by a marble spiral staircase or elevators complete with vases holding fresh flowers. With a vast collection of 800,000 volumes and three million government documents, it is a superb research source for the legislature, state employees, and the public. Of special note are the California section and an extensive collection of past and present California newspapers on microfilm. The library also features a government publications section, law library, state information reference center, and general reading room with golden pillars, studded leather doors, and a large mural of early Californians painted by Maynard Dixon.

A little-known feature of the California section is its collection of thousands of photographs from California's past. The collection was started in 1850 and includes daguerreotypes, tintypes, stereoscopic views, albumin prints, color slides, and conventional black and white prints. The public may browse through the collection, and for a fee the library will provide copies. The state library also maintains the Braille and Talking Book Library at Sixth and Broadway. It supplies tapes and books in braille for the vision-impaired.

The octagonal fifth-floor meeting room, paneled with highly varnished carved eucalyptus, was designed originally to house the state supreme court, which instead decided to occupy chambers on the ground floor. If the doors are locked, you can get the key from the state librarian's office. Hidden by an acoustical tile ceiling is a twenty-foot dome. Discovered only recently by librarians, the rotunda is emblazoned with the state seal at its zenith. Portraits of four California pioneers, including Captain John Sutter and Bret Harte, anchor the four corners. A group of librarians hopes to raise funds to restore the building, including the dome, to its original grandeur.

Information on self-guided tours of the building may be picked up in the California section; the state library phone number is 322-4570.

California State Archives

Housed in a massive three-story concrete building at 1020 O Street is the California State Archives, repository of the documentary history of California. The collection of some fifty-five thousand cubic feet of historical paper—an estimated 110 million individual documents—officially traces California's history. Although there are some records of the Spanish and Mexican period (most were destroyed during the 1906 San Francisco earthquake and fire), most of the documents relate to California after 1848. The archives contains the original and official records of the legislature for all its sessions since 1849, including the original state constitution of 1849, written on animal skins in both English and Spanish, and the 1879 constitution. (Until 1879, a provision required all laws and regulations to be in English and Spanish, since nine of the state's forty-eight founding fathers were Hispanic.) There are election reports, census records dating back to 1852, military records, prison registers, court cases, public school reports, land grant maps, and other documents. The heart of the archives complex is the vault, which contains not only the constitutions and land grant records but also volumes of the only remaining copies of laws passed by California's first legislative sessions.

Most of the researchers who use the archives are scholars or legislative aides researching bills, but the documents are available to the public as well. Although none of the holdings can be removed, copies are available for a small fee. Displays of original documents, maps, and photographs are regularly featured in the exhibit hall, which provides an introduction to the state archives. The archives and exhibit hall are open weekdays, and the more valuable documents are available for viewing with advance reservations (445-4293).

Stanford Home

The juxtaposition of the old and the new in downtown is evident at Eighth and N streets, where the elegant Victorian Stanford Home is dwarfed by the sixteen-story State Water Resources Building behind it. The home was built in 1857 as a two-story brick and plaster structure and purchased by Leland Stanford in 1861 along with two planted lots for $8,000. That fall Stanford was elected governor, and on inauguration day the city was flooded. So the resourceful Stanford traveled to the inauguration in a rowboat and returned home through a parlor window.

Leland Stanford, Jr., was born in 1868 in his mother's bedroom. He died of typhoid in Italy at the age of sixteen, and it was in his memory that his parents built Stanford University. The house underwent an extensive remodeling project beginning in 1871. Under the guidance of architect Nathaniel D. Goodell, the brick house was jacked up one full story and a ballroom was placed underneath. It was topped with another story that included a mansard roof and deeply set dormered windows. The front porch was enlarged and embellished with Corinthian columns and an imposing horseshoe staircase. The furnished home included sixteen-foot ceilings, carved oak and walnut panels, and a total of forty-four rooms. The Stanfords remained here until 1874, when they moved to Nob Hill in San Francisco. Mrs. Stanford gave the home to the Roman Catholic diocese in 1900 in memory of her son, and since then it has housed a program for troubled youth run by the Sisters of Social Service. The home is now owned by the California Department of

Parks and Recreation, which has plans for an estimated $1.5 million refurbishing job to restore the vintage residence to its original 1857 splendor. The Stanford Home will be run as a museum much like the Governor's Mansion, offering a rare glimpse of original period silver, crystal, and mahogany.

Crocker Art Museum

The block of O Street between Second and Third is distinctive for two important reasons. Not only is it the site of the oldest public art museum west of the Mississippi, it is also the location of one of Sacramento's oldest homes. The Hastings-Crocker Home was designed by architect Seth Babson in 1853 for banker B. F. Hastings. Facing Third Street, the three-story classicist brick and stucco house was purchased in 1868 by Judge Edwin Bryant Crocker, brother of railroad tycoon Charles Crocker, legal counsel to the Big Four and a state supreme court justice appointed by Governor Stanford. Crocker hired Babson to remodel the home into an elaborate Italianate residence. The refurbished house was completed in 1869 and included six chimneys and wide, one-story wooden verandas on all sides. Inside, the walls were decorated with frescoed panels with gold leaf ornamentation and divided by long mirrors reflecting ornate chandeliers. Mrs. Crocker had a well-known conservatory of exotic plants in a bay on the south side of the home.

In 1869 Judge Crocker, his wife, and his four daughters travelled to Dresden, Germany, to purchase art for a museum he had started building adjacent to his home. Included in their purchases were one thousand drawings by old masters and more than seven hundred paintings. To complete the museum, Crocker brought skilled artisans back from Europe to do the cabinetwork in mahogany, rosewood, and walnut with matched panels of myrtle and maple. A ballroom was built with parquet floors of Spanish cedar and white fir, and tiled floors imported from England. Incorporated into the addition were a billiard room, two bowling alleys, a rollerskating rink, and a third floor devoted to the display of paintings. The building also featured twin curving staircases and extensively painted plaster decorations. The splendid addition was completed in 1871 at a cost of $200,000 and served as a family social center as well as a museum.

Judge Crocker died in 1875, and in 1884 his widow, Margaret Rhodes Crocker, presented the museum to the city. The home was used as a home for girls and later was vacated and vandalized. The city purchased the house in 1911 and ten years later renovated it as a gallery annex. Over the years the Hastings-Crocker Home became hidden behind numerous remodelings of the long, architecturally nondescript annex building cast of the gallery, which was used for storage. A $22 million master plan to improve the museum includes a $7.5 million reproduction of the Hastings-Crocker Home and the construction of a pavilion to link the house with the gallery.

The Crocker Art Museum has been restored and is listed on the National Register of Historic Places. The modern R. A. Herold Wing was added in 1969 to provide more exhibition space. Since 1885 the gallery has been expanded to display a growing collection of paintings and art objects from all over the world. The distinguished old master drawings collection is world renowned and includes works by Dürer, Rembrandt, Boucher, Fragonard, David, and Ingres. The museum's California art collection is superb; it includes numerous works by local artists purchased by Judge Crocker. Two of the most famous are *Sunday Morning in the Mines* by Charles Nahl and *Great Canyon of the Sierras* by Thomas Hill. More recent acquisitions include works by well-known Northern California artists such as Wayne Thiebaud, Robert Arneson, Roy De Forest, William Wiley, and Joan Brown. The collection includes sculpture, furniture, Oriental art, Korean ceramics, Greek vases, pre-Columbian art, contemporary art, and photography.

Besides the permanent collection, the museum has changing exhibits drawn from its own collections as well as outside sources. The museum hosts exhibits, lectures, films, Sunday afternoon concerts, and art festivals. The annual Festival of the Arts is held on a weekend in early May in the Crocker Sculpture Park, adjacent to the museum. The museum gift shop offers an impressive line of art books as well as handcrafted silver and ceramic pieces, antique Oriental jewelry, museum replicas, posters, and post cards. Guided tours are available, and the museum is wheelchair accessible. The Crocker Art Museum is open Tuesday through Sunday; a nominal admission fee is charged. Call 449-5423 for more information.

Southside

One downtown Sacramento neighborhood with a strong ethnic identity is Southside, bounded by R, Broadway, Sixteenth, and Front streets. More than half of the residents are Asian, of whom a third are foreign-born immigrants. Although Southside has been a predominantly Chinese community since the 1930s, a large number of people of Japanese descent live here, and many Southeast Asians have moved in as well. The remainder of the population is made up of whites, Hispanics, and blacks.

The area was called Southside as early as 1906, when the city bought a parcel of land here to create a park. The city paid $19,000 for the land, on which stood a peach orchard, a Chinese vegetable garden, a small lake, a refuse dump, and a sewage canal. One of the people in charge of landscaping the park was John McLaren, a well-known landscape architect who had designed San Francisco's Golden Gate Park. Improvements included filling in the sewage canal and enlarging and deepening the lake. A number of the homes facing the park date to Sacramento's earliest period, including homes at 2114 Tenth, 1926 Eleventh, and 519 U streets.

Southside Park (Sixth and T) today is downtown's largest community park, with twenty acres that include a swimming pool, tennis, basketball, and bocce courts, a fishing lake, jogging track, clubhouse, showers, and picnic facilities. A large amphitheater with a colorful mural as a backdrop is the site of outdoor events, including the annual Cinco de Mayo festival.

Southside's Asian community is concentrated within Tenth, Seventeenth, S, and W streets. Most of the businesses owned or operated by Asians are located along the main streets, Tenth and Sixteenth. Mei Heung Foods at 2030 Tenth Street is one of the larger markets catering to Asians in the area. Two other large markets, Mekong and G. T. Sakai and Company, are located on Broadway between Thirteenth and Fourteenth. The Senator Fish Market at 2215 Tenth specializes in Japanese products, including fish used in sashimi and various imported goods. Throughout the neighborhood are herbalists, acupuncturists, and Chinese family association halls (meeting places of fraternal groups that sponsor social and cultural events). The Sacramento Chinese Community Service Center at 1412 S Street offers a variety of services and classes for the Chinese community.

Before World War II, the neighborhood along Fourth and Fifth roughly between K and P streets was predominantly Japanese. In 1942 these citizens were sent to concentration camps; after the war, most returned to the neighborhood. They were forced to move again in the late 1950s as a result of the city's redevelopment program, and they scattered throughout the city. One block of Tenth Street between V and W has a concentration of Japanese businesses, including a gift shop, a restaurant, and a bakery called Osaka-Ya. The bakery sells Japanese sweet rice cakes along with other Japanese baked goods and specializes in flavored shaved-ice cones. These are made with a machine and flavored syrups imported from Japan and are unlike any frozen dessert you've ever tasted. During the summer, lines of people spill out of the tiny shop onto the sidewalk outside.

Tucked away on R Street between Tenth and Eleventh in a primarily industrial area is a collection of businesses offering a shopper's delight. The Building, a converted 1914 brick warehouse that once housed the Fuller Paint and Kelley Display companies, houses eight shops offering a diverse selection of goods and services. These include fine women's clothing, gift items, sporting goods, handmade jewelry and stoneware, leather goods, and fiber arts supplies. The Building is also usually open Sundays, so you can have brunch next door at the Fox & Goose, a traditional British pub, and then while away the rest of the day shopping.

R Street has its own claim to fame in the annals of Sacramento history, for it follows the route of California's first passenger railroad, the Sacramento

Valley Railroad, which ran east to Folsom. Ground was broken in 1855 at Third and R for the railroad; the site is now a state historical landmark. Plans for Sacramento's light-rail system call for it to follow R Street for a short distance, along the same route as the old Sacramento Valley Railroad.

Sacramento City Cemetery

Judge E. B. Crocker and his wife, Margaret, are among the many illustrious Californians who are buried in the Sacramento City Cemetery at Broadway and Riverside, today a state historical landmark. In 1849, John Sutter, Jr., is believed to have donated the original ten acres for the cemetery, which was later increased to forty acres. Underneath large pine, elm, and magnolia trees on high rolling ground stand obelisks, figures on tall pedestals, tombs, and hundreds of granite and marble headstones.

Sacramento's first cemetery no longer exists. Called New Helvetia Cemetery, it was established in 1848 by Captain John Sutter near his fort. The site, on Alhambra between I and J streets, is now occupied by Sutter Junior High School. Nearby at Thirty-third and K is the site of California's first

John Sutter, Jr., grave, Sacramento City Cemetery

Jewish cemetery, established in 1850. Both sites are state historical land-marks.

A casual stroll through the cemetery, open daily during daylight hours, can provide an abbreviated history lesson, for many of the gravestones read like a Who's Who of early Sacramento and California history. You can pick up a self-guided walking tour map at the cemetery office at the main entrance at Tenth and Broadway (office hours vary, so call first—449-5621). The cemetery has separate sections for fraternal organizations, state officials, and pioneers. Many of the graves are pre-1900; much of the cemetery had been filled by that time. However, there is a veterans' plot with graves from the 1930s to 1950s, and some other graves date from as recently as the 1960s. The area immediately south of the cemetery is occupied by the Odd Fellows and Masonic cemeteries.

Some six hundred victims of the tragic cholera epidemic of 1850 are buried here in long trenches, with as many as fifty in a common grave. Because no death records were kept during the epidemic, the names of the dead and the locations of the graves are not known. If you walk down the center of the cemetery to the southern border, you'll see a large grassy plot on your left with veterans' grave markers set in the ground. Near the walkway is a simple stone marker that reads, "To the memory of the cholera victims—1852." It is believed that beneath the graves of the veterans may be the mass graves of the cholera epidemic victims. No one knows for certain, however, since cemetery records weren't kept until 1858.

Nearby, toward Riverside Boulevard, is a plot for veterans of the Spanish-American War that includes a unique monument. During the war, the U.S. battleship *Maine* was sunk at Havana Harbor in Cuba in 1898. The ship was later raised and taken apart and the pieces distributed to U.S. veterans organizations. Sacramento received two; one is at this site, and the other, marked with a flagpole, is near the north entrance of William Land Park near Twelfth Avenue.

The Sacramento City Cemetery also contains the final resting places of California Governors John Bigler, William Irwin, and Newton Booth; John Sutter, Jr., considered the founder of Sacramento; Mark Hopkins, cobuilder of the Central Pacific Railroad; and many other state and local notables.

Midtown

While Sacramento's central business district has been undergoing a dramatic revival, the midtown area has been quietly developing a unique identity of its own. Midtown includes the Fremont and Marshall neighbor-hoods, which generally fill the area between F, R, Sixteenth, and Thirtieth streets. The neighborhoods are named for the turn-of-the-century schools that still stand there. Since the mid-1970s, midtown has seen an influx of young, educated, and upwardly mobile residents. Today some eight thousand people live here, attracted by the quiet, tree-shaded streets, dignified Victorians, proximity to workplaces, and successful blending of small retail and close-knit residential sections. The commercial resurgence brought about by the area's changing tastes is reflected in midtown's conglomeration of refurbished Victorians, apartments, specialty shops, offices, corner groceries, restaurants, single-family homes, and bed and breakfast inns.

The heart of this cohesive, colorful, and progressive neighborhood is J Street, dubbed the "Rue de J" by one Sacramento writer. J Street has been compared loosely with chic Union Street in San Francisco, known for its refurbished Victorians, boutiques, and chichi restaurants. On the stretch of J Street between Twenty-first and Twenty-ninth streets, you can find everything from brie, baguettes, crepes, and gelato to tacky gifts, inventive toys, art supplies and bicycle parts. You could easily spend an afternoon along J Street, eating and window-shopping your way from one end to the other. Here are just a few of the places you'd see; many are left for you to happily discover on your own.

Established in 1910, Newbert Hardware at 1700 J has been at this location since 1950. With an inventory of about 200,000 items, Newbert's claims to have things nobody else has, like blacksmith's anvils, Italian crystal, fifteen different kinds of pot handles, and tools to roll logs. The Italian Importing Company at 1827 J is a mom-and-pop general store offering imported cheeses, pasta, olive oils, and bulk seasonings. Located in a restored Victorian, the First Sacramento Women's Building at 2224 J houses Lioness Books (the city's only women's bookstore) and the Sacramento Women's Center. In the 2300 block of J you can get rich and creamy gelato (a very dense Italian ice cream), frozen yogurt, and creative clothes for kids.

How Tacky, at 2525 J, offers punk and funky objects such as plastic pink flamingos, leather ties, bizarre greeting cards, and unusual gift wrap. Next door is Willie's Playground, an adult toy store—five rooms crammed wall to wall with monkeys, old-style tin toys, remote-control boats and jeeps, and what the owner claims is the largest collection of small windup toys in the world. Willie's sells gourmet coffee by the bag or cup as well. You can choose from more than one thousand different take-out sandwiches at Bon Air Sandwiches next door, which has been at the same location since 1947. Beverages, hot food, and desserts are also available. Down in the next block is Taylor's Art Center, with three shops catering to artists and art lovers.

Throughout midtown you'll find pockets of small, unique retail shops and professional offices—gourmet wine shops and small law practices, boutiques and public relations firms. Here's a sampling of what you might find if you venture north or south of J Street. Frank's Meats at 1609 F is an old-fashioned deli where the butcher behind the counter will sell you everything from filets to oxtails to pigs' heads. Weatherstone Coffee & Tea at 812 Twenty-first Street is a coffee-lover's heaven. Bulk coffee and tea are sold here, and you can sip freshly brewed coffee and enjoy a pastry at a table.

South of J Street is West of the Sun, 2131 K, with a great collection of stylish hats, gift items, and other goodies. For funky vintage clothes, there's Cheap Thrills at 1217 Twenty-first and Flashback at 1729 L. For a taste of Old Sacramento without the crowds, there's Gray's General Store at Eighteenth and Q. It's an 1874 building that was moved from Front Street to this location around 1905. The store has had past lives as a grocery, a deli, and an antique store and currently sells homemade giant sandwiches to go. During the summer you can sit at outdoor tables.

State Indian Museum

At the time of first contact with Spanish colonists in 1769, some 300,000 Indians were living in California. They lived in about 120 tribes organized according to language and common territory. After thousands of years of living in physical and spiritual harmony with the land, they had become superbly adapted to their environment, living a mostly peaceful life as hunters and gatherers. By 1846 when white settlers began arriving, there were only an estimated eighty-eight thousand Indians left; by 1900, only about fifteen thousand. They were effectively crushed in numbers and spirit in a variety of ways, many of which came about because of the encroachment of whites during the Gold Rush. The mission system, which stripped the Indians of their culture, took its toll, as did diseases such as cholera, malaria, and smallpox. The natives' numbers were further reduced by wars and massacres and the expansion of white settlements and industries, which diminished the Indians' food resources.

Archeologists have uncovered many ceremonial and everyday articles of the California Indians; much has been learned from these objects about the Indians' way of life. Many of the artifacts can be seen at the newly renovated State Indian Museum at 1618 K Street, behind Sutter's Fort. The four-thousand-square-foot museum depicts the lifestyles of California Miwok, Hupa, Pomo, Yurok, Maidu, Yokuts, and other tribes. Museum relics are grouped according to three themes: family life, spiritual life, and balance with nature. Among the displays is one of the finest Indian basket collections in existence. The California Indians excelled in basketry, using their woven creations for a variety of purposes, from storage to headgear. The women who made the baskets often decorated them with shells and seem to have delighted in making tiny—almost microscopic—baskets for the sheer challenge of it. Many of these minute baskets, as well as larger ones, are on display in the museum. Exhibits also include weapons, pottery, tools, featherwork, dress, jewelry, tule boats and redwood dugouts, mythology, dances, and ceremonies.

Special events on weekends include a slide show and movies on the Indian way of life, Indian legend puppet shows for children, acorn-grinding demonstrations, and live-action exhibitions of other Indian skills. A gift shop next door sells artifacts and jewelry made by Native Americans. The museum is open daily (445-4209).

Sutter's Fort

Sacramento is one of the few U.S. cities whose first permanent building is still standing. A two-story adobe-walled building, it forms the nucleus of Sutter's Fort (2701 L Street), the Sacramento Valley's first white settlement. The fort was built in 1839 by Captain John Augustus Sutter, a German-Swiss immigrant who claimed to have been a captain of the Royal Swiss Guard. Sutter had fled Switzerland after several unsuccessful business ventures resulted in his creditors getting out a warrant for his arrest. In 1834, at the age of thirty-one, he came to America to seek his fortune. He left behind his wife and four children whom he would not see for another sixteen years.

After spending five years making his way across America from New York in the company of trappers, soldiers and traders, Sutter decided to try his luck in California. To avoid the heavy winter snows and bellicose Indians, he headed for California via a long and circuitous sea route that began in the Oregon territory and included stops in the Sandwich Isles (Hawaii) and Alaska. While Sutter was in Hawaii, King Kamehameha had taken a liking to him and assigned him ten Hawaiians (Kanakas) as bodyguards. After reaching Monterey in August 1839, Sutter led an exploration party in three vessels up the Sacramento River and then up the American. On August 12, 1839, Sutter and his small party landed in Sacramento at the south bank of the American River. (The landing site today is a state historical landmark, about two hundred feet north of the marker at Twenty-ninth and B streets.)

NEW HELVETIA

On a knoll about a mile inland, Sutter established a settlement and called it New Helvetia (New Switzerland) after his parents' native homeland. The Kanakas built grass houses with tule roofs and the Indians, whom Sutter had befriended, made adobe bricks for his personal quarters. A two-mile path was cleared to a landing site on the Sacramento, which was unofficially named Sutter's *embarcadero* (Spanish for landing). In the spring of 1840 Sutter began building his fort, designed to accommodate one thousand people, largely using Indian labor. The walls were about three feet thick and fifteen to eighteen feet high. In order to qualify for a Mexican land grant, Sutter became a Mexican citizen and in 1840 Governor Alvarado gave him nearly forty-eight thousand acres.

Agriculture, cattle, fur trading, and a brandy distillery helped to establish Sutter's little empire, which was Central California's sole outpost of civilization. The fort was almost entirely self-sufficient, with facilities for carpentry, blacksmithing, candle- and soapmaking, tanning, coopering, and alcohol distilling. It became a profitable trading center and a place where weary immigrants from the eastern U.S. stopped after their long journey across the continent. Sutter was the consummate host, always ready to provide food and shelter for travelers. Among his guests were Captain John C. Fremont and his guide, Kit Carson, and General Vallejo of Mexico. In 1846 the forty-seven survivors of the ill-fated Donner Party were brought here to recover from their ordeal in the Sierra snows.

By 1847 agricultural and commercial activity were thriving in Sutter's domain. With the promise of new immigration coming steadily, Sutter planned a new city called Sutterville about three miles south of the fort. He needed lumber for its houses and stores, so he sent James W. Marshall to build a sawmill on the south fork of the American River, about fifty miles to the east. In January 1848 Marshall accidentally discovered gold nuggets, which he brought to Sutter's Fort to be tested by Sutter for authenticity. It was the real thing and Sutter tried to keep the discovery a secret, but the news leaked out and California history and Sutter's fortune were to change dramatically.

THE END OF A DREAM

Drawn by the lure of riches, thousands of goldseekers began using the fort as a wayside station and as a trading post for miner's supplies. Sutter's employees had deserted him to seek their own fortunes, leaving his crops unharvested and businesses idle, and unscrupulous partners had swindled him. Hungry miners had stolen and butchered his cattle, and squatters had taken over much of his land. By the end of 1849 the fort was sold to help pay Sutter's immense debts, and by 1852 he was bankrupt and unable to reclaim his property. Sutter retired to his Hock Farm on the Feather River near Marysville with his wife and family. He spent his last years petitioning Congress for compensation for his losses and even moved to Pennsylvania to be near Washington, D.C. On June 16, 1880, Congress adjourned without passing a bill that would have reimbursed Sutter. The man who in less than a decade had transformed an isolated, uncivilized wilderness into a thriving commercial and trading center died in poverty two days later at the Mapes

Living History Days, Sutter's Fort

Hotel near the U.S. Capitol. Sutter is buried at the Moravian Brotherhood Cemetery in Lititz, Pennsylvania.

By the late 1850s, all that was left of Sutter's Fort was the central building. The land was sold for farming and the fort served a variety of functions such as a schoolhouse, a hog farm, and a relief camp for refugees from the 1906 San Francisco earthquake. The fort was donated to the state in 1891 by the Native Sons of the Golden West, who had purchased it the year before. Reconstruction began the same year.

Today hand-held radio wands are supplied for self-guided tours of exhibits depicting daily life in 1848, including blacksmith, carpenter, cooperage, and saddle shops as well as a prison and living quarters. Throughout the courtyard are handsome old wagons and implements, including an old cannon that is fired daily. Sutter's Fort is the only place in the state where the Mexican flag flies every day. If you can arrange it, try to visit the fort on Living History Day, held several times during the year. The fort comes alive as volunteers dressed in period attire take on the identities of pioneers of the 1840s. You can see demonstrations of candle making, bread baking, weaving, and rifle shooting. Participants are well versed in the history of the period, so they're a good source of historical information. You can talk to them, but they remain completely in character. If you're visiting the fort on a typical day in 1846 and you ask Captain Sutter about the Gold Rush, he'll no doubt look at you quizzically and dismiss your frivolous question with a gruff reply (remember—the Gold Rush didn't begin until late 1848). Sutter's Fort is open daily (445-4209).

While you're there, take a walk behind the fort to the tree-shaded duck pond, an ideal spot for a picnic. It's on the site of an old slough that filled up during the winter and allowed small boats to travel directly from the fort to the river. Look for an old cottonwood tree near K Street; it's believed to be a relic dating back to Sutter's time. Some say that when the light is just right, you can see a face in the gnarled bark of the tree trunk.

Victorian Home Tour

Some of Sacramento's greatest treasures are sitting right on the city streets, available for view by anyone who happens by. They are the city's grand old Victorians, standing tall and proud as monuments to a bygone era of opulence and unabashed displays of wealth. At one time the downtown was dotted with hundreds of elegant homes built during the Victorian era (1840–1900). During this period, there were at least nine distinct neighborhoods graced by these lavish houses whose styles included Gothic, Italianate, Queen Anne, Stick, Greek Revival, Eastlake, and High Victorian. Some incorporated several different styles. During the city's early days, as gold became more plentiful and the city grew eastward from the Embarcadero, homes became larger and more elaborate, flaunting the wealth of their owners. As more women joined their husbands in the formerly rough frontier town, they added civilized touches to their homes, such as elaborate gardens, courtyards, and numerous trees. According to one estimate, there may have been as many as one hundred to two hundred grand homes that could be called mansions, making the Governor's Mansion pale by comparison.

Many of the grandest Victorians are now gone, having fallen victim to the ravages of fire, vandalism, old age, and progress. Because of downtown redevelopment on the west end during the 1950s, all the Victorians on Capitol Mall, which once was lined with houses from the 1850s, were demolished. The efforts of preservationists and historians have helped to preserve the city's remaining Victorians possessing historic and/or architectural merit, of which there are an estimated 150 to 200. A leisurely stroll through any of the neighborhoods to the north, east, and south of the capitol will yield a bounty of lovely Victorians—some renovated to their original grandeur, others in a sad and forlorn state of disrepair. As in many other cities, a strong preservation movement has taken hold in Sacramento's downtown. Individuals and families are moving back to the area and restoring older structures to their former beauty. Some are still residences; others now house offices, restaurants, and various other businesses. Groups such as Sacramento Heritage and the Sacramento Old City Association are working to protect and save these irreplaceable treasures. The Old City Association sponsors an annual Victorian Home Tour each September. Watch the newspapers for dates and details, or write SOCA at P.O. Box 1022, Sacramento, CA 95805.

You don't really need to know much about architecture to appreciate Sacramento's Victorians, many of which are embellished with dormers, gables, towers, columns, bay windows, friezes, latticework, leaded glass, and whimsical fans, brackets, and spindles. Three of the city's most outstanding Victorians—the Crocker Art Museum, the Stanford Home, and the Governor's Mansion—have already been discussed. The following Victorians provide a representative sampling of Sacramento's historic homes; there are many more for you to discover on your own.

ALKALI FLAT

Alkali Flat, Sacramento's oldest neighborhood, has numerous historic homes that still remain. The area is listed on the National Register of Historic Places. Bounded by Seventh, Sixteenth, B, and G streets, Alkali Flat was named for the powdery white alkaline deposits left by the flooding rivers. The first homes were built here during the 1850s, when it was a lively neighborhood whose residents included governors and a supreme court justice. Many homes featured formal gardens and fences—necessary to keep out the sheep herded through the streets every spring on their way to grazing grounds. Many frame houses were built later by Southern Pacific employees.

Alkali Flat today is one of the city's most diverse neighborhoods, with a large Hispanic population, an equal number of whites, and a mix of blacks and Vietnamese. Redevelopment efforts have resulted in low-income and senior housing, new street lighting, and preservation and restoration of the area's many historic homes. The following four homes are located in the Alkali Flat neighborhood. While you're exploring, you might want to visit Jalisco Mexican Foods, 318 Twelfth Street, for a good selection of ingredients for Mexican food as well as Spanish-language magazines and piñatas. Jalisco's tortilla factory next door is Alkali's oldest business.

517 EIGHTH STREET

This High Victorian home at 517 Eighth Street was built around 1894 for Mary Mesick, whose husband was an attorney representing Sutter in his land claims. The architect was Nathaniel Goodell, who designed the Heilbron home and the Governor's Mansion. These three homes, along with the Stanford home, are the only remaining houses in Sacramento with mansard roofs, which are tall and intricate with arched and deeply hooded windows. The home had been gutted by fire and was slated for demolition when Sacramento Heritage stepped in and purchased it in 1979. It was restored, sold, and now has a mixed residential-commercial use.

1010 F STREET

Reportedly the second oldest home in Sacramento (the oldest is believed to be the Crocker home), this three-story brick structure at 1010 F Street was built in 1856. The builder was I. M. Hubbard, the son of a sea captain, who had helped to build the first continental telegraph and the first railroad bridge across the American River. The large square bricks of the walkway leading to the castle-like home were made in China and used as ballast in the holds of ships bound for the Pacific Coast. Hubbard's daughter Adelaide and her husband, Lauren Upson, lived here for many years along with Lauren's twin brother, Warren Upson, the famous Pony Express rider who was the first to cross the Sierra. Completely gutted by fire, the Upson home was acquired by Sacramento Heritage in 1978, restored, and converted to offices.

917 G STREET

The two-story brick Italianate home at 917 G Street was built in 1860 for Anthony Egl, a Hungarian who had arrived in Sacramento in 1855 and owned a successful wholesale fruit, nut, and confection business on J Street. A unique feature of the home was the kitchen, which had been built separately from the main house to prevent the heat of cooking from overheating the house during Sacramento's hot summers. One of the city's few brick homes of the Victorian period, the Egl home has been restored as an office building.

925 G STREET

The restored brick Italianate at 925 G Street was built in 1869 for Albert A. Van Voorhies, a successful Sacramento businessman whose many ventures included the manufacturing of harnesses, saddles, horse collars, and other leather goods. Before coming to Sacramento, he had run a prosperous leather store in Placerville during the Comstock rush. The home has been restored and converted into an office complex.

917 H STREET

Surrounded by modern office buildings, the 1885 stick-style home at 917 H Street sits in what was once the fashionable Merchant's Row neighborhood. Bounded by Sixth, Sixteenth, G, and I streets, Merchant's Row had many mansions built by wealthy merchants and lawyers, as well as the Governor's Mansion. A number of grand houses once lined H Street between Seventh and Sixteenth.

This home was built for Sacramento pioneer Llewellyn Williams, who sold it in 1891 for $30,000 in gold to flour magnate Halsey G. Smith. The hand-carved mahogany staircase was ideal for grand entrances at the lavish parties often held here. Things quieted down a bit when the home was converted to a funeral home in 1907 but picked up again when it was leased for a time by the University Club in 1971. Now known as Mory's Place or The Victorian, the home is privately owned and available for private parties, weddings, and receptions. Lunch is served to the public during the week (443-1691).

704 O STREET

The ornate home at 704 O Street sits in what was known as the Capitol Park district, developed in the 1870s after completion of the capitol. Many beautiful homes once stood on L, M, N, and O streets between Second and Fifteenth. This house was built in 1881 for August Heilbron, a German immigrant who was a successful merchant and butcher along with his brother. This lovely home, with a mansard roof and ornamental cornices on the bay windows and porticoes, had its main floor built eight feet above the street. (Although many believe the elevated main floor was a precaution against flooding, this is not the case. It was a universal design feature of the period and had nothing to do with flooding.) The main floor had thirteen-foot ceilings with two parlors, a dining room, library, kitchen, pantry, and toilet. A large dance floor was built in the attic. The home was later converted to a restaurant and now houses a savings and loan office.

1931 TWENTY-FIRST STREET

Located on one of downtown's few hills, this neighborhood was once known as Poverty Ridge, named for the flood victims who would take refuge here during winter flooding. Later, when the land was developed, real estate developers decided the name wasn't conducive to selling property, so they changed the name to Sutter's Terrace. At the turn of the century, the area between Twenty-first, Twenty-third, S, and X streets was one of the city's ritziest, and some of the most elegant downtown homes remain here today.

With the exception of the Governor's Mansion, the Mason home at 1931 Twenty-first Street is probably the most photographed and sketched home in Sacramento and has been featured in several movies and TV programs. From the Late Victorian period, this beautifully restored home is a real eyecatcher, with its predominant corner tower supported by Tuscan columns, ornate wooden corner posts on the stairs, balconied round portico above the front porch, and unusual leaded stained glass. The shingled Queen Anne house was built of brick and wood in 1900 for Fred Mason, who owned Mason's Haberdashery and Mason's Steam Laundry. The two large parlors were divided by Roman Ionic columns, and the dining room had a fireplace and dark wood paneling. Upstairs was a dorm for the male servants. The Masons' bedrooms had such features as built-in window seats, bird's-eye maple, imported glass, and glass-beaded windowshades. They whistled into a speaking tube to summon the servants. Many of the furnishings were purchased by the Masons during their European travels.

Fred Mason died in 1901 and his wife, Caroline, remained here until 1942. The home was purchased and restored in 1968 and remains a private residence. Many of the original furnishings remain, and the home has been returned to its original turn-of-the-century decor.

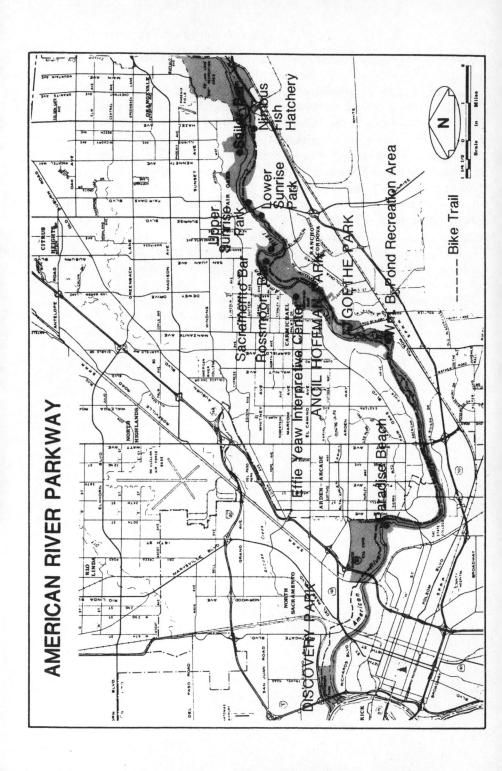

AMERICAN RIVER PARKWAY

Nimbus Fish Hatchery

Lower Sunrise Park

Upper Sunrise Park

Sailor Bar

Wm B Pond Recreation Area

GOETHE PARK

Rossmoor Bar

Sacramento Bar

ANCIL HOFFMAN PARK

Effie Yeaw Interpretive Center

Paradise Beach

DISCOVERY PARK

RANCHO CORDOVA

ARDEN - ARCADE

NORTH SACRAMENTO

NORTH HIGHLANDS

CITRUS HEIGHTS

ORANGEVALE

RIO LINDA

American River

Scale in Miles

N

------ Bike Trail

4

Exploring Sacramento County

Sacramento offers many attractions outside the central city. The Sacramento River Delta region is perhaps the largest and best-known, occupying the southwest portion of the county (see chapters 5 and 6). In addition, there are a number of large county parks (including the American River Parkway), several museums and rural communities, the city of Folsom, and Folsom Lake State Recreation Area.

American River Parkway

The five-thousand-acre American River Parkway is Sacramento's answer to San Francisco's Golden Gate Park and New York's Central Park. More than five times larger than either, the heavily wooded parkway extends twenty-three miles through the heart of Sacramento, from the confluence of the Sacramento and American rivers at Discovery Park to just below Folsom Lake. The twelve-square-mile greenbelt is a haven for outdoor activities such as picnicking, nature study, bicycling, hiking, jogging, boating, fishing, horseback riding, and rafting. Run by the Sacramento County Parks and Recreation Department, the American River Parkway is the county's most popular recreation area, attracting more than three million visitors annually.

The park encompasses twenty major recreation areas along the river, including three large parks—Discovery, C. M. Goethe, and Ancil Hoffman, all of which have ample parking. Major parking areas are also located at Howe and Watt avenues, William B. Pond Recreation Area, Harrington Drive, Sacramento Bar, Upper and Lower Sunrise, and Sailor Bar. You'll see a wide variety of flora and fauna; stately old cottonwoods and oaks grow along the riverbanks, and cottontail rabbits, ground squirrels, deer, raccoons, and beavers make their homes in the dense underbrush. In the late summer, you can even pick wild blackberries along the river.

Although it is not illegal, swimming in the river is discouraged because of whirlpools, snags, and strong currents. Jumping into the river from any of the bridges that cross it is illegal. Dogs must be on leashes, and roller-skating, skateboarding, and riding motorized vehicles are prohibited on the trails. Fires are permitted only in designated barbecue areas, and hunting is not allowed. There are daily parking fees, with all-day and annual passes available. Senior citizens receive a discount; disabled persons are admitted free. For more information on the American River Parkway, including a brochure and a map, call the Sacramento County Parks and Recreation Department at 366-2061. The following are some of the more outstanding features of the parkway, including recreational opportunities.

JEDEDIAH SMITH MEMORIAL BICYCLE TRAIL

The Jedediah Smith Memorial Bicycle Trail is a scenic, two-lane paved bike trail that runs thirty-three miles from Old Sacramento to Beals Point on Folsom Lake, where there's a special campground for bicyclists. The trail was named after explorer and trapper Jedediah Smith, who camped along the American River in 1827 and called it "the Wild River." An estimated four hundred thousand bicyclists use the trail annually—about ten thousand every weekend. From Old Sacramento the trail continues to Discovery Park, where it runs along the north side of the parkway to the William B. Pond Recreation Area. There a foot/bicycle bridge crosses the river, and the trail continues along the south side of the parkway to Hazel Avenue. A three-mile addition to the trail crosses the Hazel Avenue Bridge and continues along the north bank. On the way, it passes through the Cal Expo grounds and the Sac State campus.

One note of caution: although the bike path is patrolled by local law enforcement agencies, it's a good idea for women cyclists and joggers to go in pairs or groups, as there have been instances of harassment, mugging, and purse snatching along certain sections of the trail.

The trail is relatively flat for much of the way, so you don't need to be a marathon cyclist to have a good time. There are one-mile markers along the trail, along with restrooms, plenty of picnic spots, and water fountains. If you plan to go on a summer weekend, try to go early before the weather heats up and the trail gets crowded. Bring along the kids, a picnic lunch, and a blanket and you'll have a pleasant, low-cost outing with lots of beautiful scenery. Call the county parks department for a detailed map of the trail. You can rent bicycles at the American River Bicycle Center, 9205 Folsom Boulevard (corner of Folsom Boulevard and La Riviera, between Watt Avenue and Bradshaw Road). Hourly and daily rates are available at the Bicycle Center, which is near the bicycle trail (363-6271).

RAFTING

If visions of white water and shooting the rapids send shivers of excitement up your spine, take heart; there's a section of the lower American River that's just for you. Although it's feasible to float down the entire twenty-two-mile stretch from Nimbus Dam to Discovery Park, most rafting is done between Sunrise Boulevard and Goethe Park. That trip averages about three hours depending on the river flow, which is controlled by water releases from Folsom Dam.

On hot summer weekends, upwards of fifteen thousand people head for the American to cool off, filling the river with bumper-to-bumper rafts, kayaks, and canoes. The season generally runs from April through September, when most of the raft-rental operations are open. The Sunrise–Goethe Park section of the river is rated Class 1, which means flat water, small waves, and no serious obstacles. There are several small rapids for thrillseekers, including the colorfully named Suicide Bend, San Juan Rapids, and Arden Rapids. All along the river are places where you can put in your raft (called a "put-in") and take it out (yes, a "take-out"). Shuttle bus services transport rafters between the starting and stopping points on both sides of the river for a fee.

If you don't happen to own a raft, you can rent one at one of the many raft rental agencies in the area (check the Yellow Pages under "Rafts"). Rafts are available to hold from two to fourteen people, and fees range from around $10 to $50, including paddles and life jackets. The largest raft rental company in the area is American River Raft Rentals at 11257 South Bridge Street in Rancho Cordova (off Sunrise Boulevard just south of the Sunrise Bridge), 635-6400. In addition to raft rentals and a shuttle bus service, they have a small store selling deli items and a park with picnic tables, a barbecue grill, and restrooms.

Although you don't have to have rafting experience, you should, of course, exercise caution. Wearing your life jacket is extremely important, as most of the drownings that have occurred on the river have involved people who were not wearing them. You should leave infants at home and probably leave your alcohol at home as well, as it's a major factor contributing to accidents and drowning. It's a good idea to bring along hats and a good sunscreen, as well as a pair of old tennis shoes to prevent cut feet, which are common along the river.

For water flow information, call the California Department of Water Resources (322-3327) for a recorded message. The California Department of Boating and Waterways publishes a useful map and guide to river rafting on the American and offers river safety classes (445-2615).

FISHING

Although there are hundreds of fishing spots along the American River Parkway, a few are especially popular. For salmon and steelhead, try Discovery Park, behind Cal Expo, Paradise Beach, the Watt Avenue Bridge, Goethe Park, Sailor Bar, or downstream from the Nimbus Dam. The area on the north side of the river from Discovery Park to Cal Expo is private property, although the county is planning to purchase it. Ponds along the river, stocked with sunfish, black bass, crappie, and catfish, are also popular with anglers. These ponds are located at Sailor Bar, Sacramento Bar, and the William B. Pond Recreation Area. Fishing hours are one hour before sunrise to one hour after sunset; remember that you'll need a fishing license. The river is closed to all fishing and boating from Ancil Hoffman Park to Nimbus Dam from October 16 to December 31 each year because of salmon spawning.

Numerous car-top boat launch sites are located along the river, with the area upstream from Cal Expo the most suitable for this type of boat. Water-skiing on the river is not allowed, as there is a 5 m.p.h. speed limit. There are currently no fishing boat rentals available along the waterways in the vicinity of the central city. You'll have to bring your own boat or go to the Sacramento Delta region to rent one.

HORSEBACK RIDING

Equestrian trails follow both sides of the American River Parkway from Discovery Park to Nimbus Dam (a full day's ride). It's about a two-hour ride from the Sunrise Bridge to Goethe Park. Discovery Park has a fully developed staging area with hitching posts, water troughs, and horse trailer parking. Additional trails are located at Sailor Bar, Mississippi Bar, Sacramento Bar, and Ancil Hoffman Park, which also has a small horse arena and hitching posts. Horse rentals are available at Shadow Glen Riding Stables, 4854 Main Avenue in Fair Oaks (near Mississippi Bar). It's a good idea to make reservations by calling 988-9966.

EPPIE'S GREAT RACE

Billed as the world's first triathlon, Eppie's Great Race is easily the biggest and most popular annual event at the American River Parkway. Held the second Saturday in July, the well-organized event is a run-bike-kayak race through the heart of Sacramento, following the American River between the Guy West Bridge at Sacramento State and the Sunrise Boulevard Bridge. Proceeds from the charity event go to Sacramento County's Recreation for the Handicapped Program. The highlight of the day's activities is the traditional post-race picnic held at Goethe Park. Information on the race is available at most Sacramento bicycle and river recreation shops.

Discovery Park

Located at the confluence of the Sacramento and American rivers, Discovery Park marks the downstream terminus of the American River Parkway and the Jedediah Smith Memorial Bicycle Trail. This 275-acre park has a boat launching ramp and loading dock, grassy picnic areas, a bicycle concourse, two archery ranges, and access to the riding and hiking trails.

Named for the discovery of gold and the important role both rivers played in the Gold Rush, Discovery Park is the site of the historic Indian village of Pushune. Inhabited by the Nisenan, part of the Maidu tribe, it was the most signficant Indian village and burial ground in the region and is a state historical landmark. During the 1840s, the Nisenan had strong economic and cultural interaction with Sutter's Fort. Discovery Park, which is usually closed during the winter because of flooding, can be reached by taking Richards Boulevard off I-5.

Between Discovery Park and C. M. Goethe Park are a couple of areas popular with swimmers and sunbathers. Located off Carlson Drive across the river from Cal Expo is Glen Hall Park, a city park with baseball diamonds, picnic tables, a swimming pool, tennis courts, and showers. Adjacent to the park is Paradise Beach, a wide strip that's a popular sunbathing spot. The smooth white sand draws a largely teen and post-teen crowd to socialize over rock music. Several years ago, the beach gained notoriety as a nude beach, but city officials hastily proclaimed a ban on baring it all on Sacramento beaches. About three miles upriver, you'll find a pebbly beach area under the Watt Avenue Bridge, with access from La Riviera Drive. The beach is popular with swimmers, sunbathers, and fishermen during the summer. Rafts and car-top boats are launched at this park, which has restrooms and parking.

C. M. Goethe Park

C. M. Goethe Park is a 272-acre riverside park located on Rod Beaudry Road off Folsom Boulevard in Rancho Cordova. The heavily wooded park was named for Sacramento conservationist and philanthropist Charles Mathias Goethe (pronounced GAY-tee). The park features grassy picnic areas shaded by large oaks, riding and hiking trails, and easy access to the Jedediah Smith bicycle trail, which crosses the river here on a graceful pedestrian and bicycle bridge. The park is also a popular spot for rafters and fishermen.

Ancil Hoffman Park

Located off California Avenue in Carmichael on the north side of the American River, Ancil Hoffman Park is the busiest of the parkway parks. It was named for the former county supervisor who was also known for managing world heavyweight boxing champion Max Baer. The 386-acre park has an eighteen-hole golf course rated as one of the top fifty public courses in the nation (used by nearly 100,000 golfers annually; 482-5660). The park has oak-shaded picnic areas, game fields, equestrian trails, and a horse arena.

An outstanding feature of the park is the Effie Yeaw Interpretive Center, an eighty-five-acre nature study area (489-4918). Named for a Carmichael teacher who stressed the importance of nature to her students, the center offers a variety of programs for children and adults. The center contains exhibits of flora and fauna native to the area, with live animals such as spiders, turtles, frogs, and snakes as well as dioramas featuring mounted animals and birds. There are educational games, campfire programs, films, a puppet theater, demonstrations, and two self-guided walking tours along the nature trails. During the summer, there are special activities for kids. Free guided tours are available by reservation.

About two miles upriver near the San Juan Rapids at Rossmoor Bar is a steep bank. Known as the Swallow-Cliff Observation Point, it's a nesting place for three different kinds of swallows. Many other varieties of birds can be observed here, including goldfinches, sandpipers, barn owls, humming-birds, mallards, wrens, terns, flycatchers, and killdeer. You can see the nesting spot from the water or from the shore, which is accessible from the bicycle trail via footpaths.

Nimbus Fish Hatchery

The Nimbus Fish Hatchery is at the eastern end of the American River Parkway, just below the Nimbus Dam. From Sacramento, take Highway 50 to the Hazel Avenue exit, then turn left and proceed to the Nimbus Fish

Hatchery sign. The hatchery was built to compensate for the loss of salmon and steelhead spawning grounds inundated by Folsom Lake. Every fall, beginning around October, thousands of salmon make their way from the ocean up the Sacramento River to the mouth of the American and up to the hatchery. The fish swim up a fish ladder into a holding pond and then a tank where they are anesthetized, killed, and their eggs removed. Although it may sound inhumane, this ensures survival of the species, for without the hatchery the salmon would die without spawning.

During the height of the annual spawning season (around mid-November), as many as two thousand salmon a day are processed. The eggs are fertilized and stored until they reach smolt size, about three and a half inches long. Up to thirty million salmon are raised here every year, many of which are released into the Sacramento River near Rio Vista. Thousands of pounds of salmon are donated to charitable organizations, and those not suitable for human consumption are given to zoos for use as bear food. Next to the salmon hatchery is the American River Trout Hatchery, which raises about half a million yearling steelhead annually. Both are run by the California Department of Fish and Game (355-0666). The hatchery is open to the public year-round during daylight hours; October is the best time to visit. You can take a free self-guided tour and buy cups of food to feed the young fish.

FOLSOM SOUTH CANAL RECREATION TRAIL

Beginning at Nimbus Dam, the Folsom South Canal Recreation Trail is a popular bicycling and hiking trail. It parallels the Folsom South Canal, which supplies cooling water for the Rancho Seco nuclear power plant and will eventually extend seventy miles south to supply industrial and irrigation water. The paved trail stretches fourteen miles to Sloughhouse Road and has picnic tables, restrooms, and phones along the way, but no drinking water.

Folsom

Nestled in the northeast corner of Sacramento County about twenty miles northeast of downtown Sacramento is the city of Folsom (pop. 16,000), which straddles the American River. Founded as a Gold Rush town and sustained first by its position as a major crossroads leading to the diggings and later by the railroad, dam, and prison, Folsom today is largely known as a bedroom community for Sacramento and the home of Folsom Prison.

That image is changing, however, as this friendly small town is on the brink of another Gold Rush of sorts. The booty is not gold chips but microchips. Within the last several years, Folsom has been eyed as a relocation site by a number of high-tech firms; four to six of them have settled in the south-

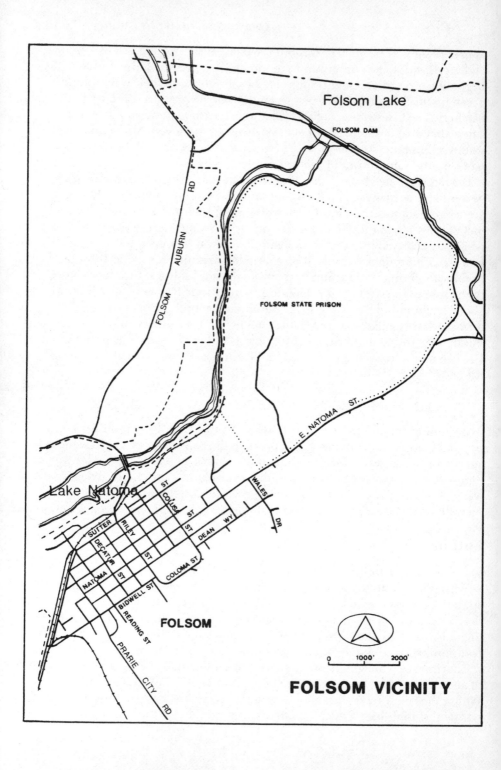

Folsom Lake

FOLSOM DAM

FOLSOM STATE PRISON

E. NATOMA ST.

AUBURN RD

FOLSOM

Lake Natoma

ST
COLUSA
ST
ST
WALES
DR

SUTTER

RILEY

DEAN WY

DECATUR

ST

COLOMA ST

NATOMA

ST

BIDWELL ST

COLOMA ST

FOLSOM

READING ST

PRARIE CITY RD

0   1000'   2000'

FOLSOM VICINITY

western section of town. At least three industrial complexes have been or are being built, and many housing developments are following to supply housing. Folsom is now the ninth-fastest-growing city in the state. Since 1970, its population and housing have doubled—the biggest jump in Sacramento County—and by the year 2000 the population could grow to forty thousand or sixty thousand. Newer subdivisions with expensive homes in the hills on the north and south sides of the American River have been dubbed "New Folsom" by old-timers. Folsom city officials have been actively seeking industrial growth as a means of becoming economically self-sufficient and providing residents the opportunity to live and work in the same community. They insist that they want to preserve the town's historical Old West character. But the town's motto, "Where the West came and stayed," might nonetheless have to be changed to "Where Silicon Valley came and stayed."

GOLD RUSH BEGINNINGS

Folsom's decision to maintain and preserve its historical significance is a wise one, for the town is firmly rooted in the California Gold Rush. Folsom is usually left out of descriptions of the gold country, perhaps because of its distance from Highway 49, but it played a crucial role just the same. First inhabited by Maidu Indians who thrived along the banks of the American River, the area was later part of a thirty-five-thousand-acre Mexican land grant known as Rancho de los Americanos. The land was owned from 1844 to 1848 by William A. Liedesdorff, a native of the Danish West Indies. Folsom began as a small mining camp called Negro Bar, established in 1850 by a group of black miners on a wide bar in the American River. When the camp flooded, it was rebuilt as Granite City. The land grant property was purchased from Liedesdorff's heirs by Captain Joseph L. Folsom, who had come to California during the Mexican War. Folsom hired Theodore Judah to engineer a railroad line from Sacramento to Folsom and lay out plans for a new community. By 1856 the new town at the northeastern tip of the land grant was finished, and the lots were auctioned off in one day. It was renamed Folsom in honor of Captain Folsom, who had died a year earlier in Mission San Jose.

Although few of the '49ers found great riches in the Folsom area, there was plenty of gold around. Much of it was concentrated at Negro Bar, although it was found as far south as the Nimbus Dam area. Many other gold mining towns sprang up; some of them disappeared after the gold played out, and others were inundated by Folsom Reservoir in the mid-1950s. Little or nothing remains of the mining camps of Ashland and Prairie City, once thriving towns. Ashland was located across the river near the present intersection of Greenback Lane and the Folsom-Auburn Road. Originally called Big Gulch, it was still lively in the 1860s, with miners' cabins and a few saloons. It was the focal point of two railroads that were put out of business in the mid-1860s by competition from the transcontinental railroad. You can still see portions of the roadbeds of both railroads in the Ashland area and along the Folsom-Auburn Road. The area was later used for cattle grazing and in the early 1900s for olive orchards and vineyards. Some of the olive orchards remain today.

Much quartz mining was done south of Folsom and at Prairie City, located near the present intersection of Highway 50 and Prairie City Road. At the height of its prosperity in 1853, Prairie City was a center for trade and boasted fifteen saloons, ten boarding houses and hotels, and two stagecoach lines that operated daily. During the 1850s, a quartz mill costing $50,000 operated here. Today a historical marker is all that remains at the site of this once-bustling town of twenty-five hundred. One short-lived gold camp was Texas Hill, located about a mile below Folsom. After the mines played out, enterprising miners went into the cobblestone business, shipping many of the "Folsom potatoes" to Sacramento and San Francisco via the Sacramento Valley Railroad. Some of these cobblestones remain in Old Sacramento and in the downtown streets of San Francisco.

Construction and filling of the 11,500-acre Folsom Dam and Reservoir during the mid-1950s inundated some twenty-four ghost towns. The lost towns that now lie under the lake had colorful names like Salmon Falls (one of the largest), Red Bank, Maple Ridge, Condemned Bar, Negro Hill, and Mormon Island. Many cemeteries had to be moved during construction of the reservoir. The largest of these, with about a hundred graves, was at Mormon Island. The Mormon Island Cemetery was moved to its present site on the eastern side of Folosm Lake on Green Valley Road, about three miles east of Folsom. Buried here are early pioneers from Mormon Island, Negro Hill, and Salmon Falls.

During construction of Folsom Lake, archeological digs attempted to salvage the area's historic Indian artifacts. A great deal of farmland was lost, and 142 parcels of land were affected by the construction. Fifty-one buildings had to be torn down or moved, and it is believed that there is still gold under the lake.

In 1856, when the twenty-two-mile Sacramento Valley Railroad line from Sacramento to Folsom was completed, Folsom became the foothill terminus of the West's first railroad and the center of trade between Sacramento and the foothill camps (and later the Comstock Lode of Nevada). That same year, Folsom got its first newpaper, the *Telegraph,* which is still published (the fourth oldest weekly in California). Because of its accessibility to the railhead, Folsom became the western terminus for the Pony Express in 1860. After the mail reached Folsom, it was sent to Sacramento by train. A historical marker on Sutter Street near Decatur commemorates Folsom's role in the Pony Express.

Although Folsom thrived as a commercial center, the search for gold in the region continued. By 1865, millions of dollars' worth of gold had been dug or panned from the Folsom area. Dozens of small tunnels still remain under and around Folsom. The thousands of mounds of rocks surrounding the city are tailings (debris) stacked by the bucket line dredgers that began surface mining in the late 1890s. These huge, steam-powered monsters, sometimes two hundred feet long, were built on barges floating in man-made ponds. Five-ton, fifteen-cubic-foot scoops could dig deep into the ground and dump the extracted rocks into a cylinder, where they were washed and their gold-bearing particles separated out. As many as thirteen dredgers operated around the clock, slowly working their way along the American River between Sailor Bar and Mormon Island. By 1962 local dredger mining operations were stopped because of the high cost of production. Nearly thirty thousand acres of land had been dug, washed, and stacked in tailings, and more than $100 million in gold had been mined. With the increase in housing construction in the area, these large rockpiles are slowly disappearing, their contents used for construction sites.

FOLSOM TODAY

As modern shopping centers and housing tracts spread away from the Sutter Street area to Natoma and East Bidwell streets, the old section of town began an economic downslide. To preserve the city's historical character, a four-block stretch of Sutter Street was restored beginning in the 1950s, complete with gaslights. The result is the charming Historic Sutter Street, a shopping area with more than 120 shops in historic buildings in a Gold Rush setting. Sutter Street is the site of numerous art events and antique shows, including the annual Sutter Street Flea Market in April, the Arts and Crafts Fair in May or June (a festive arts and music event), and the Peddler's Fair in September. For information on current events in Folsom, call the events hot line at 351-0824.

The recently renovated Folsom Hotel (1885) at 703 Sutter is a historic hostelry that still rents rooms and has a restaurant and saloon with weekend entertainment (985-2530). The Sutter Gaslight Theater, on Sutter near Wool, presents classic melodrama every weekend (the plays are changed every three months). It's adjacent to the Sutter Club, a restaurant and bar where you can dine before the show. For information or reservations, contact the Sutter Club, 720 Sutter Street, Folsom, CA 95630, 985-2093. Across from the theater at 717 Sutter is Patsy's, an authentic old-fashioned soda fountain. In business since 1905, the pink and frilly parlor serves traditional fountain goodies along with breakfast and lunch. Nearby at 727 Sutter is Emiliano's, an elegant restaurant serving California cuisine with a Mexican touch. Lunches and dinners are served on linen-topped tables in surroundings of oak paneling, cranberry carpets, and etched glass. Entrees include *carne asada* tacos, salmon with *salsa tomatillo,* and duck in orange and tequila sauce. For reservations call 985-7333.

Old Folsom has several historic structures worth seeing. The Wells Fargo Assay Office, 823 Sutter (on the west end of the street), was originally built in 1860 and served as a financial center for the region. Gold from all over the territory was brought here to be weighed, and the office was also a stage depot and the terminal for the Pony Express. In 1959 the building was torn down to make way for a gas station that failed shortly thereafter. The office was rebuilt using doors, bricks, and granite blocks salvaged from the original building and is now occupied by the Folsom Historical Society; its museum of Gold Rush memorabilia is open on weekends (985-2707).

The Folsom Chamber of Commerce is housed in the old Southern Pacific Depot at 200 Wool Street (985-2698). Formerly called Folsom Station, the depot was built in 1906 on the site of the terminus of the Sacramento Valley Railroad. Recently added to the National Register of Historic Places, the building houses displays of railroad, mining, and farming artifacts of the area. On the grounds of the depot are authentic replicas of a blacksmith's shop and a miner's cabin. Nearby at 305 Wool is the Pacific Western Traders Gallery of American Indian Art. Here you'll find contemporary paintings, pottery, sculpture, basketry, jewelry, and beadwork by Native Americans.

Located at Liedesdorff Street adjacent to the Rainbow Bridge is the old Folsom Powerhouse, the first in the world to generate long-distance transmission of electricity. Pressure for its water-powered turbines was supplied by the first Folsom Dam, completed in 1893. On July 13, 1895, a General Electric Company official threw the switch that sent electrical power over twelve copper wires from the powerhouse to light up the city of Sacramento twenty-two miles away. That September the citizens of Sacramento celebrated with a grand electric carnival, which lighted the California State Fair with twenty-five thousand incandescent lamps and six hundred arc lights. The original generating plant remained in continuous operation until 1952, when it was donated to the state by Pacific Gas and Electric Company. Now a state historical landmark and listed on the National Register of Historic Places, the old Folsom Powerhouse is part of the Folsom Lake State Recreation Area. Contact the park for hours and tour information: 988-0205.

A popular swimming and picnicking spot is located just across the Rainbow Bridge, which was built in 1918. Negro Bar Campground is on the north bank of Lake Natoma and is part of the Folsom Lake State Recreation Area. The site features picnic areas, camping, and a boat ramp; waterskiing on this lake is not allowed. Just upstream is an unusual configuration of rocks that makes for a popular swimming hole, although no lifeguards are on duty. Fishing for trout between the Rainbow Bridge and the bluffs in this area is particularly good.

High on a bluff overlooking Negro Bar is Tosh's (9900 Greenback Lane, 988-6674), a popular restaurant with gold mining decor. Lace curtains and a cozy fireplace make this a romantic spot for Sunday brunch. Folsom has many fine restaurants, including two with very different styles. Set in Folsom's foothills, Koya's (6693 Folsom-Auburn Road, 989-4926) serves fine Continental food in a pleasant environment of polished oak and chandeliers. In addition to a fancy Sunday brunch, lunch and dinner are served.

As you explore the back streets of Old Folsom, you'll find many gracious old Victorians, some dating back to the late 1850s. Many of Folsom's early merchants built lavish homes in the area around Scott and Figueroa streets, known as Folsom's "Nob Hill." Probably the most famous of these is the Cohn house at 305 Scott Street. The original structure, which is now the kitchen, was built in the 1860s. Part of the home, which is listed on the National Register of Historic Places, is occupied by the present owner's law firm. Two other Victorians occupy the same hill overlooking Sutter Street. Built in 1889, the Burnham house at 602 Figueroa is typical of late Queen Anne architecture. The three-story house was gutted by a fire in 1975 but has been restored by its present owners. Next door at 603 Figueroa is the baroque Hyman house, built in the mid-1880s.

One of Folsom's oldest structures is St. John the Baptist Catholic Church at Sibley and Natoma streets. Built in 1857, the old church was recently refurbished and once again holds Sunday services. Surrounding the church is the Catholic cemetery, established in the mid-1850s for early pioneers. Nearby at the end of Natoma Street off Folsom Boulevard is a complex of pioneer cemeteries that is now a part of the modern Lakeside Memorial Lawn Cemetery. Several cemeteries are located in this complex, including a Jewish cemetery and the Cook cemetery, probably the first burial ground here. Close by is the Chinese cemetery, which contains the graves of four hundred to five hundred Chinese. In the early days, Folsom had a large Chinatown of more than twelve hundred in this area. Back over at Figueroa and Wool is the Trinity Episcopal Church, built in 1858 and still conducting services.

Located just northeast of the old town on Natoma Street, Folsom City Park is a pleasant recreation area for kids and adults. In addition to playground equipment and shady barbecue spots, there's a small zoo, a miniature train, and riverbank trails.

Affectionately nicknamed "the misfit zoo," the Folsom Zoo provides a home for many animals that no one else wanted. The zoo began in 1963 when a badly burned black bear named Smokey was taken in by the city after a fire destroyed the forest where he was born. Since then the zoo has provided a haven for animals injured in the wild or raised as pets and then donated to the zoo. Although the zoo specializes in native species such as bears, cougars, wolves, bobcats, coyotes, foxes, and tule elk, there are a few exotic imports. The zoo is open every day except Monday, and admission is free. Feeding time is in the morning, and the public is invited to watch. For more information, call the city at 355-7200.

On weekends and holidays a miniature train runs alongside the park, pulled by a replica of the 440 Diamond Stack, the first engine to run between Folsom and Sacramento on February 22, 1856. Championship rodeos are held in April, July and October in the Dan Russell Arena adjacent to the park. The Folsom Rodeo is known throughout the rodeo world and boasts one of the largest purses in the nation for its major events, the largest of which is the annual Fourth of July Rodeo sponsored by the Folsom Chamber of Commerce.

Folsom Prison

Johnny Cash immortalized it. Hollywood romanticized it. Yet, standing outside the cold gray granite walls of Folsom Prison, just east of town on Natoma Street, one quickly realizes that this isn't a movie set and there's nothing romantic about it. Nicknamed "the end of the world" by inmates, it holds some of the state's most troublesome and violent prisoners, the majority of whom are doing time for robbery, homicide, and narcotics, in that order.

The original prison complex was built in 1880 to relieve the overcrowded conditions at San Quentin. During the early years, Folsom Prison was known for its cruel and inhumane treatment of inmates. Severe punishment was meted out routinely, meals were scant, baths and clean clothes were a rarity, and medical care was provided only to the dying. Inmates worked in the nearby rock quarry; when the quarry was shut down in the late 1940s, some 150,000 tons of rock had been cut there to be used on the prison grounds and various construction projects around the state. Ninety-two executions by hanging took place at the prison until 1937, when executions by gas were instituted at San Quentin.

With the advances of prison reform came more humanitarian measures. For a while the prison was an autonomous, self-contained little community with its own dairy and farmlands providing food for inmates. All that's gone now, and except for a few vocational and remedial education programs, the atmosphere at Folsom remains highly controlled. One of the reasons for this is the serious overcrowding that has existed until recently, resulting in highly explosive conditions and the constant threat of violence. Although the prison was designed to house 2,000 inmates, at times there have been more than 3,600 crowded inside the walls. In order to alleviate the crowded conditions, the state constructed a new maximum-security facility next to the prison, designed to accommodate another 3,000 inmates.

Main Gate, Folsom Prison

Looking like a medieval castle with rough-hewn walls on three sides and turrets at each corner, Folsom presents a formidable appearance. The fourth "wall" is formed by a series of barbed-wire fences along the American River. Above the main gate, fitted into a gothic arch, is the main tower, a rock cylinder with parapets and a conical top. Visitors are allowed to go through the heavy iron main gate to visit the prison's hobby shop. Open daily, the shop sells the work of inmates, including jewelry, fine woodwork, small wooden toys, and paintings. (The prison is well known for its May and October art shows featuring artwork by inmates. The shows are open to the public.) Adjacent to the shop is the prison museum with its exhibits of prison artifacts. The most popular attraction is the 10-barrel, crank-operated Gatling gun. The 750-pound weapon was mounted on a tower and used to guard the perimeter of the prison before the thirty-foot-high walls were built. No one knows if the gun—found discarded and in disrepair at the prison and refurbished by volunteers—was ever fired during its years of service.

In addition to being the subject of Johnny Cash's "Folsom Prison Blues" (contrary to popular belief, Cash never did any time here), the prison has been used as a location for several movies. These include *Reprieve, Inside the Walls of Folsom Prison, Riot in Cell Block Eleven, The Folsom Prison Story,* and *The Jericho Mile,* a TV movie starring Peter Strauss as a Folsom lifer aiming for a spot on the U.S. Olympic team. Special tours of the prison can be arranged for organizations; for information, call 985-2561.

Folsom Dam

The old Folsom Powerhouse provided electricity for the area until construction began on the Folsom Dam in 1952. Completed in 1956 at a cost of $60 million, the 350-foot-high dam is 1,400 feet long and generates a total of 162,000 kilowatts of power. The dam is the largest of two large dams and eight dikes that form a semicircle roughly nine miles long. Shortly after it was completed, the new dam's potential for flood control was realized when it saved Sacramento from being inundated by heavy rains. Since then the dam has prevented serious flooding a number of times.

Folsom Dam was severely tested early in 1986 when the Sacramento area experienced "the flood of the century" after rains dropped a six-month supply of water within a week in the heaviest rains on record. At the peak of the storm, the dam was filled to capacity, and just one more inch of rain would have caused it to overflow and inundate much of the city. Fortunately, the rains subsided, the dam held, and catastrophe was narrowly averted. Still, serious flooding damaged hundreds of homes in Sacramento and submerged entire towns in neighboring counties.

Seven miles downstream from Folsom Dam is the Nimbus Dam, which stores water released from Folsom Dam and regulates the flow into the

American River. This dam, which is 87 feet high and 1,093 feet long, is also a diversion point for irrigation water. Lake Natoma is the reservoir formed behind Nimbus Dam.

The Folsom Dam can be reached via the Folsom-Auburn Road. Free tours of the powerhouse, dam, and spillway are given weekdays (988-1707). The Folsom Dam Overlook provides a good view of Folsom Prison.

Folsom Lake State Recreation Area

Folsom Lake is part of the eighteen-thousand-acre Folsom Lake State Recreation Area, the state's most popular year-round, multi-use park. Some four million people flock here each year to fish, hike, camp, picnic, waterski, boat, swim, bicycle, and study nature. Folsom Lake, the larger of the park's two lakes, is the third largest lake in the state park system and has more than seventy-five miles of shoreline. Lake Natoma is the park's other lake, with thirteen miles of shoreline.

The terrain surrounding Folsom Lake, which is fed by the north and south forks of the American River, ranges from rolling foothills to steep, rocky canyons. The open woodlands are home to a variety of plant and animal life. There's an abundance of valley oak (the same kind of trees that proliferated in Sacramento when Captain Sutter arrived) as well as blue oak, Digger pine, toyon, California buckeye, and chaparral. Watch out for poison oak, which is everywhere. During the spring the ground is colorful with wildflowers, including Indian paintbrush, California poppy, larkspur, lupine, morning glory, and monkey flower. Some of the more common animals in the park are black-tail deer, ground squirrel, raccoon, skunk, opossum, gray fox, rabbit, and bobcat. There are also occasional sightings of mountain lions and coyotes. Many varieties of resident and migratory birds abound in the park, including as many as ten thousand Canada geese that migrate to the area early in the fall. Great blue herons nest in the Digger pines of Anderson Island, a ten-acre natural preserve sitting in the north end of the lake.

Three major campgrounds surround Folsom Lake. Located one mile north of Folsom Dam off Folsom-Auburn Road, Beals Point offers shady picnic sites, a large sandy beach, lifeguards, wheelchair-accessible restrooms and showers, and concessions. The Peninsula Campground, on the east side of the lake about twenty-eight miles from park headquarters, is the most secluded and can be reached by car via ten miles of paved and gravel roads from Pilot Hill on Highway 49 or by boat. Flush toilets and piped water are available. Negro Bar Campground, across from Folsom on Lake Natoma, features picnicking, swimming, wheelchair-accessible restrooms, and a boat-launching ramp. These campgrounds are open year-round, with reservations available through Ticketron recommended from April through September. The campgrounds have piped water and flush toilets; Negro Bar has cold showers. Boat camping is allowed at certain areas, but you must register at the Granite Bay entrance station or at Brown's Ravine Marina. There are also twelve environmental camps with no amenities scattered around the lake.

Five launching ramp areas are located around the lake. The largest, Granite Bay, is also a popular beach for picnicking, swimming, and sunbathing. Restrooms here are wheelchair accessible. Granite Bay has lifeguards, boat rentals, and concession stands, but it gets very crowded in the summer. Access is from Douglas Boulevard east of Roseville or via the Folsom-Auburn Road. Brown's Ravine and Dyke 8 (access from Green Valley Road) offer east-side picnicking and launching facilities. Folsom Lake Marina at Brown's Ravine has boat storage and slips, tow service, and a gas dock.

Waterskiing, sailing, and windsurfing are favorite sports at the lake. Windsurfing boards can be rented by the hour at Folsom Lake. The largest inland sailing regatta in the state, the Camellia Cup Regatta, attracts as many as four hundred entries to the lake each March. Anglers can fish for a wide variety of fish at Folsom Lake, where fishing is allowed anywhere around the lake and river. You may want to ask a park ranger or visit one of the bait and tackle shops in the area to find out where the fish are biting best. The lake is full of trout, bass, crappie, some salmon, and catfish. Although you can fish throughout the year, May and June are the two best months, with bass, panfish, trout, and salmon hitting consistently. Remember to bring along a fishing license.

For hikers and equestrians, the park has eighty miles of trails. The Lake Natoma Trail follows the north shore of the lake from the Nimbus Dam to Negro Bar; the South Fork Trail begins at Brown's Ravine and ends near the Sweetwater Creek area. The park's longest path is part of the Western States Pioneer Express Trail, which runs between Carson City, Nevada, and Sacramento. There are currently no horse rentals at the lake. Bicyclists can now ride thirty-three miles from Old Sacramento to Folsom Lake on the Jedediah Smith Memorial Bicycle Trail (see the beginning of this chapter). Hike/bicycle-in campsites are available at Beals Point, the eastern terminus of the bike trail.

Folsom Lake can be reached by taking I-80 to Douglas Boulevard East, then going down Douglas to Granite Bay or Auburn-Folsom Road south to Beals Point. An alternate route is Highway 50 to El Dorado Hills Boulevard and then to Green Valley Road. The recreation area charges day-use and camping fees and an extra fee for boats and dogs. Annual passes are available, as well as wheelchair-accessible campsites and picnic sites. To obtain a handy park brochure and map, drop by or write the park headquarters at 7806 Folsom-Auburn Road, Folsom, CA 95630, 988-0205.

Other Sacramento County Parks

In addition to the American River Parkway and its parks in the Sacramento Delta, the Sacramento County Department of Parks and Recreation operates several outstanding regional parks throughout the county. They offer everything from water recreation, field sports, and picnicking to a working ranch and an off-road vehicle park.

GIBSON RANCH PARK

Located on the north side of Elverta Road west of Watt Avenue, Gibson Ranch is an actual working ranch and the county's most unusual park. This 326-acre ranch has a colorful history dating back to when it was once part of the Rancho del Paso Mexican land grant and was homesteaded in the 1870s. R. H. Gibson bought the ranch in the 1930s to raise quarter horses and ornamental birds. This is a great place to take children, who can feed and pet the domestic farm animals—cows, horses, sheep, goats, chickens, rabbits, and more. The park has early day farm equipment displays, old buggies, a blacksmith and carriage shop, and a ranch house available for group meetings. The Old Swimming Hole is popular for swimming and wading, with spacious grassy and sandy areas for sunbathing; there are showers and a changing area. You can fish for catfish, bass, sunfish, and bluegill in an eight-acre pond. If all that's not enough, there are also five miles of equestrian trails, two horse arenas, picnic areas, and facilities for day and overnight camping. The park is open daily throughout the year (991-5322).

PRAIRIE CITY OFF-HIGHWAY PARK

Fans of motocross, 4-x-4s, and mud drag racing have a park designed just for them. Motorcycle and four-wheel-drive enthusiasts have been coming to Prairie City, an 836-acre off-highway vehicle park, since it opened in 1977. The park includes two official motocross tracks, a dirt autocross track, a mud drag-racing strip, and miles of well-marked trails. There's also a quarter-midget track (quarter midgets are small cars powered by lawnmower-size engines) and a bicycle motocross track for kids. Each March, Prairie City hosts the Hangtown Motocross, a pro-am race that attracts more than thirty thousand spectators. Amenities at the park cover the bare necessities: portable restrooms, running water, first aid services, and a phone. Park expansion plans include an oval-track speedway. Admission is low, and hours vary depending on the season; call 351-0271 for information. To get there, take Highway 50 east to Prairie City Road in Folsom; the park is about six miles south via Prairie City Road.

Motocross racing is also held nearby at the Sacramento Raceway Park, 5305 Excelsior Road (behind Mather Air Force Base). This private park features Wednesday night drag racing along with Friday night motocross and all-terrain vehicle racing. Call 363-2653 for information.

RANCHO SECO PARK

If you don't mind picnicking in the shade of the twin cooling towers of Rancho Seco nuclear power plant, you can visit the county's Rancho Seco Park on Twin Cities Road east of Highway 99. The four-hundred-acre park has a 165-acre lake for sailing and windsurfing and offers boat launching ramps and docks, a beach with a lifeguard during the summer, a bathhouse, and concessions for food, drinks, and fishing tackle. The lake is stocked with bluegill, red-ear sunfish, and bass.

If you have any concerns at all about potential exposure to radioactivity, you may want to consider the following before you visit the park. The nuclear power plant has been a center of controversy since it went on line in late 1974. The plant has had more than forty "mishaps" (significant problems), with one resulting in the death of two plant workers. The plant has generated electricity only 48 percent of the time since it went into operation. Small amounts of radioactivity have regularly been released in the steam emitted from the cooling towers. Radiation has also contaminated the creeks that drain the plant's wastewater.

ELK GROVE PARK

Elk Grove Park is the county's most popular park, after the American River Parkway. Every year some 800,000 people come here to play or watch softball at the county's largest softball complex. Half of the park's twelve diamonds are lighted. The 125-acre park also features a swimming pool and bathhouse, group picnicking areas, playground equipment, a pavilion, and a lighted horse arena. A three-acre lake has pedal boats for rent and is stocked with warm-water game fish; a small island in the lake called Pirates' Island is equipped with playground apparatus. Also located here is the Rhoads School, a restored one-room schoolhouse built in 1872 that was relocated here from the Sloughhouse area. The park is the site of Elk Grove's Western Festival, held each year on the first weekend in May. The popular event features a parade, arts and crafts booths, a petting zoo, music and dancing, and food concessions. Elk Grove Park (685-3908) can be reached by taking the Elk Grove Boulevard exit east off Highway 99 to Elk Grove-Florin Road.

McClellan Air Force Base Aviation Museum

The McClellan Air Force Base Aviation Museum boasts one of the largest collections of aircraft and aviation memorabilia in the West. For the past several years, aviation history buffs at McClellan Air Force Base have been locating and restoring military aircraft. Combined with displays, photographs and other items, the planes help to tell the story of the base, a maintenance depot and supply facility opened in 1939. Located at the base near I-80 in the north area, the museum features outdoor displays of restored aircraft, many in flyable condition. These include one of the few remaining flyable Connies, the planes that flew missions out of McClellan for twenty years, and an F-80B Shooting Star fighter.

The museum collection is still being developed and includes indoor displays of old uniforms, photographs, and other memorabilia, as well as hands-on exhibits such as a World War II instrument trainer and an airplane cockpit. Programs include guided tours, lectures, and oral and visual history programs, and souvenirs are available. You can enter the base at Gate 3 (Watt Avenue), where you'll be given a pass to drive on base to the museum. Admission is free; call 643-3192 for information. (McClellan Air Force Base is also the home of California's largest Coast Guard air station.)

Sacramento Science Center and Junior Museum

The Sacramento Science Center and Junior Museum provides children with a delightful introduction to nature and science through hands-on experience. Located in Del Paso Park, 3615 Auburn Boulevard at Watt, the museum features live animals that can be petted, nature films, an action lab, library, walk-through aviary, mobile pet museum, and gift shop. A unique animal lending library lets kids "check out" a pet. A recent addition is a thirty-foot-diameter "spacearium" offering programs on the night sky and the marvels of space exploration. Bring a picnic lunch to enjoy on the picnic tables beside the pond in the outdoor picnic area. Much of the twelve-acre grounds are planted to show coast, valley, and mountain plant types of Northern California. Open daily, the museum also provides day camps and special classes for children during the summer and holidays. Call 485-4471 for more information.

Mather Air Force Base

Located about ten miles east of downtown off Highway 50 in Rancho Cordova, Mather Air Force Base is the nation's only navigator training base. Opened by the Army as an aviation training school in 1918, it was named for aviation pioneer Carl Mather, who had died that same year. The base was closed from 1923 to 1935, when funds were provided to renovate and reopen the base. Mather has two attractions open to the public—an aviation museum and a planetarium—and sponsors an air show each fall.

Opened in 1978, the Silver Wings Aviation Museum traces the history of military and civilian aviation. The museum displays an interesting collection of aircraft as well as other artifacts and memorabilia, including the spacesuit worn by Apollo astronaut M. Scott Carpenter, a replica of a 1914 airplane hanger, and a World War I display. Every November the museum sponsors a free aviation film festival, featuring some of the 150 films in its collection. Tours are available at the museum, which is free and open daily (364-2177).

The Mather Planetarium is used to train pilots in celestial navigation and is open to the public by reservation. The domed ceiling displays facsimiles of the planets, stars, comets, meteor showers, and constellations. Special tours are open to groups of fifteen or more; participants must be age twelve or older. For information contact the public affairs office at 364-2908.

Sloughhouse

Sloughhouse is a tiny farming community located in the Cosumnes River valley about eighteen miles southeast of Sacramento on Highway 16 (Jackson Road). It got its start in 1850 when Jared Dixon Sheldon built a hotel for travelers on the road to the Amador mines. Three miles southeast of Sloughhouse is the site of a grist mill he built in 1846, which is now a state historical landmark. The roadhouse soon gained prominence and became an important stage stop, boasting such illustrious visitors as Leland Stanford. On the site of the original hotel stands the Sloughhouse Inn, a comfortable country restaurant with varnished wood, antique photos, and etched glass. Serving down-to-earth meals, the restaurant also has a comfortable cocktail lounge and a large railed deck overlooking the open countryside for warm-weather dining. Reservations are not accepted, so be prepared for a wait on weekends. Lunch is also served (423-2115).

If you're looking for downtown Sloughhouse, look no farther than the Sloughhouse Inn; that's it. Although there is no town per se, many descendants of pioneers of the community that developed near the inn still live here. Some are involved in growing hops, the delicate green cones used in brewing beer. At one time, Sacramento was planted in more than six thousand acres of hops and was one of the major hop-producing counties in the country. But a decline in the domestic hops trade has reduced Sloughhouse plantings to about forty acres, and even these may be replaced soon with other crops. Hops are grown by draping the vines over eighteen-foot-high trellises, which are being left in place in the hope that the hops market will revive. If not, it will signal the end of a way of life truly Sacramentan.

If you continue east about seven miles on Highway 16, you'll reach the thirty-five-hundred-acre Rancho Murieta, a country club community about twenty-four miles from downtown Sacramento on the Cosumnes River. Surrounded by verdant meadows and gently rolling hillocks, Rancho Murieta has many recreational facilities open to the public. In addition to two 18-hole golf courses (rated among the nation's top ten), the resort has lighted tennis courts, an equestrian center offering riding lessons and horse shows, a small airport with annual air shows, and a hotel. You can swim and picnic at a small beach on the Cosumnes. Throughout the year, Rancho Murieta sponsors events such as music festivals, car shows, and bicycle and jogging races. One outstanding feature of the country club's restaurant is its sumptuous Sunday brunch. Reservations are required; call 985-7200.

About two miles farther down the road is the site of Michigan Bar, once a booming mining town. Located in the vicinity of Michigan Bar Road and the Cosumnes River, Michigan Bar was named by goldseekers from Michigan who discovered gold here in 1849. During its heyday, it had a population of fifteen hundred with a post office and Wells Fargo agency. The town, a state historical landmark, has been practically obliterated by hydraulic and dredging operations.

Elk Grove

The community of Elk Grove got its start in 1850 as a hotel and stage stop to serve travelers from Sutter's Fort. The Elk Grove Hotel was built by James Hall, who brought his family to California from Missouri in 1850. There are two versions of how the hotel and, later, the town were named. One is that they were named for the elk that allegedly roamed the area. The more likely story is that the name came from the name of Hall's hometown in Missouri.

The old Elk Grove Hotel served as an entertainment center during the Gold Rush days, with Sacramentans making the three-hour buggy ride on the upper Stockton Road to dance and party all night. A post office and general store were soon built, and by the 1870s there was a flour mill, hardware store, meat market, furniture factory, two drug stores, and a harness shop. The Elk Grove Hotel remained standing at the western edge of Elk Grove Park until 1958, when it was torn down to make way for Highway 99. The original hotel site now lies under the northbound lane but is being reconstructed nearby by the Elk Grove Historical Society. Some of the original materials were salvaged and are being used in the reconstruction.

Elk Grove today is a small unincorporated community (pop. 14,000) about fifteen miles south of Sacramento via Highway 99. In addition to Elk Grove Park—a major county park—and the hotel reconstruction, there are several historical sites in the area. The grave of Elitha Cumi Donner Wilder, a survivor of the ill-fated Donner party, can be seen at the Elk Grove Masonic Cemetery at Highway 99 and Elk Grove Boulevard. The site of the state's first free county library branch, a state historical landmark, is located at 9125 Elk Grove Boulevard. It was established in 1908 through the efforts of the principal of Elk Grove Union High School.

If you happen to be driving through Elk Grove on a Sunday morning, you may want to pull in at the county's only drive-in church. Established in the mid-1970s, the Sacramento Community Drive-in Church is located at 8555 Stockton Boulevard between Calvine and Sheldon roads and offers Sunday services that you can hear from the comfort of your car.

Just south of town is Murphy's Ranch, the site of the beginning of the American conquest of California. Also known as Murphy's Corral, the site is west of Highway 99 at the Grant Line Road interchange. On June 10, 1846, American settlers led by Ezekiel Merritt overpowered Mexican soldiers under Lieutenant Francisco Arce and took their horses from the Murphy Ranch corral on the north bank of the Cosumnes River. The Elk Grove Historical Society hopes to reconstruct the old ranch, which is a state historical landmark.

5

The Sacramento River Delta: A World Apart

For a long time, the Sacramento–San Joaquin Delta was one of the state's best-kept secrets. Not that anyone planned it that way; it's just that over the years it's been overlooked or bypassed by travelers lured to old standbys like Lake Tahoe, Yosemite, the Big Sur coastline, San Francisco, and the wine country. It's even possible for native Californians to have heard of the delta but have no idea of where or what it is. Of course, there are those who might just as soon see the delta kept secret. These are the folks who've found the great beauty, timelessness, and tranquility of the delta unmatched by any other spot.

The delta has caught the eye and imagination of photographers and filmmakers. Samuel Goldwyn, Jr., producer of the 1960 film version of *The Adventures of Huckleberry Finn,* said he chose the Sacramento Delta for location shooting because "it looks more like the Mississippi than the real thing." It has been the setting for many films and television programs that require Midwestern or Southern scenery. You may recognize the delta in such films as *All the King's Men, Porgy and Bess,* and *Cool Hand Luke.*

The Lay of the Land

Only the portion of the delta region that lies within Sacramento County will be covered here in detail. This, however, is an arbitrary division of a

121

region encompassing roughly a thousand square miles in five counties, the major portion of which lies outside of Sacramento County. The entire region is known as the Sacramento–San Joaquin Delta or California Delta. It is a triangle of land and water with apexes roughly at Sacramento, Antioch, and Stockton. The convergence of the San Joaquin and Sacramento rivers on the floor of the great Central Valley gives rise to 1,000 miles of twisting, interlocking waterways, elevated levees, 30 diked islands ranging in size from 800 acres to 100 square miles, and many smaller islands. The islands are traversed by drainage ditches and surrounded by a latticework of river channels, sloughs, canals, and cuts. It has been estimated that if this network were stretched end to end, it would run from San Francisco to New York.

The San Joaquin, Sacramento, and Mokelumne rivers, along with their many tributaries, provide for the drainage of more than one-third of the state, and the delta is the keystone of its water supply. The proposed Peripheral Canal, which California voters defeated in 1982, would have diverted up to 70 percent of the Sacramento River's water at Hood and sent it to Southern California residences and agribusiness fields. Opponents of the plan predicted the result would be the death of the Sacramento–San Joaquin Delta, which would revert to a salty swamp, and its land—among the richest agricultural land in the world—could no longer be used for food production. Although the plan was defeated, the issue continues to be debated; new plans are proposed every year.

Most of the major delta islands are used for agriculture. The rich peat soil is famed for growing tomatoes, pears, sugar beets, field corn (used for livestock feed), and alfalfa. The delta is unsurpassed as a water recreation area, a great place for camping, and a paradise for fishermen and birdwatchers (the region is on the Pacific Flyway). Depending on the time of year, it's possible to spot herons and egrets, mallards and teal, geese, red-winged blackbirds, and mudhens.

The delta has changed very little during the last century, due largely to its inaccessibility. Perhaps the most dramatic change is the reclamation of what once was a vast swampland consisting of rivers, sloughs, backswamps, tules (bullrushes), and peat bogs. The reclamation was achieved primarily by the building of levees, which began shortly after 1850 by pioneer settlers who saw the vast agricultural potential of the land if it could be made safe from flooding.

The Early Days

Historians believe the first Europeans to see the delta were members of a small Spanish party led by Gov. Pedro Fages and Father Juan Crespi on March 30, 1772. They were exploring the area to find a suitable location for a mission. From Mt. Diablo, they saw a body of water three times the size of

Lake Tahoe. It was no great inland lake, however, but the delta country flooded by the tide and the Sierra's heavy spring runoff. The land was teeming with wildlife—wildcats, mountain lions, antelope, bears, wolves, tule elk, deer, land otter, mink, and beaver. Lieutenant Gabriel Moraga, a Spanish explorer, is credited with naming the Sacramento River in 1808 in honor of the holy sacrament.

The portion of the delta that lies within Sacramento County was the domain of the Miwok and Maidu indians. Because there were as many as five or six different tribes in the delta, it is difficult to determine exact boundaries where one tribe's domain ended and another's began. It has been estimated that the delta was home for 3,000 to 15,000 Indians, most living in *rancherias* or aboriginal villages. The largest villages were located on Sherman and Staten islands, with as many as one thousand people each. There were many different tribes, each with its own territory, name, and dialect. Spanish explorers took to identifying them by the name of a major village or by the river whose valley they settled.

"Miwok" is not the tribal name, but is the native word for people. Unfortunately, little is known of the Miwok civilization. They were of rather short stature and sturdy, with reddish skin and long, coarse black hair. They wore few clothes but decorated their faces with tattoos and their bodies with jewelry made of bones and shells. When the weather turned cold, they smeared thick layers of mud on their bodies or wore deerskin blankets. Women wore two-piece skirts made of tules, buckskin, or willow bark.

Tules (pronounced "TOOL-ees") and other marsh reeds played a central role in Indian technology. They were used to make conical huts, roofing, rugs, baskets, mattresses, duck decoys, cordage, and *balsas,* which were reed canoes and rafts. They built *temescals,* or sweat houses, where the men slept, and family dwellings, where women and children lived.

The Miwok were hunters and gatherers, with acorns the staff of life. Their diet was supplemented with bread made from cattails, arrowhead tubers, roots, seeds, and pollen. Hunting for wildfowl, deer, elk, and rabbit was done with spears, bows, and arrows. The Miwok were also skilled fishermen, using nets, spears, and bone hooks. Meal was ground with wooden *manos* and stone *metates* (mortars and pestles). They used clamshell disks as currency. Their dead were usually cremated in funeral pyres, and shamans, or medicine men, performed a variety of functions as priests, herb doctors, magicians, and psychiatrists.

After discovery by the Spanish, the Indians' days were numbered. The missionaries recruited them for slave labor and forced religious conversion on them. Most of the Plains Miwok—the group that inhabited the delta—came to be under mission control. In 1832, the mission system ended when Mexico attained independence from Spain. After the Spanish padres left the missions, the missionized Indians were stranded with no protection against secular society. Many fled to their homelands or died of disease; during the summer of 1833, a malaria epidemic destroyed 70 percent of the population.

Between the missions, which effectively stripped the Indians of their culture and removed them from their ancestral land, and the diseases, most likely introduced by Europeans, their population was drastically reduced by the time gold was discovered. Those who were left were doomed by and large to treatment as horse thieves and slaves by the delta settlers. The law required an Indian to produce upon request a certificate showing he was employed by a white man or risk getting shot as a thief. The only remnants of the Indians' culture are the mounds that at one time proliferated in the delta. They are composed primarily of middens (refuse heaps) and can provide some clues as to the natives' culture and lifestyle. Most of the mounds, however, have been destroyed over the years by levee construction and agriculture.

EARLY SETTLEMENT AND RECLAMATION

The delta was the crossroads for early settlement of California's interior. In the decades after the first Spanish explorations, small groups of explorers, mountain men and trappers traversed the delta's marshes. During the 1840s, farmers known as "rim landers" settled on the edges of the delta to raise wheat and cattle. Supplies for the settlers were delivered by sailing ships that had begun to navigate the delta's waters. With the discovery of gold in 1848, the Sacramento River became the main route for the masses of gold-hungry adventurers on their way to the diggings via Sacramento. By 1850 miners began to drift into the delta to farm or do business in the towns that were beginning to appear on the riverbanks. After California gained control of the delta from the federal government under the 1850 Swamp and Overflow Act, the swampland was sold for $1 an acre; an original selling limit of 320 acres was raised to 640 acres in 1859. In 1866, after the counties assumed control of the delta, all restrictions on delta land purchases were lifted, and the speculators moved in. By 1871, nearly all of the delta had been grabbed up.

The peat soil of the delta was immensely fertile, but it needed to be protected from inundation. The first crude levees were made from stacks of tule sod, which didn't hold for long. An act in 1861 organized reclamation districts and assigned engineers to drain the islands, but by 1885 only eight thousand acres in the delta were effectively reclaimed and free from flooding. Every few years, winter flooding would break the dikes, and the delta would once again become a swamp.

Upon the completion of the transcontinental railroad in 1869, thousands of Chinese laborers came to the delta to build the levees using shovels and wheelbarrows. They were paid thirteen cents per cubic yard for their labor.

The Chinese were treated like serfs, as were the other ethnic groups that succeeded them, including Japanese, Hindus, Filipinos, and Mexicans.

At about the same time that the Chinese workers arrived from working on the railroad, the clamshell dredge was developed. With its giant teeth, it could scoop up large amounts of river-bottom mud and deposit it on the levees, thus speeding up the delta's reclamation along with deepening the waterways for commercial shipping and pleasure boating. Reclamation of the marsh for agriculture was not completed until the 1930s. After the levees were built, the island basins within their confines were drained, leaving very fertile peat soil.

RIPRAPPING

From an environmental point of view, one of the more disturbing events to take place in the delta was the U.S. Army Corps of Engineers' systematic defoliation of the levees, beginning in the mid-1950s and lasting nearly ten years. Riprapping is a method of strengthening a levee by using piles of stones. The levees were once fringed with oak, willows, walnuts, sycamores, and cottonwoods, some of which grew to one hundred feet. Despite strong protests from local groups, the Corps of Engineers proceeded to knock down the trees with cranes and bulldozers, also removing the groundcover of cane, grape, blackberry, and California wild rose. One of the more vocal opponents of the riprapping was the late Erle Stanley Gardner, a former attorney and author of the Perry Mason books. He spent many years on a houseboat in the delta and wrote several books about his experiences there.

It wasn't until 1966 that the Corps began to reassess its policy. In 1972 it announced that trees would be saved whenever possible and foliage that had been stripped from the levees would be replaced by new trees and shrubs. Unfortunately, the results of riprapping can still be seen along miles of delta shoreline: stark piles of grey rock where thick vegetation once grew.

The Riverboat Era

Captain John Sutter's chartered schooner, the *Isabella,* was the first vessel to travel up the Sacramento River from San Francisco, bringing supplies to Sutter and his men. The golden age of the delta riverboats began with the discovery of gold in 1848 and lasted another twenty-five years or so. Life in the burgeoning city of Sacramento and in the diggings depended on the riverboats for its existence, and steamboats were in great demand to transport the supplies and miners to Sacramento.

Just a few months after the gold discovery, the first large steamers to navigate the delta's Steamboat Slough arrived from the East Coast via Cape

Steamboat race staged for the 1935 movie Steamboat 'Round the Bend *(courtesy R. F. Reynolds Collection, City of Sacramento, Museum and History Division)*

Horn, and by the end of 1850 there were twenty-eight steamboats on the San Francisco–to–Sacramento run. Steamboat Slough was a safer route because it was shorter and had fewer snags and shoals than the Sacramento River. In 1848, the elegant, 219-foot, 750-ton sidewheeler *Senator* arrived on the scene. Built in New York, it began regular service between San Francisco and Sacramento; a one-way trip took ten hours and cost $30 to $65 for the 125-mile voyage. Before competition for passengers put an end to the high prices, the *Senator* was grossing as much as $50,000 for a one-way trip and probably earned more money than any other steamboat in history. Fierce competition led to races among the different vessels, and Steamboat Slough was a favorite drag strip. Several of these races resulted in boiler explosions, killing passengers. Competing steamship companies often hired "runners" to create disturbances on their rivals' ships. Initial efforts to organize the steamboat owners to regulate the fares failed because there was always at least one renegade who would begin a price war. Finally, the formation of an association called the California Steam Navigation Company in 1854, organized by the owners of most of the steamboats, curtailed the breakneck competition.

In a short time the steamboats became downright luxurious. One of the most famous of these floating palaces of opulent luxury was the *Chrysopolis* (Greek for Golden City), carrier of the elite and the aristocrat of the river. Not only luxurious, the *"Chrissy"* was also the fastest boat on the Sacramento, setting the speed record from Sacramento to San Francisco in five hours and nineteen minutes in 1861.

The golden age of riverboats began its decline in 1873 when the Central Pacific Railroad bought the California Steam Navigation Company. Although the railroad continued to operate the runs for a number of years, its emphasis was on railroading. The ships were still being used to transport large amounts of Sacramento Valley produce and other products to market. Although the railroads cut deeply into the river trade, paddlewheel navigation was dealt the final blow by a combination of improved roads, trucks, and automobiles.

Passenger travel on the Sacramento was revived for a time beginning in 1926 with the arrival of the paddlewheelers *Delta King* and *Delta Queen*. Built in Scotland at a cost of $1 million each, they were the largest, swiftest stern-wheelers to navigate the delta. The four-deck, 250-foot vessels provided daily overnight passenger service between Sacramento and San Francisco until 1941, when they were retired due to construction of bridges and modern highways. During the 1920s a round-trip ticket cost $1.50, and rental of the staterooms, which were of solid oak with mahogany and walnut trim, ranged from fifty cents (lower deck berth) to $5 for an upper deck stateroom with twin beds and a bath or shower. The social hall had a domed stained-glass ceiling hung with crystal chandeliers and tapestries and was the site of dances with live music and elegant meals. The *Delta King* has been restored and is now permanently docked at Old Sacramento. The refurbished *Delta Queen,* now based in Cincinnati, Ohio, plies the waters of the Mississippi.

Riverboats are once again plying the waters of the Sacramento Delta. Although not the luxurious paddlewheelers of yesterday, the cruise ships offer a glimpse into the delta's rich history and scenic beauty. Delta Travel Agency operates one-way weekend cruises to and from San Francisco and Sacramento, with return by bus. The only catch is that the routes go through the Deep Water Ship Channel, so you won't be able to see all the little towns along the Sacramento until you get to Rio Vista. The ships hold about five hundred passengers and make the one-way trip in approximately eight hours. Food and drinks are available, and the cruises, running from April through October, are narrated by local historians. Exploration Cruise Lines also offers four-day cruises of the delta. For more information, contact Delta Travel, P.O. Box 813, 1540 West Capitol Ave., West Sacramento, CA 95691, 372-3690.

The Delta Today

The Sacramento Delta has its own brand of distinctive, haunting beauty. It's not the kind of grandeur that knocks you over, like your first view of Yosemite Valley or the Mendocino coastline. Its charms are more likely to creep up on you, like the tule fogs wending their way upriver. You have to take your time here and use a little imagination in order to fully appreciate the region's serene moods and subtle hues. A hurried sightseeing drive through the delta may prove disappointing, as all you are likely to see are miles and miles of agricultural flatlands, interrupted at times by sleepy little towns, and few visible landmarks.

Most of the activity in the delta revolves around the levees, because the levees and the land directly behind them are the only parts of the islands available for settlement. Elsewhere, the light, waterlogged peat soil—eighty feet deep in some areas—cannot bear the weight of many buildings. As it is, the islands are sinking under the weight of the levees at a rate of two to three inches a year.

For the uninitiated, a levee is a dike or continuous mound that is used to keep water away from land. Because the land of the delta's islands lies six to twenty feet below the waterways, it would be subject to constant flooding if not for the levees. They are made from peat, sand, river silt, and gravel. The roads on top of them are as much as thirty feet above the water and fifty feet above the land. A levee break in delta country is serious business, because it can mean flooding of residential areas and farmlands.

Northern California's unrelenting storms in early 1986 and subsequent flooding, called the worst in a century, attest to the delicate balance between man and nature in the delta. More than twenty thousand acres of farmland and three hundred homes in the Sacramento-San Joaquin Delta were inundated due to levee breaks and overflowing rivers. Numerous businesses, farms, and ranches were destroyed, and many delta marinas were severely damaged or destroyed.

Of course, all this water has its benefits, too. For irrigation all the farmer has to do is activate a siphon or raise a sluice gate. In fact, the ready availability of water and the rich peat soil, composed of decayed tules and other organic matter, have been prime factors in making the delta one of the most productive agricultural areas in the state, with more than thirty crops grown commercially.

With nearly seven thousand acres of pear orchards, Sacramento County is the center of the Bartlett pear industry; in a good year, the delta produces up to 116,000 tons of pears or about 85 percent of the county's pears. Asparagus, sugar beets, and tomatoes are also grown here. In fact, the delta's tomato crop accounts for nearly all the tomato paste and half the catsup consumed in the U.S.

Existing side-by-side with the agricultural life of the delta is the water-oriented life. The delta is a mecca for enthusiasts of houseboating, fishing, waterskiing, pleasure boating, ferries, and drawbridges. When it comes to the best way to see the delta, the answer you'll get depends on whom you ask. Freelance writer and self-proclaimed "river rat" Hal Schell, also known as

"Mr. Delta," says you need to see it both by boat and by car. Along with his delta map, Schell's books, *Dawdling on the Delta* and *Cruising and Houseboating the Delta,* cover everything you need to know about the thousand miles of delta waterways. (These books can be purchased at many delta establishments or can be ordered directly from Schell Books, P.O. Box 9140, Stockton, CA 95208, 209/951-7821.)

HOUSEBOATING

Houseboating on the delta is a relatively recent phenomenon; it has gained popularity only within the last twenty years or so. Nothing else compares with floating lazily down a river in a boat that has almost all the comforts of home. Although the slow pace of houseboating may take some getting used to, it's an ideal family vacation. Along the way, there are a number of marinas where you can stock up on supplies; you'll also find plenty of great restaurants where you can indulge if you need some time off from cooking.

Your floating hotel comes equipped with nearly everything you need, including running water, refrigerator, stove, dishes and other cooking utensils, flush toilet, and lifejackets. Most houseboat rental agencies require you to bring your own bedding, towels, groceries, and personal items.

You don't need a pilot's license or any boating experience to pilot a houseboat. The rental operator will give you hands-on instruction in the basics for an hour or so. For extra safety, you may want to take a free boating safety class offered by the U.S. Coast Guard Auxiliary. Never overestimate your boating skills or underestimate the power of the river. The most dangerous time for houseboating is winter and early spring, when flood-level flows cause extremely swift currents. You should know how much power you have and whether you're too underpowered for the current. You should also be familiar with the handling characteristics of the houseboat and whether the anchor is heavy-duty enough for strong currents. If the winds are over twenty to twenty-five knots (not uncommon in the delta), you're liable to get blown around a lot—possibly up on the rocks. When you anchor the houseboat at night, be sure to take the tides into account; the next morning you could end up ashore or floating downstream.

Before heading out for boating, especially during the winter, it's a good idea to call marine safety and enforcement agencies. For local river information on the delta, call the U.S. Coast Guard at Rio Vista, 707/374-6477 or 707/374-2871. The California Department of Boating and Waterways publishes several free booklets on California boating laws and safe boating tips for the delta (445-2615).

You'll need a detailed and current map of the delta, and Hal Schell's is one of the best. The U.S. Department of Commerce publishes a yearly nautical chart of the Sacramento and San Joaquin rivers, showing depths and tidal variances. Waterskiiers will be happy to learn that ski boats are easily towed behind houseboats and can be rented at many of the houseboat rental agencies.

About a dozen rental firms rent the two hundred or so houseboats available in the Sacramento–San Joaquin delta. All of the firms welcome families with children. The boats range from twenty-five to fifty feet long and can accommodate four to ten passengers. Rates vary, depending on the season and the style and size of the craft. A week-long summer outing can cost between $600 and $1,350, with off-season rates (October to May) averaging about twenty percent less. You also pay for any fuel you use. Weekend rentals are usually available only in the off-season; during the summer, rentals are usually for one week or more, and make sure you reserve your boat well in advance. One way to bring the costs of houseboating down is to share the costs among a group of friends. (Just make sure you know your friends well before you embark on a week-long houseboating trip.)

For brochures and current rates, contact these houseboat rental firms:

Delta Country Houseboats, P.O. Box 246, Walnut Grove, CA 95690; 776-1741.

New Hope Landing, P.O. Box 417, Thornton, CA 95686; 209/794-2627.

S & H Houseboat Rentals, Rt. 1, Box 514, Antioch, CA 94509; 415/757-3621.

FISHING

Fishing enthusiasts will find a tremendous variety of fish in the waters of the delta. Remember, you'll need a fishing license. You can get licenses, tackle, fishing tips, and any other information on delta fishing at any of the area's many bait shops. The Sacramento County Parks and Recreation Department publishes a handy guide to fishing in the county that includes a map of delta fishing access points (see Appendix).

Four kinds of catfish live in the delta's waters, with white catfish accounting for about 95 percent of the catch. Sardines and fresh-water clams are popular baits. If you're looking to catch yourself a really big fish, angle for the white sturgeon, the largest freshwater game fish in North America. Many of the sturgeon caught in the delta today weigh in at 40 pounds, with some as much as 250 pounds. The best time to fish for white sturgeon is December through May. Snodgrass Slough is said to be a good fishing spot.

The delta used to support a thriving crawdad (crayfish) industry, with hundreds of thousands of pounds shipped to distant markets. Crayfish look like miniature lobsters and taste a little like shrimp. You need a whole slew of them to make a meal, but it's worth it. The crustaceans are still found throughout the delta and can be caught with a simple trap, using cheap dog food as bait. You can get the traps and pointers on how to catch and cook them at local bait stores. You need a fishing license for crawdads, too.

Small fishing boats and tackle are available for rent at most of the marinas in the delta. If you're a landlubber, try bank fishing, a popular delta pastime. One way to locate bank-fishing spots is to look for parking turnoffs along the levee roads. These are a sure sign there's a bank-fishing spot nearby. Sacramento County fishing access areas are located at Sherman Island, Cliff House on Brannan Island, Hogback Island, and Georgiana Slough.

Touring the Northern Delta: Port of Sacramento to Courtland

Most of the places in the Sacramento Delta can be reached by road. State Highway 160, a designated scenic highway, follows the Sacramento's meandering course for most of the way. Most of the delta towns are found on Highway 160, a narrow and shoulderless levee road.

It's a good idea to bring along a road map of the area. Unless you stay on Highway 160, it's easy to get lost, especially at night. The California State Automobile Association's *Sacramento Valley Region* map is good (you have to be a member to get one), although it is less detailed than delta maps. Compass Maps and Murray's Maps both publish a delta map, and these are about as accurate as you'll find. The *Thomas Guide to Sacramento County* also has good detail, but it's in book format and you have to keep flipping from page to page. The U.S. Geological Survey publishes quadrant topographical maps of the area, but they're updated only about every ten years and don't reflect recent road closures or name changes; however, some fishermen swear by them.

There isn't a single ideal time to visit the delta. Delta weather is pleasant through much of the year, with windy days in the spring and early summer. March is a good time to see the pear blossoms in full bloom. During the summer, when Sacramentans may be sweltering, it can be fifteen degrees cooler on the delta. In fact, delta breezes have cooled down many a sizzling Sacramento summer day. Delta falls are perfect, and because the peak harvest time is September and October, it's an interesting time to visit. Winters are generally mild, with tule fog creeping in during December and January.

This delta tour follows Highway 160 south from Sacramento to Sherman Island, with several side trips along the way. The total distance is about fifty-five miles and would take about one and a half to two hours to drive with no stops. Several east-west roads connect Highway 160 with I-5 to the east. I-5 roughly parallels 160, so you may enter or leave the delta by any of these roads. You'll find gas stations at Courtland, Walnut Grove, Isleton, and Rio Vista. The most important thing is to take your time. Plan a picnic or try one of the delta's many restaurants.

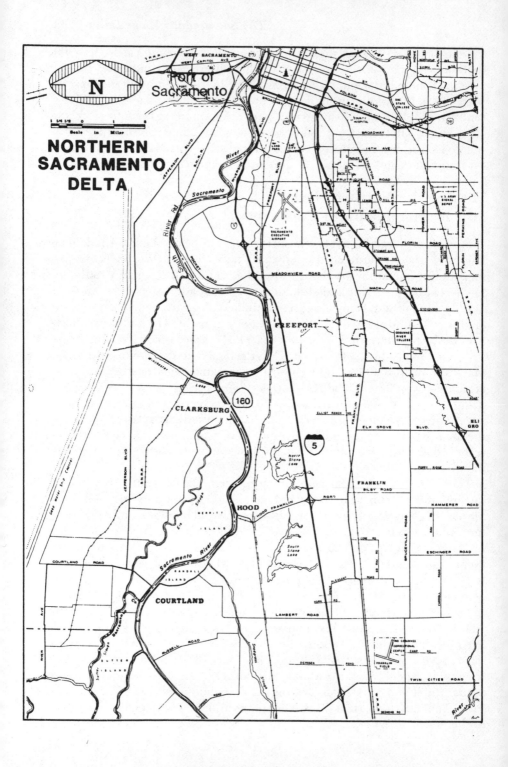

A selected, but by no means complete, listing of restaurants and resorts is included here. Dress at most of the restaurants and resorts is casual, though shoes and shirts generally are required. Be sure to call ahead to check for hours or to make reservations. Many delta establishments have different hours depending on the season.

Port of Sacramento

It's hard to imagine that one of California's major seaports lies right in the middle of the state. When you think of ports, you're more likely to think of Long Beach, San Francisco, or San Diego. Yet twelve to fifteen oceangoing ships dock at the Port of Sacramento every month. The port and harbor are connected to the San Francisco Bay by a seventy-nine-mile-long shipping route that includes a deep water shipping channel; the journey takes from six to seven hours. Since the port's opening in 1963, more than 2,600 vessels flying the flags of 41 nations have shipped 30 million tons of cargo through it. It is touted as the West Coast's finest bulk cargo shipping facility.

Visitors are welcome every day of the week and may occasionally board visiting freighters. Ask for a brochure with the self-guided port tour at the main gate. To reach the port, take Business 80 west from Sacramento to the Harbor Boulevard exit and head south to the main gate. Phone 371-8000 for more information.

WILLIAM G. STONE LOCK

The Port of Sacramento is connected to the Sacramento River by the William G. Stone Lock, the state's only navigation lock. Because the Sacramento River is higher than the harbor water level, sometimes by as much as twenty-one feet, boats entering the harbor from the river must be lowered, and vice versa. To get to the lock's overview point from the Port of Sacramento, turn right on Industrial Boulevard as you exit the port. Turn right again at Jefferson, which will take you straight to the lock and South River Road.

DEEP WATER SHIP CHANNEL

If you've ever wondered what it looks like to see a large freighter cutting through a cornfield, the Deep Water Ship Channel is the place to see it. The channel was completed in 1963 and extends nearly forty-three miles from the harbor to the mouth of the Sacramento River at Collinsville. The direct route from Rio Vista, where it leaves the Sacramento, cuts off sixteen miles from the river route. The channel is one of the few waterways in the delta with no perceptible current. It can be reached via Jefferson Boulevard from West Sacramento.

A more scenic route would be to continue south on South River Road from the Stone Lock and turn right at Burrows or any of the other roads that connect South River Road with Jefferson. This side of the river is more scenic than the east bank and it's the only road that follows the river between Sacramento and Freeport. Because there isn't as much traffic, the road is good for bicycling, although you always need to be alert for traffic on these narrow levee roads. Once you're on Jefferson, follow it south until it parallels the Deep Water Ship Channel. This is the best spot to watch for passing freighters and pleasure boaters, who also make use of the channel. From Jefferson you can head back to South River Road and continue to the Freeport Bridge, which joins Highway 160 on the west bank of the Sacramento, or continue along South River Road to Clarksburg. Along this stretch of levee road you

Silver Bend Christmas Tree Farm

may notice some rather fantastic-looking mailboxes. They're the handiwork of a retired delta farmer who fashions custom-made mailboxes out of a variety of materials such as old horse-drawn plows, hand pumps, grinding wheels, and drill presses. Just north of Clarksburg is Pumphouse Road, leading to Winchester Lake, a popular waterskiing spot. Located in a rural area, the lake has a slalom course, a ski jump, and a picnic area.

For an old-fashioned holiday family outing, there's the Silver Bend Christmas Tree Farm, located on South River Road just north of Pumphouse Road. Only fifteen minutes from downtown Sacramento, Silver Bend is part of a one-thousand-acre farm dating to the Gold Rush. Visitors can wander among 125 acres of fragrant Monterey pines and choose and cut their tree. Starting in October, you can reserve a tree and return later to cut it down. Wagons pulled by Percheron draft horses will help you transport your tree, or you can ride an antique steam train. Afterwards, you can warm up next to a pot-bellied stove, sip hot cider, and browse through the selection of homemade gift items. Silver Bend is open year-round and offers fresh produce (including sweet corn and tomatoes), horse-drawn hayrides, buggies and surreys for special occasions, picnic grounds, and a pumpkin patch. Call 665-1410 for more information.

Clarksburg

Located in Yolo County, the sleepy little town of Clarksburg (pop. 360) is one of two delta towns situated entirely on the west bank of the Sacramento (the other is Rio Vista). More than three thousand walnut trees provide shade for this charming village, which has an antique store, a market, and a hardware store. Clarksburg may soon gain national recognition as a wine grape–growing region; the twenty-five growers in the area are now able to market their grapes under the Clarksburg name. Clarksburg's chenin blanc grapes are considered among the finest in California. About three thousand acres of wine grapes are planted in the region, which stretches from West Sacramento to Walnut Grove.

There are two bonded wineries in the Clarksburg area. R & J Cook Winery, two and a half miles from Clarksburg on Netherlands Road, is a small family winery with four hundred acres of vineyards. The Cooks' tasting room is open Monday through Friday, and informal tours are given on request. A picnic area has tables and benches overlooking Elk Slough. For more information call 775-1234. Bogle Vineyards (744-1139) has 350 acres planted in grapes. The winery is open for informal tours by appointment. Bogle Vineyards is about three miles south of Clarksburg on Road 144, which parallels Elk Slough.

Freeport

Highway 160 is the main route from Sacramento to the delta country. From the capitol, it follows along 15th Street and Freeport Boulevard south for nine miles where it meets the Sacramento River at Freeport (pop. 100). This is where you get your first view of the river and where the road becomes a levee road, called River Road; it was made a public highway in 1863. Portuguese commercial fishermen were among Freeport's early settlers. Living on the river in houseboats, their lives revolved entirely around the river. A large Portuguese population still lives in the delta.

A. J. Bump's Freeport Saloon (665-2251) is housed in a venerable two-story building built in 1863, the town's only restored historic building. The building once served as the town's first general store and post office. It is now a saloon and restaurant and also serves as an unofficial museum, with early day delta photos covering the walls. It's a popular spot for boaters and serves lunch and dinner daily.

The Freeport Bridge is one of the many bascule bridges in the delta. These open like drawbridges, using massive concrete counterweights weighing more than one hundred tons to raise each half of the span. (The London Tower Bridge is a bascule bridge.) Many of the bridges in the delta, including those at Paintersville, Isleton, and Walnut Grove, are also bascule-type bridges.

The Walnut Grove Bridge, typical of the bascule bridges found throughout the delta

Hood

Seven miles south of Freeport lies Hood (pop. 300), a railroad town named in 1909 for William Hood, the chief construction engineer for the Southern Pacific Railroad in the 1880s. Southern Pacific once ran a spur into Hood, and until recently the town was a pear shipping point on the railroad that ran to Isleton. Today Hood has a restaurant called the Rusty Hook, a bar, a grocery store, and a post office.

Of the many elegant, grand old delta homes that once graced the riverbanks, only a few survive. Of those, the only one listed on the National Register of Historic Places is the Rosebud Mansion on Highway 160 just north of Hood. The Italianate Victorian mansion was built in the 1870s for State Senator William Johnston and designed by architect Nathaniel Goodell, who also designed the Governor's Mansion. The grounds are filled with fruit trees, camellias, towering palms, and a magnolia. Although the house is not open to the public, it can be seen easily from the road.

Courtland

About a mile and a half south of Hood, the road leaves the levee to go around Randall Island and returns to the levee just north of Courtland (pop. 521). From the looks of this somnolent little town, it would be hard to guess that it was once a thriving riverside community with several fish canneries, an important steamboat landing, a prosperous pear and asparagus industry, and a large Chinatown. This section along the river is the number one pear-producing area in the country, and Courtland is the heart of it. During the 1870s, farmers who were having a hard time making a profit growing wheat found that growing pears could be far more lucrative. The first pear orchards were planted by the Chinese, who have lived in Courtland since it was founded. They lived primarily in buildings erected on stilts, overhanging the river bank at the north end of town. After a fire in the 1930s, most of the Chinese moved to other delta towns.

A handful of the remaining buildings still stand, though most are abandoned and in disrepair. You can still see Chinese lettering on some buildings in the north section of town. One such building, the Wo Chong and Company store, was for a short time the residence of Lin Sen, the first president of the Republic of China. Courtland was also the site of a large meeting convened by Dr. Sun Yat-sen. He was in the area to gather economic support from Sacramento area Chinese workers for the revolution that in 1911 toppled the Manchu Dynasty and established the Chinese republic. In support of Sun Yat-sen, local Chinese purchased ten to twenty airplanes to be sent to China. They were stored on a wharf below Hood but were destroyed by arson before they could be shipped.

Courtland also felt the effects of the tong wars that took place during the mid-1930s. Chinese tongs, fraternal associations much like clans, can experience bitter rivalries. Members of two tongs from San Francisco fled to the delta, and armed Chinese patrolled Courtland for a mile around.

A popular spot for socializing was a store run by Chong Chan, who provided a traditional free meal for Chinese laborers every Sunday. Chan's son, Lincoln Chan, for many years ran a large delta farming operation that is still headquartered behind the old Chinatown.

Courtland has a good market, a pharmacy, and a post office. There's also an impressive colonnaded building that served as the Bank of Courtland before the stock market crash of 1929. It now houses government offices. The biggest event in Courtland is its annual Pear Fair in July. The one-day event features an art fair, road races, historical displays, a parade, a carnival, and more. A popular event for the farmers is the largest-pear contest. And of course there are pears everywhere—pear pies, pear frappes, and pear crepes.

PAINTERSVILLE

Just south of Courtland near the Paintersville bridge is the site of the former steamboat landing town of Paintersville, named for Levi Painter, who founded the town in 1852. The town consisted of a store, a saloon, and a hotel. Painter gained notoriety on the river for his "post-hole bank." On moonless nights, he would bury the money that was left in his safekeeping by friends under selected fence posts around his property. Paintersville met its demise after the riverboats stopped calling at the wharf. The site is occupied today by J. M. Buckley and Sons, a trucking firm established in 1918.

6

The Heart of the Sacramento Delta: Steamboat Slough to Sherman Island

After leaving Courtland, Highway 160 follows the ribbon-like Sacramento for about thirty-three miles until it cuts through Sherman Island at the southern tip of Sacramento County. This is the heart of the delta country, a patchwork of reclaimed islands that don't look like islands, sleepy little towns hugging the levees, quiet, tree-shaded waterways, and no-frills roadside cafes where good grub sticks to your ribs and your coffee cup is never empty.

Steamboat Slough

Highway 160 crosses the Sacramento River at the Paintersville bascule bridge and follows the west bank of the river to just north of Isleton, where it crosses back to the east bank. Just south of the Paintersville Bridge, the road crosses the northern end of Steamboat Slough, which connects with the Sacramento. Used during the steamboat days as a shortcut, Steamboat Slough is now exclusively a playground for fishermen, waterskiers, and boaters. Running between Grand and Ryer islands, the twelve-mile-long slough reveals sandy beaches for sunning during the low tide.

Steamboat Landing (775-1058), open year-round, is on the Sacramento River at the Steamboat Slough Bridge on Grand Island. The landing has guest

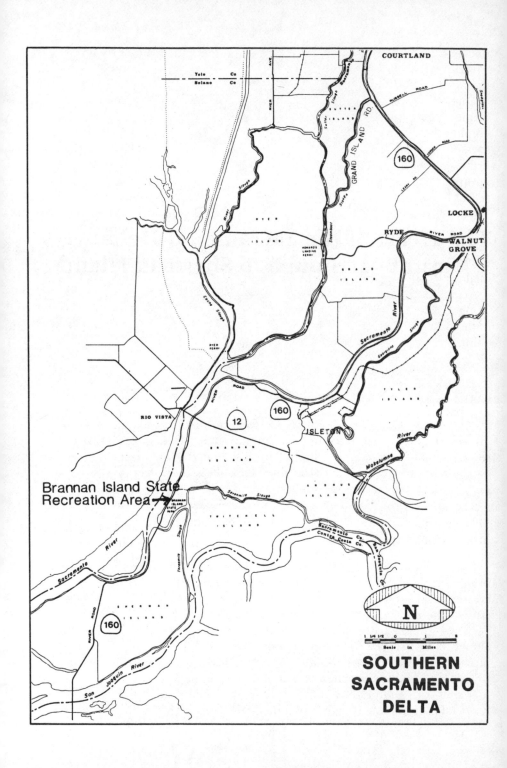

Brannan Island State
Recreation Area

**SOUTHERN
SACRAMENTO
DELTA**

docking, a fine sandy beach open to the public for a fee, and a restaurant specializing in seafood and Sunday brunch. Pig roasts are sometimes held on the nearby beach.

One of the first people to settle Grand Island was Reuben Kercheval, a former gold prospector who later became a state senator. Kercheval employed the Maidu Indians who were living on the island when he arrived (possibly as early as 1849) to build one of the first levees in the delta. Only a few feet high, the levee was made from blocks of peat cut from the wet ground. The peat shrank after it dried, leaving crevices that caused the levee to leak during the flood of 1852. Undaunted, Kercheval continued building levees that continued to be destroyed by flooding. Thirty years of hydraulic mining in the gold fields, which wasn't outlawed until 1893, dumped two billion cubic yards of "slickens" (a mixture of fine silt, sand and stones) into the Sacramento River system, elevating the river beds faster than the levees could be raised.

At this point, you can continue south along Highway 160 or take a side trip along Grand Island Road, which follows the east bank of Steamboat Slough, to the Grand Island Mansion. It's a pleasant ride on a rustic road fronted by palms, eucalyptus, oaks, and old farmhouses.

GRAND ISLAND MANSION

About three miles down Grand Island Road, the Grand Island Mansion comes into view. With an entrance graced by four thirty-foot Corinthian columns, this twenty-four-thousand-square-foot, fifty-eight-room mansion could easily be taken for a Mediterranean villa in the south of France. It has four stories, a terra-cotta roof, and spacious balconies with intricate iron railings. The mansion was built in 1917 at a cost of $350,000 for Louis Meyers, an eccentric German financier whose wife missed the glamour and excitement of San Francisco.

Listed on the California Registry of Historic Homes and reputed to be one of the largest privately owned homes in the United States, the mansion has a past that is shrouded in mystery and romance. It was the site of the state's first senatorial inaugural ball and was said to be a hideaway for society's elite during the Prohibition years. Actress Jean Harlow made frequent visits here, as did author Erle Stanley Gardner. More recently, the mansion has hosted formal events attended by such guests as Ronald Reagan, Jerry Brown, and Walter Mondale. It has been used as a location for films and magazine layouts, as well as private events such as political and charitable fundraisers, weddings, and parties.

Currently valued at $3.2 million, the mansion has changed hands several times and has been operated on and off as a restaurant and cocktail lounge. It has been remodeled several times as well and is now truly a showpiece, with

Grand Island Mansion

its eighteen bedrooms, eleven bathrooms, bowling lane with automatic pinsetter, billiard room, eighteen-seat cinema, gymnasium, ballroom with beveled mirrors on the walls, gilded columns, and two massive mahogany bars. The mansion also boasts an old-fashioned, eight-seat soda fountain, a library, chartroom, stellar observatory, tiled swimming pool, and tennis courts. And everywhere there is marble, velvet, hardwood, ornate fireplaces, tiles, and Persian rugs. Situated on four acres of land surrounded by pear orchards, it even has its own yacht harbor and heliport.

The present owner has opened the mansion to the public on weekends from March to December, serving a lavish Sunday brunch. It is not open for tours, although you may park on the levee road in front to see it from the outside. Call 775-1705 for more information.

RIDING THE DELTA FERRIES

Continuing south on Grand Island Road, you'll come to a farm road, where you can return to Highway 160 at Ryde. For a nostalgic diversion, you may wish to try riding one of the four public ferries in the Sacramento River Delta region, especially if you have children along. You'll see the Howard Landing ferry on your right just before you reach the road that goes to Ryde.

Before the bridges were built, the only way to get across the rivers and sloughs was by ferry. These are the only river ferryboats in Northern California and they're free, operated by state and/or local agencies. The state-run Howard Landing ferry crosses Steamboat Slough to Ryer Island. Called the *J-Mack,* it is a diesel-powered, steel-decked ferry that pulls itself across the slough by a greased cable anchored to each bank. When the ferry is not in use, the cable lies on the slough bottom so as not to interfere with passing boats.

Ryer Island is an excellent spot for bicycle riding, for you can circle the entire island on its levee road. Once you cross the slough, you can ride south on Ryer Road to the Ryer Island ferry, which crosses Cache Slough. Named *The Real McCoy,* the sixty-five-foot, steel-hulled, free-running diesel ferry is steered by the captain from a pilothouse. As you ride, you may see oceangoing vessels going by, since they take this route to and from the Deep Water Ship Channel.

You can turn right around and take the ferry back to Ryer Island, or you may continue south to Rio Vista and Highway 12. If you drive east on Highway 12 about ten miles to Terminous, you'll come to the Staten Island ferry, another free public ferry in a setting right out of *Huckleberry Finn.*

HOGBACK ISLAND RECREATION AREA

Just south of Howard Landing on Steamboat Slough is the county-maintained Hogback Island Recreation Area. Located on a tree-shaded berm that is actually a small island linked to the land, it's one of the nicest spots in the delta. It includes many pleasant picnic sites, restrooms, a four-lane boat launching ramp, a parking area, and an extensive beach for fishing and other water activities. During the riverboat era, many steamers went aground here because of the slough's shoals and low water. The area was developed during the 1960s by the Army Corps of Engineers and given to the county in 1967.

Locke

To get to Locke and Walnut Grove, you can continue south on Highway 160 from the Steamboat Slough Bridge and cross the Sacramento River at the Walnut Grove Bridge, or you can take the River Road, which follows the river's east bank. Locke (pop. 60) is the only town in the nation founded and settled entirely by Chinese, and it was the last community established in the delta.

By 1852, twenty-five thousand Chinese had been drawn to the state by the Gold Rush. Threats of violence from greedy and prejudiced whites forced most who made it to the diggings to leave or to work on less profitable mines. Thousands of Chinese were later employed to build the transcontinental railroad, and many stayed on to construct levees in the delta, settling in

Chinese camps along the river between Sacramento and Rio Vista. After the levees were completed, they remained to clear and work the reclaimed farmland.

Walnut Grove was one of the first Chinese settlements in the delta. Its two groups of residents spoke the Chungshan and Choysan Cantonese district dialects, and the two factions did not get along. After a fire in 1915 destroyed the Chinese section of Walnut Grove, members of the Chungshan decided to establish a settlement of their own. Two Chungshan families had been living about a mile upriver in the tiny hamlet of Lockeport on land owned by rancher George Locke. A group of Chungshan businessmen approached Locke and persuaded him to rent them ten to twelve acres on one of his pear orchards. The contract was finalized by a simple handshake. The Chinese were not able to purchase the land outright because the California Alien Land Law of 1913 prohibited aliens who were ineligible for citizenship from owning property (the law was declared unconstitutional and repealed in 1952). The entire town of Locke was built practically overnight and now has a total of fifty-nine buildings.

Walking down Locke's worn wooden sidewalks shaded by spindly wooden balconies, one gets the feeling of being in a Western ghost town or on a movie set. The tongue-and-groove wooden buildings touch each other; cross-through alleys and rickety stairs allow pedestrians to move east and west. Only two blocks deep, the town was built thirty feet below the levee top, with the second story at the same level as the levee. Because the state reclamation laws forbade building on the levees, the Chinese built a few feet inside the levee and attached wooden ramps to bridge the gap between second-story porches and the levee road. The buildings all look alike because an American contractor built most of the major buildings and back-street homes hurriedly, one right after the other. He remained in Locke and during Prohibition converted his two houses to brothels, hiring white madams and prostitutes.

The residents of Locke wanted to be sure that their wooden town would not suffer the same fiery fate that other delta Chinatowns had. They hired a night watchman to watch all night for fire. After completing each circuit of the town, he sounded the "all's well" by knocking a stick against a hollow wooden block called a *bok bok*. Locke was the only Chinese community in the delta to be spared by fire, thanks to the *bok bok* man.

The town soon prospered, growing rapidly. At one time it had a population of four hundred and boasted a church, Chinese school, post office, lodge, theater, six restaurants, five hotels and rooming houses, two saloons, five grocery stores, a dental office, two cigar stores, a shoe repair shop, pool room, and bakery. Many owners lived above their stores. Daily bus service connected Locke (the name was changed from Lockeport in 1920) with other delta Chinese villages and San Francisco. The Star Theater was built and

Star Theater, Locke

showed Chinese and American films. During the early 1930s, Chinese theater groups from San Francisco presented dramas at the Star, with the casts costumed in beautifully embroidered Chinese clothing and magnificent headdresses. The dilapidated Star Theater is still standing, its archway and wooden stairway connecting Main Street with the levee.

During Prohibition in the twenties and thirties, thousands of field workers, mostly single men from Mexico and the Philippines, sought escape at Locke's gambling rooms, speakeasies, brothels, and secret opium dens. The brothels were operated by white madams and their white prostitutes. Chinese women were not involved; few were even allowed into the country. Just before World War II, the Chinese population in the delta between Courtland and Isleton peaked with fifteen hundred to two thousand permanent residents. By the 1930s there were five gambling halls in Locke. At first they catered only to the Chinese, but the Filipino, Japanese, and Mexican field workers who came into the area soon became regulars at the halls, as did the whites. As bootlegging evolved along the Sacramento, the gambling houses became more crowded and it meant big business, at least until the Depression.

Of all the gambling houses in Locke, the Dai Loy (translated "a very big welcome") was the first, largest, and most profitable in the delta. It operated continuously for thirty-five years until it was closed down in 1951. The Sacramento River Delta Historical Society has restored the historic gambling hall on Main Street and operates it as a museum on weekends from April to November, 11–5; there is no phone. The Dai Loy and other gambling halls often contributed part of their earnings to community improvements such as wells, equipment for the language school, and the Baptist Mission. The museum is a faithful recreation of the gambling hall as it appeared in 1916, with gaming tables, original gaming pieces for the games and lottery, and furnishings.

In addition to the museum, several other spots in Locke are worth visiting. Of the several art galleries, the River Road Art Gallery (776-9902) is the most established. A group of local artists opened the gallery in 1973. Original watercolors, oils, acrylics, sketches, and crafts by local artists and craftspeople are exhibited and offered for sale. One room has photo albums containing historic photographs of the delta, and at the back of the gallery is an exhibit of a Chinese kitchen in its original location. The gallery is open on weekends from March to December; call to check hours.

The Locke Country Store is a boutique selling clothing and a few antiques, and Locke China Imports specializes in imported Chinese gift items and bric-a-brac. Locke Garden Restaurant, serving Chinese food, is located in Locke's first and oldest building, a beer parlor built in 1912. A plaque commemorating Locke's historical significance was placed on the building in 1970 by the Sacramento County Historical Society.

One of the most popular eating spots and bars in the delta is located on Main Street in Locke. The legendary Al's Place (776-1800), still known fondly as "Al-the-Wop's," was Locke's first Caucasian business. It was named for Al Adami, a bootlegger from Collinsville who bought the building in 1930. You enter Al's through an ancient saloon, its twenty-foot ceiling dotted with thumbtacked dollar bills. (The bartender will show you how he gets the bills up there—using *your* dollar!) You can eat at the aged mahogany bar or in the bench-and-table dining room. Lunch is served daily and consists of steak sandwiches only; the jars of peanut butter and marmalade on the tables are for spreading on the sandwiches (the taste combination actually grows on you after a while). Steaks with all the trimmings are the only dinner fare, but you'll get plenty to eat. Al's is a favorite with boaters, delta ranchers, and Sacramentans. Saturday nights can be a bit crowded and rowdy.

Just across the street is another Locke landmark, the Yuen Chong Market, established in 1915. The market has always had a large clientele comprised of local Chinese, delta residents, and boaters; it was a favorite hangout for author Erle Stanley Gardner, who lived on a houseboat in the delta for several years. The market still sells Chinese vegetables and herbs grown in the neatly tended home gardens of Locke. The long building on the riverbank, completed in 1921 almost three decades after construction began, was originally a storage shed for produce transported by riverboat. It is now known as the Boathouse (776-1204) and provides guest docks, fuel, launch services, and marine supplies.

Even a cursory tour of Locke and its sagging old buildings points out the fact that this is a dying town. All of the young people have left for higher education and better opportunities, leaving behind the fragile old people, mostly in their eighties. The town has for several years been caught in a legal mire, its fate tossed like a hot potato between public agencies and private developers. Several years ago the land was bought by the Asian City Development Corporation, a Hong Kong company. Its plans to turn Locke into a Disneyland-like park were rejected by the state, which in 1981 had appropriated money to acquire and develop the area as a state park. The plans fell through, however, and Locke's future is as uncertain as ever.

According to Connie King, long-time Locke resident and unofficial vice-mayor of the town, Locke is a popular stop for tour buses, tour boats, and tourists in cars. King's primary concern is that visitors respect the elderly Chinese people, who are frequently photographed for "character shots." She asks photographers to get permission from their subjects before they start snapping pictures. Locke also has a litter problem, and no public restrooms are available in town. Try to park along the levee road if possible, because parking is tight and limited along the narrow little Main Street. In these days of amusement parks and authentic replicas of historic towns, it is often hard to keep in mind that a town like Locke is a real town inhabited by real people. However old and dilapidated it may appear, it is still their home, and the town and its residents deserve respect and sensitivity.

THE MEADOWS

Directly behind Locke is a lovely area accessible only by boat. Called "the Everglades of the West" by Erle Stanley Gardner, its quiet, tree-shaded waterways blanketed by pond lilies and water hyacinths are the last remnants of the pristine delta wilderness. Snodgrass Slough, Lost Slough, and the Delta Meadows are thick with overhanging vegetation and serve as home to abundant animal and plant life, including more than one hundred species of birds. The Meadows is a favorite overnight anchorage for cruisers and houseboats. The Delta Meadows and Lost Slough are great wild blackberry spots. The berries grow along the water throughout the delta, and you can pick them right from your boat. Blackberry season begins around Memorial Day and lasts into late August. A large portion of the Delta Meadows property has been acquired by the California Department of Parks and Recreation. Plans include the creation of a state park, with a portion of the land to be set aside as a preserve to protect the area's scenic beauty, wildlife habitats, and archeological resources.

Snodgrass Slough is linked to the Sacramento River by the Delta Cross Channel, which was dug for flood control. It has two gates that are sometimes closed to regulate water flow. Fishing skiffs can use the channel when the gates are raised, but the clearance will not accommodate houseboats.

Walnut Grove

As you head south along the Sacramento River, Walnut Grove (pop. 936), twenty-nine miles from Sacramento, is the first town with a sizeable population. It's the only town south of Red Bluff that sits on both sides of the river. East Walnut Grove is primarily the business district, with several markets, stores, and a gas station. This section, also known as Old Town, is the site of the delta's first Chinese settlement as well as a Japanese settlement. Across the river, West Walnut Grove is primarily a newer residential area, with many large, suburban-style homes on neatly manicured lawns shaded by numerous trees. The two halves of Walnut Grove are connected by a counter-weight bascule bridge built in 1952.

The town was founded in 1851 by John W. Sharp and his family and was one of the earliest settlements in the delta. Sharp began farming, raising crops and dairy cattle. He also founded Walnut Grove's first general store, owned and operated the first ferry on the river, was the blacksmith and postmaster, and ran a hotel. By 1865, Walnut Grove was a major shipping point for produce, grain, and fish. It was also a popular stopover for miners, gamblers, and businessmen traveling between San Francisco and Sacramento.

After Sharp died in 1880, Mrs. Agnes Brown of San Francisco purchased the hotel and ran it with the help of her son Alex. Alex went into the fruit business, opened a general store, and was the first to grow asparagus in the area. Along with his son John he established a small bank named the Bank of Alex Brown. Although Brown died in 1923, his descendents continue the family enterprises, including the Bank of Alex Brown, which has branches in other communities. The original bank building built in 1916 is on the east bank on River Bend Road and now houses an insurance office.

The delta's first Chinese settlement in Walnut Grove burned down in 1915 and again in 1937. The remains of the old quarter are located at the north end of town. A number of Western movies have been filmed in this section. Some of the descendents of the early Chinese population still live and work in the area. Ping Lee, a second-generation Locke resident and son of one of the founders of Locke, has owned and operated the Big Store in Walnut Grove for more than thirty years. His grocery store occupies the building built after the 1915 fire destroyed the Alex Brown general store.

East Walnut Grove is also the site of one of the delta's two primary early Japanese settlements (the other is in Isleton). The Japanese began arriving in large numbers some time after 1884, when Chinese immigration was restricted by Congress. They helped build the levees and later worked in the fields. When some began to prosper and acquired their own farms, they hired fellow Japanese to work the farms. This posed a threat to the white farmers who had large operations; they were afraid of losing their cheap labor supply. The small farmers didn't like the competition either, and the wage workers were upset because the Japanese farmers usually hired only Japanese workers.

These three groups pressured the state government, and in 1913 the California Alien Land Law (the Webb Act) was passed, prohibiting Japanese or any aliens from owning land. By 1915, 75 percent of the delta was being cultivated by tenant farmers, of whom 75 percent were reported to be Oriental. The whites still resented the Japanese's economic progress and continued to pressure their state legislators, resulting in a 1924 ban on Japanese immigration. By this time, the white farmers had found a new source of cheap labor from Mexico and the Philippines.

Walnut Grove's Japanese population shared the Oriental district but had its own section bounded by A, C, Market, and Tyler streets, later extending to Grove Street. The Japanese section survived the 1937 fire, and many of the original buildings are still standing, some occupied by the same Japanese

Weathered buildings, Walnut Grove

owners. The Hayashi Company market, specializing in Japanese foods and fish, has occupied its B Street location since the early 1920s. The Walnut Grove Market on A Street, a grocery and hardware store, stands on the site of the Japanese theater where traveling Japanese companies performed Kabuki and other forms of theater. Several Japanese bathhouses were located in buildings that once stood on B Street; some were still in use as late as the 1960s. These bathhouses served the same function as the Chinese meeting halls and were the heart of the Japanese quarter. Here the Japanese men could gather to relax and share the latest news and gossip.

The Walnut Grove Buddhist Church on Pine Street serves the town's Japanese residents. Its ceremonial furnishings came from the Buddhist church in Isleton, which never reopened after World War II. The church sponsors an annual bazaar near the Fourth of July weekend and the Obon Festival, a religious festival featuring dancers in traditional clothing, also in July. Next door is the Gakuen Hall, which is listed on the National Register of Historic Places. It was built in 1928 with donations from the Japanese community and served as the Japanese community center. Among other uses, it served as a school for Japanese children, who were required by the state to attend separate schools as a result of the 1921 Oriental Segregation Law.

Among the notable buildings still standing is the old Grove Theater on Market Street, built in the 1920s and operated into the 1960s. It was originally called the Imperial Theater. Up on River Road is the Valley Oak Food and Deli, owned by Alex Brown's great-grandson Stanford Brown. It stands on the site of the first Alex Brown Store, which burned down in 1915. Also on River Road is First San Joaquin Savings and Loan, built on the site of the first hotel built by the Sharps and the second hotel built by the Browns in 1918. The three-story, Tudor-style hotel cost $120,000 to build and furnish. It was destroyed by fire in 1969.

Walnut Grove is a popular stopover for boaters, who can dock at the Walnut Grove Merchant's Dock on the east bank or the Deckhand's Marine Supplies on the west bank. The Deckhand's has rentals of waterskiing gear, fishing boats, and jet skis. There is also a market and gas station on the west side. Tony's Place (776-1317) is just across from the merchant's dock on the east bank. Over the course of thirty years, Tony Enos's restaurant and cocktail lounge has earned its fine reputation and faithful following. New York steaks and Portuguese beans are the specialties; dinner is served Saturday and Sunday only (reservations are recommended), and lunch is served weekdays. The cocktail lounge is open daily.

East Walnut Grove occupies the northern tip of Tyler Island, one of the areas in the Sacramento Delta hardest hit by the disastrous flood of 1986. A break in the levee along the Mokelumne River covered the island's 8,200 acres with 300,000 acre-feet of water, causing $14 million in damage to homes, businesses, and farmland. Walnut Grove's industrial area was the hardest hit; fortunately, the major portion of the residential section of town was saved from inundation, thanks to frantic, round-the-clock efforts to strengthen the remaining levees.

Walnut Grove has the distinction of having two of the tallest man-made structures in the world. The two television towers, owned by Sacramento TV stations, are among the few visible landmarks in the delta. The tallest and newest is the two-thousand-foot KCRA transmitter tower, twice the height of the Eiffel Tower and taller than New York City's World Trade Center. The ride to the top in the two-person cage elevator takes about half an hour. About a mile and a half away on the bank of the Delta Cross Channel is what locals refer to as the Walnut Grove television tower. Built in 1962, the 1,549-foot tower owned and operated by KOVR and KXTV was the tallest structure in the delta until KCRA's tower was completed in 1984. If the towers don't seem exceptionally tall, that's because there are no other structures nearby with which to compare them.

WALNUT GROVE ROAD

From Walnut Grove there's easy access to I-5 via Walnut Grove Road. Along the way are several restaurants and marinas worth mentioning. The Walnut Grove Marina (776-1181) provides guest docking, houseboat rentals, marine services, fuel supplies, groceries, and snacks. Just down the road is Giusti's landing, bar, and Italian restaurant, another delta landmark, located at the confluence of the North Fork of the Mokelumne River and Snodgrass Slough. The original building, which still stands and serves as the back section of the present restaurant, was built in 1896. This was a favorite hangout for Erle Stanley Gardner and continues to be a favorite for locals and boaters. Giusti's serves lunch, dinner, and Sunday brunch during the summer and is famous for its New York steaks as well as its seafood, shellfish, ravioli, and veal cutlets. Giusti's (776-1808) offers guest docking and fuel.

The next spot down the road is Wimpy's (209/794-2544), about two miles east of Walnut Grove and three and a half miles west of I-5. Located on the Mokelumne's South Fork, it is a year-round resort area with a marina, guest docking, camping, a bait shop, and a warm, friendly restaurant and cocktail lounge. Breakfast, lunch, and dinner are served daily, along with a popular Sunday brunch. Lunch and dinner fare includes hamburgers, hot crab sandwiches, steak, prawns, prime rib, and homemade desserts. New Hope Landing next door offers houseboat rentals, an R.V. park, fuel and propane, and groceries.

GEORGIANA SLOUGH

Continuing south on River Road along the east bank of the Sacramento in Walnut Grove, you'll come to the north end of Georgiana Slough, which connects the Sacramento and San Joaquin rivers via the Mokelumne. The scenic, winding twelve-mile cutoff was once used by riverboats plying the waters between Stockton and Sacramento. Jack London, who spent much time in the delta, used to write while drifting down the Georgiana in a houseboat during the day; at night he'd visit friends in the river towns. In recent years the slough has become a well-traveled thoroughfare for boaters and fishermen. Fishing along the brush-lined banks is good, with access to both banks for much of its length.

Georgiana Slough is another of those delta waterways that is perhaps best seen by boat, but unlike the Delta Meadows, it is accessible by car. From Walnut Grove, take River Road to the swing bridge, which leads you to Andrus Island Road and the west bank of the Georgiana. Tyler Island Road also offers access. A couple of miles or so down Andrus Island Road is the county-maintained Georgiana Slough Fishing Access. It's a small, grassy park with a few trees on a bend of the slough. You can bring a picnic lunch, fish, and watch the boats go by. The day-use-only park provides a car-top boat launch and restrooms. Until recently, there were no commercial enterprises along the Georgiana. This changed with the development of the Ox Bow Marina at the southern part of the slough near Isleton. It is a deluxe marina and mobile home park with covered berths, a clubhouse, private launching, a yacht brokerage, guest docking, and other facilities. Future plans include a restaurant and motel.

In an attempt to regulate boat traffic in the delta for safety and environmental reasons, Sacramento County imposed wake and speed controls on Georgiana Slough in 1983. Waterskiing is not allowed anywhere in the channel. On the upper two miles of the channel, boats may not leave wakes, and on the lower two miles, a five-miles-per-hour speed limit is in effect.

Ryde

The little town of Ryde (pop. 60) is located on Highway 160 about three miles west of Walnut Grove. The first thing you'll see is the tall black water tower looming over the Ryde Hotel, Ryde's main (and only) attraction. The town was named by Thomas H. Williams, who had come to Grand Island and set up a ranching operation. When the post office was built in 1893, Williams suggested the name Ryde, after his hometown on the Isle of Wight off the south coast of England.

During Prohibition the Ryde gained notoriety up and down the Sacramento River. The hotel was renowned for its elegant rooms and sumptuous

Ryde Hotel

meals, and its basement speakeasy was the site of the hottest action for miles around. You had to have connections or know the password to gain entrance to its large dance hall and casino, which included slot machines. The original door, complete with peephole, is now located in the hotel lobby. The mahogany and walnut bar had been brought in from San Francisco and now graces the main dining room.

A secret tunnel connected the speakeasy with a back building where bootleg whiskey, wine, and gin were made. Packaged bottles of whiskey were sold from a secret room. Ryde's leading bootlegger was Al Adami, who later founded Al's Place in Locke. In an ironic turn of events, Herbert Hoover, a strong supporter of Prohibition, announced his candidacy for president during a political rally at the Ryde in 1928. No one knows if he was aware of the goings-on in the basement.

The place was raided several times, and the tunnel was sealed in 1930. With the end of Prohibition in 1933 and the end of the riverboat era, the mystique and glamour of the Ryde faded and soon disappeared. In the ensuing years it had several different owners and served as a migrant labor camp for a time. The three-story, fifty-room hotel was restored and reopened in 1972. The hotel, restaurant, and bar are open from April through December. Some rooms have shared baths, and prices are reasonable. A basement club called—what else—the Speakeasy has live rock music and dancing on Friday and Saturday nights. The quaint dining room, with lots of potted plants and a river view, serves breakfast, lunch, and dinner on weekends and a Sunday champagne brunch. Private dining rooms and guest docking are available. Special events include an annual Halloween costume party and a New Year's Eve bash. For room rates and hours of operation, call 776-1318.

Isleton

Isleton (pop. 923) is the only incorporated city lying within Sacramento County's delta region. The chamber of commerce, located at the Isleton City Hall, can provide information on the town, including the booklet *The Heart of the Delta* that is available for purchase (100 Second Street, P.O. Box 758, Isleton, CA 95641, 777-6082).

Dr. Josiah Poole, a Mexican War veteran, founded the town in 1874. He built a drugstore, the first shipping wharf, and downtown buildings, and also served as the town's first postmaster. The town was flourishing by the 1880s when a hotel, stores, and a livery stable were added, and it was an important riverboat stop.

Quo Wo Sing Co., Isleton

Isleton had its own Chinatown, located to the south near Jackson Slough. Like the other delta Chinatowns, its closely spaced wooden buildings were not immune to fire, and the section burned down twice. After the second fire in 1926, the Chinese rebuilt at the north end of town using tin, brick, and asbestos shingles. Most of these buildings are still standing, and some of the original businesses are still operating. Quo Wo Sing Co., also known as the Isleton Bait Shop, is a general merchandise, hardware, and sporting goods store affectionately referred to as "Isleton's K mart." After the 1940s, this section became a Mexican barrio and a source for farm labor when agriculture was Isleton's mainstay. Isleton also had its Japanese quarter, where sumo wrestlers would compete for prizes in a ring first purified with salt. Large numbers of Filipinos also settled here to work in the canneries.

The town flourished as a canning and farm center; by the 1920s, three large canneries had followed the rail line to Isleton. During Prohibition, Isleton was known as "the Little Paris of the Delta." Gambling and prostitution were big business in Isleton's Chinatown, providing diversions for the large numbers of farm workers who lived there. With the onset of the Depression, the town entered financial hard times. The canning industry began to decline, riverboat traffic was disappearing, and new railroads and highways bypassed the area. A redevelopment effort aimed at attracting the recreation trade to bolster Isleton's sagging economy is now afoot.

Isleton today is a quiet little river town that's worth visiting for its picturesque old buildings. You'll also find all the amenities, including groceries, bait, sports equipment, boat repair, a post office, gas stations, a drug store, restaurants, and bars. There's the Hotel Del Rio (777-6033), a newer hotel with a bar and lounge, restaurant, and friendly cafe. The Chuck Wagon Restaurant at the hotel is known for its prime rib. Another well-known delta attraction and hangout for locals is Ernie's restaurant and saloon (777-6510). The dinner specialties are sirloin steak and broasted chicken; lunches and sandwiches are served during the day. Ernie's has an overnight guest dock with electricity.

Isleton's residents have put on their May Festival every year since 1974. The two-day event held in early May is a real down-home, small-town celebration with a parade, dance groups, ethnic food booths and cultural booths, contests, and games.

About two miles south of Isleton on Highway 160 is Vieira's Resort (777-6661), located on a small wooded berm called Ida Island. It's a full-service resort with picnicking, camping, boat launching and docking, boat rentals, RV parking, and cottages with kitchenettes. Seafood is the specialty at The Store (777-6562), the restaurant at Vieira's. Choose from hearty breakfasts, fifteen kinds of lunch sandwiches and specials, and dinner entrees ranging from mahimahi, lobster, and abalone to steaks, veal, and fried chicken.

ANDRUS ISLAND RESORTS

Several miles south of Isleton via the Jackson Slough or Terminous roads lies the tip of Andrus Island, fronted by the San Joaquin and Mokelumne rivers. Here you'll find the largest collection of riverside resorts in the Sacramento County delta area. At the fifteen or so resorts, boaters and motorists will find a variety of services, including RV and mobile home parks, camping, boat launching and docking, groceries, fuel, yacht sales, fishing, waterskiing, cottages, and restaurants.

The B & W Resort Marina (777-6652) is located at the Highway 12 bridge and has twenty-three housekeeping cottages, a cafe, boating facilities, and even a hair salon. Painted white with red trim, Moore's Riverboat (777-6545) is a 156-foot riverboat converted into a floating restaurant and cabaret in 1965. Owner John Moore spent five years almost single-handedly converting and preserving the old freighter *Sutter.* Open March through December, the restaurant serves breakfast, lunch, and dinner; such specialties as steak, fish, delta crawdads, and fresh sourdough bread are served. The bar is hopping on weekends, and there's dancing Friday through Sunday nights to live big-band music.

Korth's Pirates Lair is one of the oldest and most beautiful delta resorts. It's located in a natural harbor with palm trees shading its lawns. The cafe serves breakfast and lunch. The Andreas Cove Marina serves three meals and has guest docking and RV camping. Spindrift Marina's restaurant serves fine food from a varied menu (777-6654). It also offers dancing to live music and a cocktail lounge. The marina has groceries, liquor, marine supplies, guest docking, covered berths, and a mobile home park.

Rio Vista

To get to Rio Vista (pop. 3,200) from Isleton, take Highway 160 about four miles south to Highway 12, a major east-west route through the southern delta. The highway connects with I-5 about fifteen miles to the east (from there it's thirty-five miles to Sacramento). To get to Rio Vista, take Highway 12 west across the Rio Vista tower drawbridge, which is the busiest drawbridge on the Sacramento River.

Sportfishing is the name of the game in this busy Solano County city. Bait and tackle shops abound, and licensed fishing guides are available to help you catch the big one. The city maintains a riverbank fishing access with a grassy fishing and picnic facility just south of the Rio Vista Bridge. The town's biggest event is the annual Bass Derby, held the first weekend in October and sponsored by the chamber of commerce. The three-day event was first held in 1933 and has been going strong ever since. The derby attracts thousands of visitors every year for its parade and carnival, crawdad races, demonstrations, exhibits, and food. For exact dates of the Bass Derby and more information on Rio Vista, call or write the Rio Vista Chamber of Commerce, 60 Main Street, Rio Vista, CA 94571, 707/374-2700.

Rio Vista is known as the crayfish capital of the western U.S. Connoisseurs of these tasty crustaceans travel long distances to buy them fresh at Delta Crayfish, located downtown at 608 Highway 12, just across the bridge (707/374-6654). The height of the crayfish season is from May to November, but you can purchase them here year-round. As many as 500,000 pounds of crayfish are caught each year in delta waters; more than three-fourths of the catch is exported to Sweden, by far the largest customer for delta crayfish.

Rio Vista is noteworthy for other reasons as well. For many years, it was the delta port-of-call for Sacramento riverboats and served as the regional trade

Mansion on "Millionaire Row," Rio Vista

center. In 1936, huge natural gas fields were discovered, some of the largest in the world and the richest in California. A number of leases in Rio Vista were filed, and the fields continue to produce $25 million every year. Royalties from the gas fields made some farmers and other landowners rich overnight; Second Street is known as "Millionaire Row" because of the splendid Victorian mansions that were built by local land barons.

In 1844, General John Bidwell, who had joined forces with John Sutter at his New Helvetia fort in 1841, was granted a tract of land by the Mexican government. In 1855, he divided the land and sold it for about fifteen cents an acre, which was considered a good price, since no one believed the land to be of any agricultural value. One of the buyers was Colonel N. H. Davis, who surveyed the land around Rio Vista in 1857. The site was a couple of miles above the present Rio Vista Bridge near Cache Slough and was called Brazos Del Rio ("arms of the river"). In 1860 the name was changed to Rio Vista ("river view"). The town had a flourishing river trade until January 1862, when a flood swept away the entire town. The hardy delta settlers rebuilt their town on higher ground at its present location, renaming it New Rio Vista. Soon stores, a hotel, churches, a post office, and boatyards were built, and Rio Vista (or "Rye-o Visty," as some of the oldtimers used to call it) was on its way.

Rio Vista today is a modern little city with a shopping area offering most anything you might need, a small airport, RV and camping facilities, motels, restaurants, and boat launching and docking. The Delta Marina is a full-service marina with guest docking, berths, fuel, and a yacht shop with a large selection of nautical gifts. The Point Restaurant (707/374-5400) at the Delta Marina is considered one of the prettiest dining spots in the delta due to its luxurious atmosphere and impressive river view. The Point serves lunch and dinner, and its menu features seafood and shellfish. It also has a large cocktail lounge with a view of the marina entrance; you can watch the passing freighters from the dining room. A public address system announces information on the freighters as they cut through the Sacramento River, which is close to one thousand feet wide in the Rio Vista area.

If you prefer watching airplanes as you dine, take a short drive to the Rio Vista Airport. Near the entrance you'll see a large blue-and-white airplane with a carpeted boarding platform. It's Flying Down to Rio, a DC-4 passenger plane that has been converted into a cafe. According to the management, it's the only restaurant of its kind in the country. Until the plane was retired, it carried commercial passengers for a Brazilian airline. The owners have tried to keep everything in the airplane intact, along with adding tables and a small kitchen. You can even check out the cockpit. It's open for lunch and early dinner on weekends only from March to November. Specialties include homemade soups, sandwiches, and salads. The restaurant can accommodate private parties. Call 707/374-2423 for reservations.

SANDY BEACH COUNTY PARK

Sandy Beach is located at the south edge of Rio Vista's city limits and is maintained by Solano County. Although it is relatively new and somewhat bare of shade, the forty-acre recreation area is popular with boaters and fishermen. The park has campsites, twenty-five RV sites, picnic tables, barbecues, showers, restrooms, boat launching, and fishing access. A sunbathing beach is located here, but swimming is not advisable.

CALIFORNIA RAILWAY MUSEUM

A recommended side trip for railroad buffs is the California Railway Museum, located about twelve miles west of Rio Vista on Highway 12. It's run by the non-profit Bay Area Electric Railroad Association, whose volunteers have restored some eighty pieces of rail stock, including freight cars, passenger cars, streetcars, and steam, diesel, and electric locomotives. Much of the equipment is in running order and can take passengers for frequently scheduled two-mile rides. Picnicking is invited on the tree-shaded lawns, and you can browse in the railroad bookstore and gift shop. One of the more recent additions to the museum's collection is the old No. 46 Pacific Gas and Electric streetcar that plied T Street in Sacramento until it was retired in 1938. It had been sitting forgotten under trees and bushes on a lot overlooking the American River in Fair Oaks for more than forty years.

The museum, which is open weekends only, hosts an annual Spring Railway Festival on the last weekend of April. Call first to check on hours and admission rates; 707/374-2978.

Brannan Island State Recreation Area

About three miles south of Rio Vista on Highway 160 is the lush, tree-studded Brannan Island State Recreation Area (777-6671). It is the only state campground facility in the Sacramento Delta, with camping, picnicking, boating, fishing, and swimming.

The 336-acre campground is located on a hummock, or knoll, in the southwest corner of Brannan Island. The area was built up with earth from river dredging and has an elevation of twenty-five feet, making it the highest ground in the delta. The park was developed during the 1950s by the state. Trees are plentiful, including willow, cottonwood, eucalyptus, oak, and pine. The spring wildflowers put on a spectacular show, and wildlife and birds abound, among them ground squirrels, jackrabbits, meadowlarks, and mockingbirds.

The 102 family campsites have stoves, tables, drinking water, and restrooms. Six group campsites accommodate up to thirty people each, and an RV rally site with no hookups can handle up to 45 RVs. Trailers up to thirty feet long can be accommodated; a trailer sanitation station is located near the park entrance. The Delta Vista Boat Camp is ideal for delta boaters in small or medium-sized crafts. It has thirty-five open berths adjoining twenty-five walk-in campsites that are available for non-boaters as well. The camp also has several picnic areas with tables and barbecues, including group picnic sites with overhead shade. Swimming is good at the beach on Seven Mile Slough at the northeast end of the park, and lifeguards are on duty from Memorial Day to Labor Day. A boat ramp is located on Three Mile Slough. The park's Visitor's Center sells publications relating to the delta.

Frank's Tract is part of this state recreation area. Located about five miles southeast of Brannan Island in Contra Costa County and accessible only by boat, it has been set aside for water recreation, including waterskiing, boating, and fishing. The area is farmland that was flooded, leaving only 300 of its 3,507 acres above water. There are no facilities.

Sherman Island

Directly across Three Mile Slough from Brannan Island via Highway 160 lies Sherman Island, a reclaimed island about seven and a half miles long and three miles wide. It was named for Sherman Day, California's U.S. surveyor general from 1868 to 1871. The only town that existed on Sherman Island was the tiny hamlet of Emmaton. Located at the spot where Highway 160 makes a sharp southern turn to bisect the island, it was swept away by floods in 1878 and never rebuilt. The island is now used primarily for farming. The only major flood to hit Sherman Island in recent times occurred early in 1969. Residents had to wait as much as eight months before they could return to their homes, and Highway 160 and the Antioch Bridge were closed for eleven months.

As you head south on Highway 160, to your right you'll notice a small island at what is called Horseshoe Bend. This is Decker Island, part of Solano County and formerly the place where part of the Rio Vista Army Depot's mothball fleet was anchored. The island is presently in agricultural use. Across the river are rolling grasslands known as the Montezuma Hills, which geologists believe were created by deposits of river silt deformed by faulting and folding. You can get large hamburgers and delicious brown beans at the Bean Pot cafe, located at Horseshoe Bend and a popular spot for locals. Limited guest docking is available.

The county maintains a public boat ramp in this area with boat launching, fishing, swimming, and picnicking. For years it has been known locally as Sandy Beach (not to be confused with Rio Vista's Sandy Beach) and may be reached by taking the Sherman Island levee road that meets Highway 160 where it turns south at Horseshoe Bend.

The lower portion of Sherman Island is known as the Sherman Island State Wildlife Area, a 3,200-acre multi-purpose area managed by the California Fish and Game Department. Two-thirds of the island is actually a flooded tidal marsh. The area is popular for fishing, nature study, waterskiing, and boating. Birdwatchers will delight in observing the one hundred species of birds that inhabit the island. Winter is the best time to observe migrating waterfowl.

Part II

THE GOLD COUNTRY

7

Introduction to the Gold Country

California has always conveyed the image of a land of golden opportunity. One California historian has called it the "jackpot psychology"—the idea that with a little effort and a lot of luck, one can strike it rich beyond his or her wildest dreams. California has been the mecca for the hopefuls seeking fame and stardom in the backlots and drug stores of Hollywood, for the lost souls seeking themselves in the hot tubs of Esalen or on the Beverly Hills shrink's couch, for the high-tech entrepreneurs looking to make a killing in Silicon Valley.

One need look no further than the great seal of the state of California. Right at the top is the word "Eureka," which is Greek for "I have found it!" And just below is a miner with a pickaxe and a shovel, hard at work. You can be sure he isn't digging for truffles. And California's nickname, "the Golden State," isn't a reference to its golden poppies or sun-bleached hills. We're talking real gold here, that shiny, precious metal that turned an entire nation upside down and inside out for about a decade during the last century.

California's Gold Rush took place in what is known as the Mother Lode, a region a couple of hundred miles long on the western slopes of the Sierra Nevada. The term *Mother Lode* is a translation of *la Veta Madre,* a term coined by Mexican miners. They were referring to an incredibly rich vein of gold about 120 miles long, stretching from Bear Valley to Auburn. In later years, the term has come to describe the entire gold region from Mariposa to

Downieville. There were other gold-producing areas besides the Mother Lode—in the Southern California hills and the Shasta-Trinity-Siskiyou area, for example—but this was the major gold region and the scene of most of the action.

The gold country today is a living museum where you can readily experience the history, folklore, and tradition of the miners who toiled here. Time and the elements have taken their toll on many of the mining camps that once flourished, but the region has remained mostly unchanged over the years, and it is still possible to recapture the flavor of the Gold Rush. Everywhere are remnants of a bygone era, from deserted mines to cemeteries overgrown with wildflowers and weeds. There are towns like Sonora and Nevada City that have survived and prospered and are a delight to visit, and towns like Angels Camp, forever immortalized in the writings of Mark Twain and Bret Harte, who both spent time there. You'll find cozy little antique shops, art galleries

Remains of the North Star 60-stamp mill, Grass Valley

displaying the wares of local artisans, small museums, interesting little cafes, and historic bed and breakfast inns. For lovers of the great outdoors, the area presents numerous opportunities for camping, hiking, horseback riding, fishing, skiing, water sports, bicycling, and picnicking. There are wineries open for tours, apple farms selling freshly baked apple pies and hot cider, train rides, Christmas tree farms, and places to pan for gold (see chapter 10).

The gold country ranges in elevation from rolling grassland about seven hundred feet above sea level to elevations over twenty-five hundred feet. It's a bucolic region characterized by small, grassy hills dotted with pine, poplar, eastern maple, and blue oak, the most conspicuous tree in the Sierra foothills. It has lakes and rivers, mountains and small prairies. Colorful wildflowers abound, especially in the spring, carpeting the landscape with Scotch broom, lupine, wild daisy, sweet pea, California poppy, baby blue-eyes, Mariposa lily, and owl's clover. The region is traversed by Highway 49, officially designated the Mother Lode Highway, which follows the burro paths of the '49ers and stretches 325 miles between Oakhurst in the south and Vinton in the north. The highway passes through nine key counties and many small ranches, sleepy little Western towns, and small cities. Tourism and recreation are major industries, along with lumber, gold mining, livestock, and agriculture.

Before setting out on a tour of the Mother Lode, let's take a look at what took place here. A little background information and a vivid imagination can go a long way in increasing one's enjoyment of a visit to the gold country.

The Great Adventure

January 24, 1848, was a day just like any other for Henry Bigler, a workman at John Sutter's sawmill under construction on the American River. The winter in the Sierra Nevada foothills had been cold and rainy, but work on the mill was nearly done. That day Bigler wrote a short entry in his diary: "Monday 24th this day some kind of mettle was found in the tail race that looks like goald first discovered by James Martial the Boss of the Mill."

Without knowing it, Bigler became the first to chronicle what would soon become one of the greatest adventures of American history: the California Gold Rush. The shiny precious metal, and the search for it, directed and shaped the course of western settlement in the United States perhaps more than any other single phenomenon. The mad rush for gold that made men take leave of their senses and their families provided the impetus for the great migration that opened the West and led to California's settlement and statehood. California's gold also played an important role in the destiny of the United States. California and Nevada had been settled primarily by

Northeasterners who supported the Union during the Civil War. As a result, more than $180 million in gold from California and silver from Nevada's Comstock Lode helped to finance the Union Army between 1861 and 1864.

The Spanish had occupied California for eighty years without finding the gold. The Indians had ignored it for centuries. At the time of James Marshall's discovery, California was a sleepy Mexican frontier colony held by the U.S. as a prize from its war with Mexico. It was thinly populated with several coastal settlements, small settlements around the missions, and a few cattle ranches in the interior. The first to arrive in the gold fields were the '48ers, most of whom were settlers who were in California before the discovery. There were also large groups of Chileans, Mexicans from Sonora, and a few settlers from the Oregon Territory. It was the masses of city and village people who followed who became known as the '49ers.

Thousands of latter-day argonauts (named for the Greeks who sought the Golden Fleece) came by three arduous routes: a thirteen-thousand-mile voyage around Cape Horn, a "shortcut" across the Isthmus of Panama, and a hazardous overland trek across the plains and mountains. The '49ers from the Eastern Seaboard who could afford the more expensive trip around the Horn had to endure seasickness, boredom, and illness from lack of fresh fruits and vegetables. The shortcut across the Isthmus of Panama did save time, but there was the ever-present threat of contracting malaria or cholera in the disease-infested jungle. The overland trail was the cheapest, the most dangerous, the most demanding, and the most popular route.

As word spread of the fabulous riches to be had for the taking, so did gold fever, and few were immune to it. In two short sentences, a young soldier captured the feeling of the times: "A frenzy seized my soul; piles of gold rose up before me at every step; thousands of slaves bowed to my beck and call; myriads of fair virgins contended for my love. In short, I had a violent attack of gold fever." Most of the adventurers were young men between the ages of eighteen and thirty-five; very few women initially came to the gold fields. They were farmers, doctors, sailors, lawyers, soldiers, and merchants. They were also determined chroniclers, bringing with them journals, notebooks, writing paper, portable writing desks, pens, and ink. It is for this reason that we have such a detailed and accurate account of this period in history.

Many of the '49ers joined associations or companies to share the cost of transportation and supplies. These groups had from a few members to several hundred members and were usually organized for a five-year term. Most, however, dissolved when the goldseekers reached California. Sacramento was the staging area for the northern mines and Stockton was the staging area for the southern mines. Those who arrived by ship in San

Francisco still had to get to Sacramento or Stockton. If they didn't get there by boat, they walked, because few could afford to pay for a wagon or a horse.

Tall tales of easy riches abounded. A man was sitting on a rock, moping in discouragement. He stood up and kicked the rock; it rolled aside to reveal a gold nugget. A Coloma man found $2,000 worth of gold under his own doorstep. Three Frenchmen pulled up a tree stump in the middle of the Coloma road and dug $5,000 in gold from the hole.

One of the best stories involves the funeral of a miner who died near Carson Hill. His friends decided to give him a proper burial, preacher and all. When the preaching kept on and on, some of the miners got restless and started running their fingers through the dirt from the grave. Suddenly one of them yelled, "Color!" Sure enough, there were traces of gold in the dirt. The preacher roared "Congregation dismissed," the body was removed from the grave, and the mourners quickly set about digging. The body was eventually laid to rest in another less profitable hole. With stories like these circulating, it's no wonder the '49ers expected to find great piles of gold without having to work for it, and for many, this was the case. But the vast majority of goldseekers soon learned that mining was incredibly hard work and luck played a big part.

LIFE IN THE DIGGINGS

Placer gold was the kind of gold that miners were searching for during the first years of the Gold Rush. This was loose gold in the form of nuggets, dust, and flakes that had been eroded by the rivers and streams from the outcrops of the yet-to-be-discovered Mother Lode. Placer gold was deposited in the riverbeds of the Feather, Yuba, Merced, American, Stanislaus, and Tuolumne rivers as well as the smaller streams that fed them. The primary tools of the placer miners were the pan, the cradle, long tom (a long wooden trough), and sluice, which all helped to separate the heavy gold particles from the lighter sand and dirt. Gold was worth $16 an ounce in San Francisco in 1849. In order to make enough just to get by, a miner had to find at least half an ounce to an ounce of gold a day. Miners were lucky to average $10 a day. This was barely enough to pay the vastly inflated prices for such basic necessities as food and supplies. Butter and cheese were $6 a pound; blankets went for $50 to $100; shirts were $16, and horses cost from $100 to $150. There were few fruits and vegetables, and most miners subsisted on pork (pickled or cured and usually fried), as well as beans, sourdough bread, and flapjacks. Few miners ever struck it rich, and they often abandoned a claim to look for a better one.

During the early days of the Gold Rush, crime was practically nil. There was an unwritten code of honor among the miners. Each miner was allowed

Rough and lonely life in the diggings (courtesy California State Library Collection, City of Sacramento, Museum and History Division)

one claim, and all that was needed to stake a claim was to leave one's tools on the spot. Gold was left lying around in tents and cabins with no fear of theft. It appeared there would be enough for everyone. There was also a strong spirit of camaraderie, and when someone was down on his luck, others would often join to help him out. The emotion that brought the miners together was homesickness. The arrival of mail from home was a great occasion, often reducing toughened miners to tears.

Camps sprang up everywhere, often being abandoned when word of a new strike spread. They were named for anything that struck the miners' fancy—other miners, animals, mishaps, misbehavior, and luck (both good and bad). Thus camps had names like Rich Bar, Bedbug, Jackass Hill, You Bet, Delirium Tremens, Humbug, and Gomorrah. The center of the town was the camp store, which at first was usually just a tent, a canvas hut, or a log cabin. If mining in the area was successful, the store quickly expanded its function to serve food and liquor, rent sleeping space, and act as a social center where plenty of drinking and gambling took place.

Although some pleasant portraits have been painted both with paint and with words showing Chinese, blacks, Indians, and whites working peacefully side by side during the Gold Rush, this was more the exception than the rule. The truth is, intense xenophobia permeated the camps, and the victims were usually those whom the miners considered to be "foreigners." Of the eighty-five thousand men who swarmed to California's gold fields in 1849, about twenty-three thousand were not U.S. citizens. They came from Europe, China, Australia, South America, Canada, and Mexico. The local Indians suffered the most at the hands of the whites; although they played key roles as laborers in many mining fortunes, it was not considered a crime to shoot them, and thousands were indeed shot. The prevailing attitude was that California was now American and only Americans were entitled to its riches. (Of course, the white miners conveniently forgot that the Maidu and Miwok Indians had been there at least two thousand years before the Americans arrived and that Spaniards and Mexicans had also lived in this land before whites did.) Beginning in 1850, the fledgling California legislature translated these ideas into a series of laws taxing those whom it called "foreign miners." The first was a Foreign Miners Tax of $20 a month. Although it was repealed temporarily the following year, it reappeared in 1852 as a license fee of $3 per month (later raised to $4) for all foreign miners.

Curiously, very little has been written about the presence of Jews in the gold country between 1849 and 1880. One possible explanation is that their numbers were likely very small, probably not more than about six hundred, and most Gold Rush historians choose to focus on ethnic groups who came to the gold country in large numbers, such as the Chinese and Mexicans. Although their numbers were small, their contributions to the economic and civic vitality of nearly every mining camp were major.

Nearly all of the Jews who came to the gold fields were European, primarily from France and Germany, with some from Great Britain, Russia, Prussian Poland, and the Netherlands. They were businessmen—primarily merchants and tradesmen—for this was the occupation they knew best, although a few did become miners. Many brought goods to sell in California or money to buy goods in San Francisco to sell in the camps. Many of the Jews brought their families with them and immediately formed Jewish communities and organizations, conducted worship services, and established separate cemeteries as required by their faith. There are Jewish cemeteries at Sonora, Mokelumne Hill, Jackson, Placerville, Grass Valley, and Nevada City. Only two synagogues were built, in Jackson and Placerville (where there is still a synagogue).

The most famous of the Jewish tradesmen was Levi Strauss, a Bavarian immigrant who came to San Francisco from New York by ship in 1850. He was carrying with him goods from his brother's clothing shop but sold everything on the way except for a roll of tent canvas. Upon his arrival in San Francisco, he learned that the miners' pants often ripped and tore during strenuous work. He fashioned a pair of pants from the canvas and sold them to a miner, and the first pair of Levi's was born. The idea caught on in the mining camps, and Strauss started manufacturing pants, later dyeing them blue and adding copper rivets. Strauss had found a gold mine without shoveling one ounce of earth.

CIVILIZATION COMES TO TOWN

The Gold Rush reached its peak in 1852; $81 million worth of gold had been taken, and 100,000 miners roamed the 120-mile stretch of Sierra foothills and mountains between Bear Valley and Auburn. By the mid-1850s, many of the individual prospectors were replaced by large-scale mechanized companies that could handle deep-shaft quartz mining and hydraulic mining. Most of the placer gold had been mined, and it took sophisticated machinery to mine the gold-laden quartz.

With the passage of time, civilization crept into the wild and wooly camps. During the early years in the diggings, lonely miners drowned their sorrows in booze, spent their time and money at gambling halls and fandango houses (dance halls), and meted out justice with a whip and a noose. Within a few years, however, miners began sending for their wives and families, so schools were built. Stagecoaches began making regular runs, allowing for easier access and swifter communication. Banks were established and fraternal lodges set up. Free libraries and volunteer fire companies were organized, and newspapers began publishing. On the heels of the new civility came the preachers and the temperance workers, who tried to make the rowdy miners clean up their act further. Traveling minstrels and performers had been visiting the gold towns almost from the beginning, providing some relief from the monotony and boredom. After a while the mines became part of the regular itinerary for many famous and not-so-famous performers.

Of the 400,000 emigrants who had come to California during the decade after Marshall's discovery, only a few realized their dreams of fabulous riches;

most found just enough gold to keep themselves alive. The real fortunes were made primarily by those who catered to the miners' needs. But it was an adventure that most wouldn't have missed for the world. They had participated in one of the greatest adventures of all time, and they knew it. By the end of the 1850s, many were still in California, having moved to the cities of San Francisco, Sacramento, and Stockton or to the valleys to farm. Some remained in the gold fields to work for the large commercial mining outfits. Some headed for other gold fields in Colorado, Nevada, Montana, and Australia. And some returned home to their former occupations with enough memories to last a lifetime.

Touring the Gold Country

This tour of the gold country will focus on the 189-mile stretch of Highway 49 between Mariposa and Nevada City. Many of the major mining camps are located on this road, which runs north and south along the Sierra foothills. Most of Highway 49 is a two-lane road. Its average elevation is about two thousand feet, except where it descends into river canyons and where it turns east and climbs through the rugged High Sierra country just north of Nevada City. Although much of the highway is wide and level, permitting high-speed driving, some sections are narrow, steep, and winding. Except for the sixty-seven-hundred-foot Yuba Pass at the crest of the Sierra Nevada in the north, which is sometimes temporarily closed due to heavy snow, Highway 49 is open year-round.

Crisscrossing the main highway are many scenic backroads that offer the leisurely traveler some great side trips. Exploring these rustic country roads that lead to deserted little ghost towns and idyllic picnic spots can provide a rewarding experience for the adventurous. Many believe that it is in these out-of-the-way towns that one can more readily recapture the Gold Rush atmosphere. In fact, many of the most historic mining camps are located on these backroads. Of the 546 mining towns that existed at the height of the Gold Rush, 297 have vanished, leaving behind crumbling adobe walls, rusty mining machinery, scarred hillsides, and mounds of tailings. These remnants dot the foothills, barely discernable to a sharp-eyed observer.

This tour focuses on the main road, however, and you'll find plenty of color and ambience in the villages and towns along the way. Even along Highway 49, you'll find variations in degrees of antiquity versus modernity. The Gold Rush atmosphere in the larger towns that serve as county seats, business centers, and major highway junctions requires a bit more exploring to find. Some of these cities, such as Grass Valley and Placerville, are bisected by freeways or major highways, and you're liable to see more than one fast-food restaurant on the main drag, which is apt to be congested with traffic during the peak season. Then again, some charming little backwoods communities seem to be untouched by progress and to exude the essence of small-town California. But wherever you go, you'll find many buildings from the Gold Rush era, museums, elegant restored homes of the Victorian period (1840–1900), and picturesque, winding little side streets lined with old homes and shops.

As you explore these towns, keep in mind that the oldest remaining buildings were built during the mid- to late 1850s, after the Gold Rush reached its peak. This is because most of the pioneer canvas, log, and board structures were destroyed by fire. So as you walk down the main street, you're not getting the true view of 1849. If you look at the back of the main street buildings from a rear alley, however, the brick-arched windows, iron shutters, and rock walls will give you a good feel for the buildings of the mid-1850s.

The gold country attracts more than one and a half million visitors annually, and the prime tourist season is between Memorial Day and Labor Day. At this time you'll find the highways and popular attractions more crowded than at other times of the year. The weather can get fiercely hot at the lower elevations, and accommodations fill up early in the day. On the other hand, this is the time when most of the local events such as festivals and county fairs take place and also the time when you'll find more shops, museums, and other attractions open on a regular schedule. Because hours and admission prices change so frequently, they have not been included here; just call before you go.

Spring and fall are ideal times to visit the gold country. As early as February and March, the foothills are lush and green and dotted with colorful spring wildflowers. The spring runoff from the Sierra fills the dry stream beds, creating the best conditions for gold panning. By April and May, the weather has lost its winter bite, and the summer crowds haven't yet arrived. The region is a delight in the fall when the leaves are emblazoned with color, especially in the north toward Grass Valley. The weather is still mild and the crowds have thinned. Even the wintertime can be a good time to visit, as long as you dress warmly. Most of the roads at lower elevations are open, and many ski resorts are located within close proximity of Highway 49. Christmas craft fairs and other seasonal events will help you get into the holiday spirit, and what could be more romantic than cuddling up with a mug of hot spiced cider in front of a cozy fire in a historic country inn?

Speaking of inns, the gold country is brimming with bed and breakfast inns, and the number is growing constantly. Each has its own unique personality and brand of hospitality. Selected inns are described here, but to find out about others you can contact individual chambers of commerce. You can also get information from a monthly newsletter on Northern California inns and an up-to-date list of gold country inns, available from Northern California Inns, P.O. Box 3383, Santa Rosa, CA 95402. The California Office of Tourism also publishes a free guide to bed and breakfast inns (see appendix).

Although you could drive the entire 189-mile distance between Mariposa and Nevada City in a day, you probably wouldn't want to. There's just too much to see and do. Even a three-day weekend isn't enough to do the area justice, and a week still wouldn't be enough to include the backroads spots. The ideal way to visit the gold country is to do it a section at a time, giving yourself plenty of time to appreciate its slow-paced, rural ambience without feeling rushed. Sacramento is an ideal base for visiting the Mother Lode, as it is only about forty-five miles west of Placerville, the geographical heart of the region. Sacramento is like the hub of a wheel; spokes connect it with much of the gold country. I-80 is a major east-west route connecting Sacramento with Auburn thirty-four miles to the east. Via Highway 16 east from Sacramento, it's about thirty-seven miles to Plymouth, just north of Jackson. From Sacramento you can also take Highway 99 south, which connects with several east-west roads leading to the southern gold country. Note: This section divides the gold country into northern and southern portions for purposes of organization. There is no other significance to this division.

The listings in this tour follow a south-to-north route beginning at Mariposa, but this is only one route for seeing the gold country. You can also plan loop trips, taking a freeway to get to the farthest northern or southern point and following Highway 49 to a point where another highway will lead you back to Sacramento.

It's a good idea to bring along a good map of the area, especially if you want to do some backroads exploring. Again, California State Automobile Association maps are good, but you have to be a member to get them. One of the best maps is published by Compass Maps; called the "Gold Map," it includes street maps of most of the major Gold Rush towns and historical information as well. You can find it at the Map Center, 631 North Market Boulevard, Suite F, Sacramento, CA 95834, 920-3661. The Golden Chain Council of the Mother Lode publishes a colorful map of the area, which is available along the Mother Lode route or can be ordered from the council at P.O. Box 1246, Auburn, CA 95603. Local historical societies and chambers of commerce provide a great deal of background information as well as information on festivals, art and antique fairs, and other special events taking place throughout the year.

The chapters that follow are by no means complete or all-inclusive. They are intended to direct you to the most interesting activities and sights, either from a historic or a human-interest point of view. You'll need a good dose of the spirit of adventure to make the most of the gold country, but after all, that spirit was what propelled the gold country into one of the most exciting periods in American history.

8

The Southern Mines: Mariposa to Amador City

With the exception of bustling Mariposa, most of the towns in this region are small, with a rural ambience. Many little towns lie to the east and west of Highway 49—some not more than abandoned ghost towns, but worthy of exploration nonetheless. Many colorful characters roamed the countryside in this region, which is also known as Bret Harte and Mark Twain country.

Mariposa

Mariposa (pop. 1,200) is the southern gateway to the gold country and the southern terminus of Highway 49. It is also located on a major route to Yosemite National Park (Highway 140) and serves as the county seat, so it's a bustling, thriving community with a large amount of tourist traffic. Mariposa was one of the few camps founded on a Spanish rancho, Col. John C. Fremont's forty-five-thousand-acre Rancho Las Mariposas. Originally called Logtown, its name was changed to Mariposa in 1852 when the town became the county seat. Mariposa was created in the spring of 1849 when miners settled along Mariposa Creek. As the placer deposits began to give out, the miners turned to mining the rich gold-bearing quartz veins. These were part of the Mother Lode veins, and Mariposa was the site of the first gold quartz

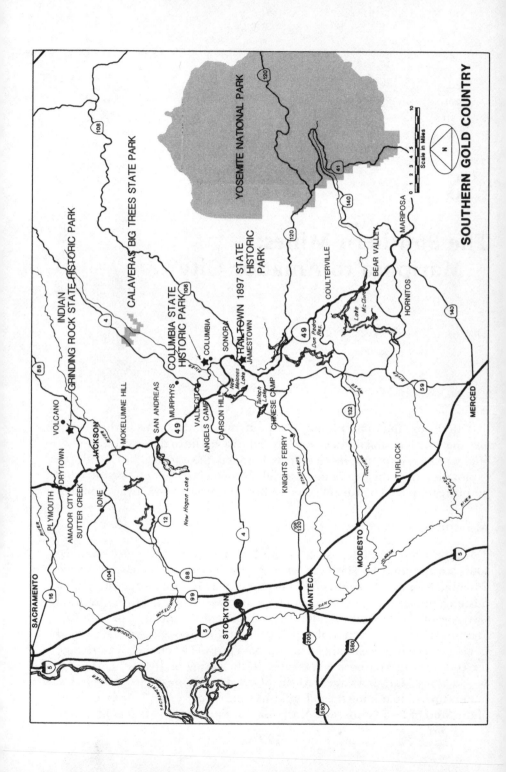

SOUTHERN GOLD COUNTRY

mining, done by Colonel Fremont. Mariposa's population grew to several thousand, due largely to the presence of the quartz mines, which could be worked year-round and thus attracted miners and their families.

Eventually the mines closed down, and much of the town was destroyed by a fire in the late 1860s. The town began to decline until Yosemite Valley became established as a popular tourist destination; Mariposa then became a key stopover for travelers.

A good source of information is the Mariposa County Chamber of Commerce, P.O. Box 425, Mariposa, CA 95338, 209/966-2456. Although

Mariposa County Courthouse, Mariposa (courtesy John R. Poss)

Mariposa has its fair share of modern motels and restaurants, many of its historic structures remain, making a stroll through town worthwhile. Just off the main street on a quiet hill at the north end of town stands one of the most beautiful structures along Highway 49, the charming, New England–style Mariposa County Courthouse. Built in 1854, it is the oldest courthouse in continuous operation in the state. The two-story, white frame structure displays a large English clock tower brought around Cape Horn and installed in 1866. The courtroom on the second floor still has many of its original furnishings. The courthouse is open daily for free public touring (209/966-2006). Nearby is the office of the Mariposa Gazette, a weekly established in 1854 and one of the oldest newspapers in continuous publication in the state.

The Mariposa History Center (209/966-2924) is one of the Mother Lode's most impressive museums. Located at the north end of town at Twelfth and Jessie streets, the combination library/museum has intriguing displays depicting life in early Mariposa. The fine collection of Gold Rush memorabilia includes a five-stamp mill (used for crushing gold-bearing quartz), horse-drawn vehicles, mining and printing equipment, an Indian village, and authentic replicas of rooms depicting life in the gold camps. Open daily during the summer; hours vary during the rest of the year.

Other historic sites of interest include the old stone jail, St. Joseph's Catholic Church, the balconied Schlageter Hotel, Fremont's adobe assay office, the Trabucco Store and Warehouse, the I.O.O.F. Hall (still in use), and Judge Trabucco's home, a stately Victorian on Jones Street. Mariposa's Butterfly Days festival takes place in May or June, and the Mariposa County Fair is held during the Labor Day weekend.

East of Mariposa and forty-five minutes from the south entrance to Yosemite National Park is Meadow Creek Ranch, a bed and breakfast inn. Located on an eighty-five-acre ranch, this 1850s stagecoach stop has five guest bedrooms and provides a country breakfast. Contact Meadow Creek Ranch, 2669 Triangle Road, Mariposa, CA 95338, 209/966-3843.

Mariposa to Jamestown

The fifty-two-mile stretch of Highway 49 between Mariposa and Jamestown passes some lovely countryside and tiny mining towns, as well as several picturesque side roads that present possibilities for side trips.

MT. BULLION

You wouldn't know it to look at it, but Mt. Bullion was the location of the rich Princeton Mine, which yielded $3 million to $4 million in gold and was one of the largest producers in the region. The Trabucco Store and Princeton Saloon are among the few old buildings remaining along the highway.

HORNITOS

Eleven miles west of Bear Valley on Highway J 16 lies the sleepy village of Hornitos. In Spanish, the name means "little ovens," possibly referring to the oven-like tombs of stone in which the original Mexican residents placed their dead. Hornitos was a Mexican mining camp founded by Mexican miners driven out of nearby Quartzburg by prejudiced white miners (who abandoned the camp soon after). According to legend, Hornitos was a rip-roaring, lawless, wild place, the scene of nearly unbelievable tales of knife duels, lynchings, and other grim escapades.

The centerpiece of many of these stories is the legendary bandit Joaquin Murieta, who supposedly spent a lot of time in his hideout here. Gold Rush historians disagree on the existence of Murieta, reputedly one of California's most notorious outlaws. Some suggest he was really a composite of several different Mexican bandits. All mysterious crimes committed by Hispanics were ascribed to him, even if they occurred simultaneously miles apart. As the legend goes, Murieta arrived in Saw Mill Flat outside Sonora from Sonora, Mexico, in 1850. In Murphys, Yankee persecutors tied him to a tree, beat him, assaulted his wife, and murdered his brother, and he swore vengeance against them. From that day on, he led a life of crime. Murieta was captured and killed in 1853 by former Texas Ranger Harry Love and a company of twenty men. To claim his reward money, Love cut off Murieta's head and stuck it in a jar of alcohol, and the gruesome prize was exhibited widely throughout the gold country. Some who saw the head on exhibit said the hair was light and curly and the eyes were blue—far from the black-haired, brown-eyed Murieta of earlier descriptions. Whatever the truth, the romantic legend of the notorious bandit lives on, and he has a permanent place in the colorful folklore of the Gold Rush. Nearly every gold country town boasts some connection with Murieta.

Seemingly untouched by time, Hornitos is one of the best preserved ghost towns in the Mother Lode, its turbulent spirit lingering in the old adobe buildings surrounding the town plaza. It had a population of fifteen thousand during its heyday, and $40,000 in gold was shipped daily from the town's Wells Fargo Express Office. Inside the old jail with its two-foot-thick granite walls is a small museum containing historic artifacts. Opposite the plaza are the remains of the Ghirardelli Store, built in 1859. This is where D.

Ghirardelli, the famous San Francisco chocolate firm, got its start. Auto maker John Studebaker got his start here, too; he earned enough money as a blacksmith to move to Placerville, where he worked at a wheelbarrow and wagon factory. The white wooden St. Catherine's Catholic Church (1862) sits on a knoll overlooking the town. The church's little cemetery is filled with crumbling gravestones, some of which are shaped like little ovens.

BEAR VALLEY

During the 1850s, Bear Valley was the headquarters of Colonel Fremont and his vast land grant. At one time it had a population of three thousand and a rich quartz mining operation. The town once included a well-known hotel, the two-story, balconied Oso House, along with a large company store and other businesses. Fremont lived in the White House, an elegant home staffed with French servants that was the site of many lavish parties. Although Fremont's home and the hotel are gone, you can still see the large stone Trabucco Mercantile building, first opened in 1862. The I.O.O.F. Hall houses the Oso Museum. (*Oso* is Spanish for "bear.") As the mines played out, the town declined, leaving only a handful of ruins as testament to the once-prosperous gold camp. In 1863 Fremont sold his Mariposa Grant for $6 million—a tidy profit, considering he paid $3,000 for it in 1847.

Granny's Garden is a bed and breakfast inn located in an 1896 Victorian farmhouse that has been home to four generations of the Trabucco family. In a country setting complete with cats and farm animals, Granny's offers two guest rooms and an upstairs suite; rates include a continental breakfast. The inn is open from mid-May through October at 7333 Highway 49 North, Mariposa, CA 95338, 209/377-8342.

Just a short stroll down the road is the Bon Ton Cafe, established in 1860 as a saloon (209/377-8229). The surroundings are intimate, with only five tables to allow for personal service. The Bon Ton features European specialties and an excellent Sunday brunch. During the summer there's outdoor patio dining next door in the ruins of an old dry-goods store.

Just north of Bear Valley, Highway 49 begins a winding, thousand-foot descent into the Merced River canyon, known locally as Hell's Hollow. Although it is rugged mountain terrain, you'll see very few trees. Near the bridge across the Merced River is a road leading to the Bagby Recreation Area, which offers camping and boating facilities. The Merced River here forms the eastern section of Lake McClure; nearby are several recreation areas, including the Horseshoe Bend Recreation Area, located five miles west of Coulterville (209/878-3452).

COULTERVILLE

Lying sixteen miles north of Bear Valley is Coulterville (pop. 142). Although only a shell of its former self, Coulterville was once a prosperous town of five thousand people, fifteen hundred of whom were Chinese, and the center of a rich and extensive mining district. At its height, Coulterville boasted ten hotels and twenty-five saloons on its main street. Despite the ravages of three fires that destroyed much of its original character, the town retains much of the aura of a once-booming mining town. The last fire in 1899 caused Coulterville's final "gold rush." Unbeknownst to anyone, a former resident of one adobe building had hidden a cache of gold coins in the walls of the now-burned-out structure; rubble from the building was used to fill potholes in the streets. With the first rains, gold coins began to appear in the road, and the entire town rushed out with shovels, picks, spoons, and any other digging tools they could get their hands on. In a short time, the main street was reduced to an impassible mire.

Today Coulterville is experiencing a rebirth as a Gold Rush town. Many of its beautiful stone and brick buildings, complete with cast-iron doors, are being restored or rebuilt. The entire town has been designated a state historical landmark, and in 1981, the Main Street area was entered into the National Register of Historic Places. You'll want to see the recently remodeled Jeffrey Hotel with its 30-inch-thick walls. Originally built as a cantina in the 1840s, it was converted into a hotel in 1852 and has been owned by the same family for three generations. One of its more prestigious guests was Teddy Roosevelt, who stayed here in 1902 while en route to Yosemite. The adjoining Magnolia Saloon is right out of a Western movie, with swinging doors, polished bar, oiled wood floor, and a fine collection of Gold Rush memorabilia. Across the street are the remains of the Coulter Hotel, once a four-story stone edifice, and the Wells Fargo Building, which served as a trading post during the boom days. Buffalo Bill Cody's brother, Nelson, ran the trading post during the 1870s.

In front of these buildings and under the remains of the local hangman's tree is a handsome steam locomotive nicknamed "Whistling Billy." The narrow-gauge engine was used around the turn of the century to haul ore from the Mary Harrison mine on a four-mile stretch of track known as "the world's crookedest railroad." The only surviving remnant of Coulterville's flourishing Chinatown is the Sun Sun Wo Company Store, at the end of Chinatown Main Street. With some of the original cabinets and the original floor still intact, the 1851 adobe structure now houses an antique store and has been designated a national historic landmark.

After gradually climbing to a summit, Highway 49 descends into the Tuolumne River valley, passing the junction with Highway 120, which leads to Yosemite. The road spans the Tuolumne River and passes the Don Pedro Reservoir to the west.

CHINESE CAMP

About eighteen miles north of Coulterville on Highway 49 lies the somnolent little town of Chinese Camp (pop. 165), first settled in 1849 by a group of Cantonese after they had struck rich claims about a mile east and were run off by white miners. The diggings here were also rich, and several Chinese mining companies were formed. About five thousand Chinese eventually settled here, planting the "lacy trees of heaven" as they did everywhere they settled in the gold country. The trees still flourish today, shading a number of well-preserved old buildings.

Stopping to take a walk through Chinese Camp is worthwhile for its many well-preserved old buildings, trees, and rosebushes. Of special interest are the old-time post office (built in 1854), the remains of the Wells Fargo Building and the Rosenbloom Store, and the beautiful St. Francis Xavier Catholic Church with its old graveyard, built on a knoll in 1855 and restored in 1949.

KNIGHT'S FERRY

A seventeen-mile side trip via Highway 108 west leads to Knight's Ferry, where in 1849 William Knight started the first ferry across the Stanislaus River on the road from Stockton to Sonora. In 1854 a covered bridge replaced Knight's ferry, but the name of the town stuck. The bridge was swept away during the flood of 1862 and the present New England–style bridge was built; it is held together by locust wood pegs. Although it is no longer in service, the historic one-lane bridge, one of the few remaining in California, may be viewed from the modern bridge built nearby. On the hill above the bridge is the Dent House, where General Ulysses S. Grant visited his brother-in-law in 1854. Other points of interest are the 1871 Hook and Ladder Company No. 1 on the restored main street, the Masonic Hall, the iron jailhouse near the covered bridge, and the remains of the flour mill that replaced the original mill that was swept away along with the first covered bridge.

Jamestown

Back on Highway 49 is Jamestown (pop. 2,206), casually known as "Jimtown" in the old days. Jamestown was founded in 1848 by Col. George James, a San Francisco lawyer who later was booted out of town for unscrupulous business dealings. The town was strategically located in the center of a rich mining district sustained by rich gold quartz deposits and

Knight's Ferry Covered Bridge (courtesy John R. Poss)

attracted a population of six thousand at one point. The area around Jamestown provided background for several of Bret Harte's stories.

Although many historic wood-frame buildings were destroyed in a 1966 fire, the Gold Rush atmosphere has been well preserved here. A number of 19th-century structures remain, including the ornate brick-and-wooden-gingerbread Emporium on Main Street, now an antique shop, and the Community Methodist Church, located on a hill one block east of Main Street. Several fine old hotels serve romantic meals in pleasant dining rooms. The recently restored Hotel Willow Restaurant (1862) has a gold mine running directly underneath and once hosted a number of dignitaries, including President William McKinley in 1901. Built in the 1850s and recently remodeled, the Jamestown Hotel is furnished with antiques and patchwork quilts. Many of the rooms have a separate sitting room, and all have private baths. A continental breakfast is served, and a restaurant and saloon are located downstairs. For more information, contact the Jamestown Hotel at P.O. Box 539, Jamestown, CA 95327, 209/984-3902.

The Country Kitchen on Main Street is known for its double banana splits; the owners keep a list of everyone who has eaten one and how long it took. Mountain Steamer Pizza, also on Main, specializes in pizza, steamed clams by the bucket, and Cornish pasties.

RAILTOWN 1897 STATE HISTORIC PARK

Just outside of Jamestown off Highway 108 is Railtown 1897, a reconstruction of the Sierra Railroad's depot, roundhouse, yard, shops, and steam locomotives in their 19th-century grandeur. The Sierra Railroad, the shortline gem of the Mother Lode, began operations in November 1897, hauling supplies and materials between the mining and lumbering towns of the foothills and the freight centers of the San Joaquin Valley. The railroad added excursion trains in 1922 as tourism increased in the area. The park closed in 1980 for financial reasons but reopened in 1983 after being purchased and refurbished by the state at a cost of $1.5 million.

The twenty-six-acre state historic park is a great stop for train buffs and families. When funding is available, several different scenic round-trip passenger excursions are offered during the season, which runs from mid-April through October. The Mother Lode Cannonball takes an hour-long, twelve-mile jaunt along Woods Creek to Chinese Camp. Two longer excursions make a more scenic thirty-six-mile trip to a point near Cooperstown and back. The Wine and Cheese Zephyr serves wine, fruit, cheese, and bread. The Twilight Limited is an evening run with cocktails and snacks aboard the train and a steak barbecue dinner at Railtown's picnic green afterwards. Tours of the functioning roundhouse are offered, and there are gift shops and a picnic area with snacks available.

Locomotive No. 3, built in 1891, is known as the *Hooterville Cannonball* from the TV series "Petticoat Junction" (in which Jamestown's water tower also appears) and is the most photographed locomotive in the world. Railtown and its trains have been used as locations for more than a hundred motion pictures and television programs, including *High Noon, My Little Chickadee, The Great Race,* and "Little House on the Prairie."

Rates, hours, and days of operation for the excursion rides vary greatly; be sure to check with the park office first. For more information, contact Railtown 1897 SHP, P.O. Box 1250, Jamestown, CA 95327, 209/984-3953.

Sonora

Four miles from Jamestown on Highway 49 is Sonora (pop. 4,100), a bustling, picturesque little city serving as the Tuolumne County seat, the commercial center of the region, and the junction for Highway 108, which provides access to the Stanislaus National Forest and Yosemite National Park. In spite of its congested streets and air of commercialism, the evidence of Sonora's robust and flamboyant past remains, especially in the many old buildings and narrow side streets threading their way along the hillsides.

Known as "the Queen of the Southern Mines," Sonora was the largest, wildest, and richest town in the southern mining district. One of the first Mother Lode camps, Sonora was founded in 1848 in two parts. The first was called Campo Sonorense by miners from Sonora, Mexico, who found rich placer deposits here. Before long the rich strike became known, and Americans began pouring into the area, naming their nearby camp Campo Americano. By the end of 1849, more than ten thousand Mexicans and four thousand Americans and Europeans were living in Sonora, which was part of the Tuolumne district that eventually produced $600 million in gold. Located near St. James Episcopal Church, the Big Bonanza Mine was one of the richest pocket (small) mines in the world, producing $160,000 of pure gold in one day. Almost from the beginning, Sonora was the most cosmopolitan town in mining territory, with adobe houses, fandango houses, strolling guitarists, lavishly decorated saloons, painted ladies, and bear-and-bull fights.

But with the American miners came trouble. They resented the "foreigners" working the rich diggings. After the state imposed the Foreign Miners Tax, aimed primarily at the Mexicans, the Mexicans banded together in defiance, and a series of violent acts between the two groups ensued. An all-out war was barely averted when some two thousand Mexicans hastily departed. Although the tax was repealed in 1851, the business community suffered hard times because of the sudden drop in population, and Sonora never regained its boomtown prominence.

Many structures of historic significance remain in Sonora. The dark-red frame St. James Episcopal Church (1860) is the most historic, charming, and photogenic. Standing at the north end of Washington Street, it is one of the two oldest Episcopal churches of frame construction in the state. Just across the street is the red Street Morgan Mansion. With its gingerbread trim, this elegant Victorian is one of the most beautiful in the gold country. Sonora has an excellent collection of restored Victorian homes, especially along its residential streets. Many of them can be seen on the Heritage Home Tour, a walking tour that begins at the Tuolumne County Museum, housed in an old 1857 jail. Among various relics from the Gold Rush era, the museum boasts a $40,000 gold collection, period costumes and old letters, photographs, and diaries. The building is also the home of the Tuolumne County Chamber of Commerce, a good source of information and brochures on the area (P.O. Box 277, 19445 West Stockton Road, Sonora, CA 95370, 209/532-4212).

Another source is the Tuolumne County Visitor Bureau, P.O. Box 4020, Sonora, CA 95370, 209/533-4420.

The oldest residence in Sonora is the beautifully restored and decorated Gunn House, built in 1850 by Dr. Lewis C. Gunn, an early civic leader. It later served as the office of the *Sonora Herald,* the first newspaper to be published in the California mining region. This romantic, two-story adobe structure is now operated as a comfortable inn, with antique-filled rooms, private baths, and a heated pool hidden in a shady court. For reservations, call or write the Gunn House, 286 South Washington, Sonora, CA 95370, 209/532-3421. Two cozy bed and breakfast inns located downtown are the Barretta Gardens Inn (209/532-6039) at 700 South Barretta Street and the Ryan House (209/533-3445), 153 South Shepherd Street.

For down-home, stick-to-your-ribs cooking, try the Cafe Europa, open twenty-four hours a day. Everything is reasonably priced and made from scratch, including the cafe's famous homemade pies and forty-five dinner entrees.

Among the many festivals in Sonora are the Square Dancers Festival in April, the Mother Lode Round-Up in May, the Mother Lode Quarterhorse Show in June, and the Mother Lode Fair in July.

Columbia

About four miles northwest of Sonora via Highway 49 and Parrotts Ferry Road is Columbia, once known as "the Gem of the Southern Mines." If you only have time to visit one place in the area, this should be it, for it's the best-preserved gold mining town in the West and the number one attraction in the Mother Lode. Run as a state historic park since 1945 and covering twelve square blocks, the business district is a living museum with the best surviving collection of Gold Rush architecture anywhere. Walking along the main street, shaded by arching trees, is like stepping back into the early 1850s, with dozens of picturesque old brick buildings housing authentic businesses of the 1850s and 1860s. You can sip a sarsaparilla or beer in a restored saloon, watch a blacksmith at work, have your photograph taken at an old-fashioned tintype photo studio, ride a stagecoach, or get a haircut at the oldest barbershop in the state.

Columbia was one of the last of the old mining towns to be founded; Dr. Thaddeus Hildreth and his party found placer gold here on March 27, 1850. First known as Hildreth's Diggings, then New Camp, Columbia proved to be one of the richest gold strikes in the state, eventually producing $87 million in gold. Word of the find spread fast, and within a month the site was a wild, sprawling tent city for five thousand goldseekers. Its fame attracted a flood of prospectors, gamblers, merchants, opportunists, prostitutes, and miscellaneous camp followers. The explosive growth continued, and in its heyday, Columbia had a population of fifteen thousand whites—plus many Chinese—and was the largest town in the southern mines region. Eight stagecoaches carried passengers along the road from Sonora to Columbia, which was solidly lined with miners' shanties.

Disastrous fires struck the wooden town in 1854 and 1857, after which the town was rebuilt of brick and masonry with wrought-iron doors and window shutters to prevent the spread of fire. For all its glory, however, Columbia faced the same fate as so many other boomtowns. By 1870 the gold was gone, and so were the miners. Although the once-sparkling, once-rowdy town remained a nearly abandoned shell, it was never completely deserted and, despite decades of vandalism and exposure to the elements, retained much of its Gold Rush appearance.

The only drawback to visiting Columbia today is that it borders on the commercial and can become terribly crowded with visitors during the height of the season, especially during its major summer festivals. You might want to see it in the spring or fall when things aren't so crowded. Commercial or not, it's a great place for history buffs, romantics, kids, and anyone else who wants a taste of the old days. Stop by the park headquarters on Jackson Street or the museum on Main Street for information and a brochure on the self-guided walking tour. Plan to spend at least a half a day here; you'll want plenty of time to explore the town and all the sights.

One of the oldest and most famous buildings in town is the two-story brick Wells Fargo Express Building (1858) with its iron shutters and fancy wrought-iron lacework balcony. The ground-floor interior has been restored and contains authentic period furnishings, including the huge, handsome gold scales that weighed out $55 million in gold dust. For a ride around town, you can catch the stagecoach or a surrey in front of the building. Housed in the Knapp Building, the Columbia Museum has a good display of gold in its different forms, along with various relics of Columbia's past and a narrated slide show. The 1861 Schoolhouse, one of California's first public schools and in use until 1937, has been faithfully restored with wooden desks, seats, potbellied stoves, old books, and a pump organ. Behind the schoolhouse is the restored Masonic cemetery, founded in 1853. Built in 1860, the Fallon House Theater is the scene of plays performed in the summer by the University of the Pacific repertory theater company, whose actors follow in the footsteps of Lotta Crabtree, Edwin Booth, and Lola Montez, all of whom performed here.

The only lodgings in Columbia are at the City Hotel, first opened in 1856 and fully restored in 1975 by state and federal agencies. Nine guest rooms are furnished with authentic Victorian antiques from the collection of the state

Wells Fargo Express Building, Columbia (courtesy John R. Poss)

parks and recreation department. Guests are encouraged to gather in the parlor and entertain themselves with conversation and games. The hotel's dining room has a reputation for superb French food served on fine china in elegant surroundings. For hotel and restaurant reservations, contact the City Hotel, P.O. Box 1870, Columbia, CA 95310, 209/532-1479. For somewhat less expensive accommodations, try the Marble Quarry Resort, a private campground a half-mile east of Columbia (209/532-9539), or the Columbia Inn Motel, adjacent to Columbia State Park (209/533-0446).

If you dare to brave the crowds, time your visit for the first weekend in May when the annual Fireman's Muster, Columbia's biggest and most famous event, is held. The colorful gathering features competition between old hand-pumped fire engines. Columbia also hosts a festive old-fashioned Fourth of July celebration as well as many other events. For more information, contact Columbia SHP at P.O. Box 151, Columbia, CA 95310, 209/532-4301 or 532-1479.

If the thought of fresh rainbow trout for dinner sounds appetizing, you might want to visit the Springfield Trout Farm, located about a mile southwest of Columbia at 21980 Springfield Road. As you head south on Parrotts Ferry Road, you'll see Springfield Road on your right just past Airport Road. Named for the springs that still feed Mormon Creek, Springfield was once a thriving town that covered a square mile and had two thousand inhabitants; all that remains now is a historical marker. At the Springfield Trout Farm you can either fish for your dinner (better yet, let the kids do it while you relax on the cool and shady grounds) or buy freshly dressed trout. Tackle and bait are furnished, there's no limit, and your catch is cleaned for you and packed in ice. Call 209/532-4623 for hours and rates. You can continue on Springfield Road to get back to Highway 49.

JACKASS HILL

Along the fourteen-mile drive on Highway 49 between Columbia and Angels Camp are several sites of interest. Just before you get to the bridge spanning the upper end of New Melones Lake, you'll see a well-marked side road leading to Jackass Hill. Here you'll find an authentic replica of Mark Twain's cabin, rebuilt in 1922 around what is said to be the original fireplace and chimney of Twain's cabin. Twain was a guest at the cabin for five months in 1864–1865, and it was here that he wrote his famous story "The Celebrated Jumping Frog of Calaveras County."

STANISLAUS RIVER

Back on Highway 49 you'll come to a bridge spanning what used to be the Stanislaus River and is now the New Melones Lake. The Stanislaus River canyon bears mentioning both for its historic richness and for the valiant fifteen-year struggle waged to prevent its flooding by the New Melones Dam, which was completed in 1979. That was the last year that the Stanislaus was a flowing river below the Highway 49 bridge, and by 1983 another sixteen miles was flooded upriver to the Camp Nine bridge. The battle to save the Stanislaus involved two congressional bills, one statewide referendum, a state bill, a Supreme Court decision, and a number of lawsuits; in the end, the federally funded and operated dam project won out.

The Stanislaus River was known as a scenic and exciting white-water rafting river. In 1981, the last year the river was rafted, more than sixty thousand people visited the river, making the Stanislaus the third most popular white-water river in the country. The area was also important for its archeological and historic resources. Evidence indicates that the Stanislaus River Canyon may have been one of the most populated river canyons in the foothills, with Indian remains dating from as far back as two thousand years ago. Archeological excavations performed before the river was flooded identified hundred of Miwok Indian sites, including bedrock mortars, village sites, and burial caves (most of which remain above the water line, which is at the 1,088-foot elevation). The U.S. Bureau of Reclamation plans to build an interpretive center near the Highway 49 bridge to exhibit some of the excavated artifacts.

The entire town of Melones now lies underwater. It was named by the Mexicans who first established the mining town for nuggets of gold found nearby that resembled melon seeds. At this site was Robinson's Ferry, established in 1848 to transport freight, animals, and miners across the Stanislaus. It is said that during the height of the Gold Rush, $10,000 in tolls was collected in a six-week period. Robinson's Ferry, Parrott's Ferry, and O'Byrne Ferry, all on the Stanislaus and all state historical landmarks, are now underwater.

CARSON HILL

Just past the north end of the Highway 49 bridge is Carson Hill—not much to look at now but considered in its heyday to have been the richest of the Mother Lode camps. In a hill above town is the Morgan Mine's huge glory hole, which produced $5 million. A 195-pound gold nugget was found here (worth $43,000 then, about half a million now). The Carson Hill tailings now lie under the New Melones Lake.

Angels Camp

About four miles up the road is Angels Camp (pop. 2,302), founded in 1849 by George Angel. Located in a rich gravel mining area that was also one of the richest quartz mining regions in the Mother Lode, Angels Camp and the surrounding areas produced more than $100 million worth of gold. A good source of information is the Calaveras County Chamber of Commerce, P.O. Box 111, 753 South Main Street, Angels Camp, CA 95222, 209/736-4444. Although there are several notable buildings worth seeing, including several old churches, the Angels Hotel on Main Street, and the Angels Camp Museum a mile north of town on Highway 49, the town's primary claim to fame is its Jumping Frog Jubilee, held every year during the third week of May. Begun in 1928, the event recalls Twain's tale of Jim Smiley's champion croaker, Dan'l Webster, who lost a jumping contest after he was secretly fed a handful of buckshot. Twain's story catapulted him to literary fame and assured Angels Camp a permanent spot on the map.

Held at the fairgrounds south of town, the Jumping Frog Jubilee coincides with the Calaveras County Fair and draws tens of thousands to the area. It's a bit commercial, and you must pay a hefty price to see the actual competition, but for some it is worth it to see grown men and women on all fours gesticulating, gyrating, and grunting their toadies on to victory. In case you're considering entering (why not—the first prize is around $1,500), the contest is open to any frog whose body is at least four inches long. The frog that jumps the farthest in three consecutive jumps is the winner. If you don't have your own frog, you can rent one at a rent-a-frog booth. If you're afraid of getting warts and don't want to touch the beast, you can hire a professional frog jockey to enter your frog for you. A recent first-place winner was plucked from a pond near the Rancho Seco nuclear power plant near Sacramento— the contest's first nuclear-powered frog (wonder if he glows in the dark?). For more information on this event, you can contact the Calaveras Fairgrounds Office at P.O. Box 96, Angels Camp, CA 95222, 209/736-2561.

Angels Camp was frequented by its share of colorful and notorious figures, such as Joaquin Murieta, the notorious Black Bart (the gentleman bandit who engineered twenty-eight Wells Fargo stagecoach robberies before he was caught and found to be a respected San Francisco citizen), and writers Bret Harte and Mark Twain. Harte came to the Mother Lode in 1855 and tried his hand at mining at Robinson's Ferry and Angels Camp. He left only two months later, critical of the harsh life in the rough camps but with enough material to last for the rest of his literary career, which focused on the frontier and the mines. His first story on the camps was "M'liss," and other Gold Rush stories followed, such as the well-known "Outcasts of Poker Flat" (believed to be set at O'Byrne Ferry) and "The Luck of Roaring Camp" (probably set in Angels Camp).

Mark Twain didn't arrive in the gold country until about ten years later, in 1864. He had first gone to San Francisco, where he met Harte, by then San Francisco's best-known writer, who hired him to work at the San Francisco *Call*. Twain's stay was brief—about five months—but it was long enough for him to leave his mark. A bronze statue of Mark Twain stands in Utica Park, a pleasant, shady park along Highway 49 that's a nice spot for a picnic.

MOANING CAVERN

Five miles east of Angels Camp on Highway 4 is Vallecito, settled by Mexican miners in 1850 and the site of a rich strike in 1852. Among the landmarks in this little settlement are the Wells Fargo Express Office, the 1851 Dinkelspiel Store next door, and a church bell on a stone monument in front of the Union Church on the main street.

Two miles south of Vallecito on Parrotts Ferry Road is Moaning Cavern, a colorful limestone cavern formed by underground water. It has one of the largest single-room caverns in California—large enough to hold the entire Statue of Liberty. Although it was discovered by miners in 1851, human bones resting beneath the floor of the vast main chamber reveal that it was known to prehistoric man at least thirteen thousand years ago. A forty-five-minute guided tour leads you down 65 feet on wooden stairs, then 100 feet down a steel spiral staircase. The strange and beautiful stalactite formations with names like Angel Wings and King Kong create a feeling of otherworldliness.

Moaning Cavern is run by the same family that runs California Caverns (also known as Cave City Caverns), located ten miles east of San Andreas near Mountain Ranch. If the steep vertical descent at Moaning Cavern is too challenging for some families and seniors, try the walk-through family tour offered at California Caverns. More strenuous spelunking tours are available at both locations. For information, write Moaning Cavern, P.O. Box 78, Vallecito, CA 95251, 209/736-2708.

Murphys

Continuing east on Highway 4 from Vallecito about four miles is the well-preserved town of Murphys (pop. 1,183). With white Victorians gracing side streets shaded by elm and locust trees and intriguing Gold Rush buildings lining the main street, Murphys is a charming blend of past and present with not much of an air of commercialism. This is one of those towns where you'll want to get out of your car and go for an unhurried stroll. A map of the town's buildings and sights is available from local merchants.

Murphys was settled in July 1848 by the Murphy brothers, John and Daniel, who came west in 1844 with the first pioneer party to cross the Sierra Nevada. Called the "the Queen of the Sierra" by early residents, Murphys was one of the principal mining communities in Calaveras County, producing more than $15 million in gold. The town's many brick and limestone buildings were built after several fires ravaged the earlier wooden structures.

The Jungle Room at California Caverns (courtesy Liz Hymans)

The most prominent old building in town is the Murphys Hotel, known in 1856 as the Sperry and Perry Hotel. In its time, it was considered the finest hotel outside of San Francisco.

Many visitors used the hotel as a stopover, as Murphys was right on the road to Calaveras Big Trees, a popular 19th-century tourist attraction. This explains why the hotel had so many notable guests. You can see a photocopy of the old register bearing such illustrious names as Mark Train, Ulysses S. Grant, Henry Ward Beecher, Horatio Alger, Thomas Lipton (the tea magnate), and Charles Bolton (alias Black Bart). You can stay in one of the hotel's nine historically authentic rooms named after the famous guests whose names appear on the hotel register. If you prefer more modern accommodations and private baths, the hotel also has a modern, twenty-room annex. The Murphys Hotel dining room serves breakfast, lunch, and dinner, with specialties including prime rib and fried chicken. The hotel saloon, reputedly the best in the Mother Lode, hops with live local entertainment on weekends (when you may have difficulty sleeping if you stay in the old hotel). For reservations or more information, contact the Murphys Hotel, P.O. Box 329, Murphys, CA 95247, 209/728-3454.

For a more traditional bed and breakfast experience, there's the Dunbar House, an Italianate-style house built in 1880 and restored as a five-bedroom inn with a traditional parlor, dining room, and gardens. Smoking is not allowed (as is the case with many bed and breakfast inns, so check first). The Dunbar House was used as a location site for the TV series "Seven Brides for Seven Brothers," much of which was filmed in Murphys, a favorite location for TV and films. For reservations, write the Dunbar House, P.O. Box 1375, 271 Jones Street, Murphys, CA 95247, 209/728-2897. For an old-fashioned soda or a homemade candy treat, try the Peppermint Stick ice cream parlor.

Across the street from the Murphys Hotel is the 1856 Peter L. Traver Building, now the home for the Old Timers Museum and its collection of Gold Rush artifacts. The Murphys Elementary School, built in 1860, was California's oldest continuously used grammar school until it closed in 1973. One of its graduates was Albert A. Michelson, who won the Nobel Prize for physics in 1907. Murphys hosts its annual Homecoming Celebration during the third week of July and its annual Octoberfest on the first Sunday of October. The local Black Bart Players perform old-fashioned melodrama on Saturday nights in April and November.

MERCER CAVERNS

A mile north of Murphys on Sheep Ranch Road is Mercer Caverns. Formed by a fissure created millions of years ago by an earthquake, the cave was once an Indian burial ground. The first white man to discover the cave was prospector Walter Mercer, who felt a stream of cold air coming from a mossy hole in the rocks on a hot September day in 1885. Guided forty-five-minute tours of the limestone caves take visitors past unusual stalactites, stalagmites, columns, curtains, and other cave formations in eight chambers. The temperature inside is a constant fifty-five degrees, a cooling respite from the summer heat, and the walkways are well lighted. For more information, contact Mercer Caverns, P.O. Box 509, Murphys, CA 95247, 209/728-2101.

CALAVERAS BIG TREES STATE PARK

For idyllic camping among the redwoods, Calaveras Big Trees State Park can't be beat. Located fifteen miles east of Murphys on Highway 4, the park's 5,437 acres contain magnificent stands of *Sequoia gigantea* ranging from 250 to 325 feet in height and from 2,000 to 4,000 years old. The park is open for year-round activities, including camping, hiking, picnicking, swimming, fishing, cross-country skiing, and tobogganing. In the summer, there are scheduled nature walks and campfire talks. During peak periods, the visitor center, with its nature and history displays and a herbarium, is open. Many of the facilities are wheelchair accessible; the Three Senses Trail for the vision-impaired was opened in 1977. Two campgrounds provide 129 campsites with all the amenities. For a snack or provisions, stop in Arnold, where there are several markets, delis, and restaurants. For more information, contact Calaveras Big Trees State Park, P.O. Box 120, Arnold, CA 95223, 209/795 2334.

San Andreas

From Angels Camp, it's about twelve miles to San Andreas (pop. 1,912), the seat of Calaveras County. The settlement of San Andreas followed the same pattern of many other gold country towns. It was first settled by Mexicans in 1849, but when the white miners heard of the rich gold deposits, they chased the "foreigners" away. After the placer deposits played out, the Chinese settled here and worked the areas abandoned by the white miners.

Not much of old San Andreas remains, but the downtown area on the historic bypass road does have some interesting structures, especially the courthouse, which is now the home of the chamber of commerce and the excellent Calaveras County Museum. Museum exhibits include Indian relics, pioneer and mining artifacts, manuscripts and documents, and a superb gem collection. There's also a garden of native plants and trees. Behind the courthouse is the old jail where Black Bart languished after his capture. On the second weekend of September, San Andreas honors the notorious robber with its annual Black Bart Days. Just west of town is the historic pioneer cemetery, dating from 1851. Across the street from the museum is the Black Bart Inn and Motel, 55 St. Charles Street, P.O. Box 576, San Andreas, CA 95249, 209/754-3808. The motel is a combination of the old Hotel Treat with twenty-five rooms and a modern, forty-room motel with a swimming pool, cocktail lounge, and restaurant serving good steaks and prime rib. If you have a hankering for homemade bagels and soups, try the Razzle-Dazzle Luncheon Parlour at 373 West St. Charles, which also serves quiche, homemade pies and cakes, and daily dinner specials.

New Hogan Lake is located about ten miles west of San Andreas via Highway 12. Run by the U.S. Army Corps of Engineers, the year-round recreation area offers fishing, boating, swimming, waterskiing, camping, and picnicking. Rental boats are available at the marina. For information call 209/772-1343.

Mokelumne Hill

Eight miles north of San Andreas is the picturesque and tranquil town of Mokelumne Hill (pop. 600), known widely as Mok Hill. Make sure you keep an eye open for signs leading you to the side road that loops through town. Since the late 1960s, when Mok Hill was almost a ghost town, residents have been preserving and restoring the original Western appeal of the village, and it is well worth a visit.

At one time, Mokelumne Hill was one of the richest and nastiest of the mining camps, with one murder a week during a seventeen-week period. Founded in 1848, the town thrived and developed a cosmopolitan flavor, with large groups of French, Germans, Chileans, Irish, and Chinese. Because of the richness of the diggings, claims were restricted to plots sixteen feet square.

Sitting on a mountaintop overlooking the Mokelumne River, the Hotel Leger is one of the loveliest and most elegant inns in the Mother Lode. Originally called the Hotel de France when it was built in 1851, it burned down and was rebuilt in 1874. The pillared and balconied palace has been handsomely restored to its full Victorian elegance. Many of the rooms have sitting areas and fireplaces, and all are decorated with antiques. Although expensive, the parlor suites are a study in Victorian opulence and comfort. Even if you don't stay in one, try to take a peek. There's also a swimming pool and porches for relaxing. For reservations, contact the Hotel Leger, Mokelumne Hill, CA 95245, 209/286-1401.

Among the many remaining structures of bygone days is the I.O.O.F. Hall at the north end of the main street. The first two floors were built in 1854 and the third was added in 1861, making it one of the first three-story buildings in the state. The building at one time housed the *Calaveras Chronicle,* where Mark Twain once worked as a reporter. The wooden Congregational Church (1856) is one of the prettiest in the gold country and the oldest of that denomination in the state. Every year the town whoops it up during its Old-Fashioned Fourth of July Celebration, featuring a real down-home Independence Day parade.

Jackson

Seven miles north of Mokelumne Hill is Jackson (pop. 2,650), a lively and progressive town that has served as the Amador County seat since 1854. Via Highway 16, it's forty-eight miles from Sacramento. The colorful central business district is located just east of the highway. The Amador County Chamber of Commerce, next to the civic center at the intersection of Highways 49 and 88, has lots of good information on Jackson and surrounding towns, including a county map, walking tours, lists of inns and restaurants, and historical information (P.O. Box 596, Jackson, CA 95642, 209/223-0350). While you're there, pick up a free copy of the *Scenic 88 Fun Times,* a monthly guide to all the goings-on in Amador County. The county is also a fine wine region, with many local wineries producing a wide range of quality wines. (See chapter 10 for details on wineries in the gold country.)

Although Jackson would later take its place as an important gold-producing center, it got its start as a key way station for traffic to and from the towns of the southern mines and the two most important supply centers in the region, Sacramento and Stockton. Placer gold was found in small amounts, but the real boom came with the rich quartz deposits discovered in the early 1850s. The most important factors in Jackson's economy were the Kennedy and Argonaut mines and several smaller quartz mines. Before the mines closed down in 1942, more than $140 million in gold was dug from the Kennedy and Argonaut. Jackson has maintained its economic vitality through tourism, agriculture, and lumbering.

Despite the inevitable march of progress, Jackson has strived to maintain its Gold Rush character. Although many of its older buildings have been modernized, it remains a picturesque town of narrow, tree-shaded streets winding past handsome Victorians and a Main Street lined with wrought iron–balconied stores and well-kept old buildings dating from the 1850s and 1860s. One of the oldest is the restored National Hotel (1862), reputedly California's oldest continuously operated hotel. Originally the Louisiana House, it was rebuilt after a disastrous fire destroyed most of the town in 1862. It has forty-four pleasant, clean, and inexpensive rooms upstairs, more than half with private baths and all furnished with turn-of-the-century antiques. The Louisiana House bar and restaurant is a gathering place for locals and a great spot to hear honky-tonk piano. There's a sing-along every Saturday night, with a usual "Saints Go Marchin' In" parade in which noisy celebrants are likely to march unannounced through the bridal suite. The cozy cellar dining room serves hearty dinners, and most of the furniture is for sale. In fact, the National Hotel is an antique lover's delight; in the basement is a sixteen-room store called Arcade Antiques (209/223-1320), filled with antique furniture for sale. The prices are so good that many Sacramentans make the trek here to find great buys and attend the store's twice-yearly auctions (call to get on the mailing list). To make reservations, contact the National Hotel, 2 Water Street, Jackson, CA 95642, 209/223-0500.

Catercorner from the National is the Wells Fargo Restaurant, on the site of the 1857 Wells Fargo Building. Also on Main Street is Stanton's Right On Main, featuring an old-fashioned soda fountain, and the Balcony restaurant, with a romantic atmosphere and fine Continental cuisine, including crepes, quiche, and salads.

The Amador County Museum is located in the historic Brown House, a two-story brick house built in 1858. In 1920 the home was used as a set by Will Rogers for the movie *Boys Will Be Boys*. Located on Church Street at the eastern edge of downtown, the museum displays original furnishings in the kitchen and bedrooms interspersed with local memorabilia of 19th-century life. Next door the carriage house displays intricate working models of equipment from local mines. The museum phone number is 209/223-6386. Across the street on the grounds of Jackson Elementary School is the site of the Mother Lode's first Jewish synagogue, dedicated on September 18, 1857 and a state historical landmark. One of the Mother Lode's most impressive architectural sights is the St. Sava Church on Jackson Gate Road north of downtown. Built in 1894, it was the first Serbian Orthodox church in the country.

Just north of town via Main Street and Jackson Gate Road is a hollow in the hills called Jackson Gate, the site of the giant Kennedy tailings wheels. Next to the Wells Fargo Building in Columbia, these fifty-eight-foot wooden wheels are probably the most photographed, sketched, and painted subjects in the gold country. Located at Kennedy Wheels Park, they were built in 1912 to lift tailings (waste gravel and sand) over two hills to an impounding dam behind Jackson. Only two of the original four wheels are still standing; the others lie in ruins. There's a pleasant picnic area at the site. Just to the west are two of the most famous mines in Amador County, the Kennedy and the Argonaut. In operation until 1942, these were two of the deepest and most productive gold mines in the United States, with vertical shafts extending more than five thousand feet into the ground. Surface tours of the Kennedy Mine are given from time to time; check with the chamber of commerce for details.

Kennedy tailings wheels, Jackson

Jackson Gate Road is also affectionately called "Restaurant Row" by locals, for there are several fine restaurants on this bucolic country lane. One is Buscaglia's Italian Restaurant, in business since 1916 at 1218 Jackson Gate Road, 209/223-9992. On weekends you can dance to live music on a lighted glass dance floor. Nearby at 1235 Jackson Gate Road is Teresa's, with fine Italian food and an extensive local wine list (209/223-1786). If you have children with you, check out the Country Squire Motel, located in a country setting near the Kennedy Mine. The motel was one of the last private gambling casinos in California; it closed in 1952. Several of the eleven rooms are furnished with antiques; the bridal suite furniture is French, dating to 1790. Ducks and sheep roam freely on the two-acre grounds that include a large barbecue grill, lawn games, and year-round gold panning in the creek. A complimentary continental breakfast is served every morning. For reservations, contact the Country Squire Motel, 1105 North Main Street, Jackson, CA 95642, 209/223-1657.

Jackson has a number of bed and breakfast inns; the chamber of commerce will give you a complete list. The Court Street Inn (209/223-0416) is located in a historic 1870s home that is listed on the National Register of Historic Places. Children are welcome at Ann Marie's Country Inn (209/223-1452), a Victorian decorated with the owner's artwork. Festivals in Jackson include the Serbian Christmas and New Year in January, the Dandelion Days Celebration and Flea Market in March, the Mother Lode Dixieland Jazz Benefit in April, and the Great Bicycle Race in September.

PRESTON CASTLE

About twelve miles west of Jackson via Highway 88 is the little town of Ione, which got its start during the Gold Rush as a supply center for the mines. There are a number of old buildings worth seeing, but by far the most dramatic is the abandoned Preston Castle, which sits on a hill at the northern edge of town off Highway 104. It was completed in 1894 to house the Preston School of Industry, the state's first attempt to rehabilitate male juvenile offenders with vocational training programs. Built with sandstone and red clay bricks mined from local claypits, it is the most significant example of Romanesque Revival architecture in the Mother Lode; it has been designated a state historical landmark and is on the National Register of Historic Places. The school opened July 1, 1894, with a group of seven teenagers transferred from San Quentin. The school was run like a military academy and was almost entirely self-sustaining, with wards raising their own livestock and produce and making their own personal items such as shoes and buttons. The 120-room "castle" was finely appointed inside, including twenty-seven tile fireplaces and handmade fixtures. All of the doors and paneling were oak, and leaded crystal windows graced the dining hall doors. There was even a swimming pool in the basement.

The building was condemned and its doors closed in 1960 after a new facility next door was completed. For more than twenty years, the castle has been brooding in a state of ruin like a forgotten, toothless hag, its windows broken, its roof leaking and partially collapsed, and its interior gutted of fixtures, many of which are now on display in state parks throughout California. A local citizens' committee has been working to preserve the building, which is owned by the state and leased to the city of Ione, from total destruction. The first step was to repair the roof and board up the windows to protect the building's interior from the elements. The eventual plan is to provide an exterior walking tour and establish a museum of memorabilia next door. The building is not open to the public, but if you drive up Palm Drive you can get within several hundred feet for a closer look.

INDIAN GRINDING ROCK
STATE HISTORIC PARK

About ten miles east of Jackson is Indian Grinding Rock State Historic Park, the state's only park devoted primarily to Indian culture. To get there, take Highway 88 east from Jackson about eight miles to Pine Grove, then follow the Pine Grove-Volcano Road about a mile and a half. The forty-acre, oak-dotted park's focal point is a huge 7,700-square-foot limestone outcropping covered with 1,185 mortar cups, or *chaw'ses*, that were used by the Northern Miwok for grinding acorn meal. Near the mortar holes are 363 petroglyphs (decorative or religious rock carvings). Before the Gold Rush, Miwok Indians gathered here in the fall when the acorns were ripe, although archeological data indicates many Indians lived here year-round as well. Using the rock and stone pestles, the women would grind nuts, berries, seeds, fungi, and acorns in this community grist mill, laughing and chatting while they worked. Because of the geological and historical importance of the rock, the largest bedrock mortar found in the western U.S., a replica is on display at the Smithsonian Institution in Washington, D.C.

The Miwok, whose territory in the Mother Lode in the 1700s extended roughly from Mariposa to El Dorado County, were primarily peaceful hunters and gatherers. Their ancestors were present as early as 2000 B.C., numbering as many as nine thousand in ancient times and living in some one hundred villages. Although most of the foothill Miwok avoided missionization, many were either killed or confined to reservations after the arrival of white men. By 1910 there were only 670 left, and only half were full-blooded Miwok.

The Amador Miwok today have taken an active role in developing the park's displays, exhibits, and audiovisual programs. You can see a round house (used by the Miwok for meetings and religious activities), a handgame house, several cedar bark dwellings, a grain storage center, an Indian football field and village, and a nature center and trail. A cultural center contains displays on Miwok heritage. Wheelchair-accessible camping and picnic facilities are available. Every year modern Miwok gather on the fourth weekend in September for their "Big Time" festival, where they perform tribal dances, play games celebrating the annual acorn harvest, and buy and sell handiwork. Contact Indian Grinding Rock SHP, P.O. Box 177, Pine Grove, CA 95665, 209/795-2334.

VOLCANO

A couple of miles further down the road is Volcano (pop. 100), considered by many to be one of the most picturesque, noncommercial gold towns left.

The town is situated in a natural cup in the mountains, but there are no volcanoes around here. Early goldseekers who came to the area found rocks and crags that resembled volcanic craters, so they mistakenly called their settlement Volcano. It once boasted a population of eight thousand, and the surrounding area yielded $90 million in gold. The town was well equipped with seventeen hotels, three breweries, a five-hundred-seat theater, and thirty-five saloons.

The camp also claimed many firsts in the state's cultural development. Volcano had the first rental library in California, the first little theater, the state's first literary and debating society and, nearby, California's first astronomical observatory. Volcano residents continue to preserve the town as a mecca for arts and handcrafts. The Volcano Pioneers Community Theater Group presents major productions, workshops, and other performing arts activities. Several galleries and shops sell artwork and hand-crafted items made by local artists and craftspersons.

Very little of the town has been restored, so what is left is the real thing, and you can see all of it on a relaxed walking tour. The three-story, balconied brick St. George Hotel (1862) is Volcano's largest structure and still offers meals and rooms to visitors (P.O. Box 9, Volcano, CA 95689, 209/296-4458). The old Sing Kee Store (1857) now houses a mineral shop. There's also the old jail, a brewery built in 1856, the I.O.O.F. Hall, the Adams Express Office, and "Old Abe," a bronze cannon that helped to win the Civil War. Unionist miners planned to use it to keep Volcano's gold away from Confederate sympathizers; the cannon was never fired. Soldiers Memorial Park, directly across from the general store, is a good spot for a picnic and for the kids to run around and climb rocks. It was once on the same level as Main Street, but the land was washed away by hydraulic mining.

DAFFODIL HILL

Three miles northeast of Volcano is Daffodil Hill, a private ranch that opens to the public daily each spring when 300,000 daffodil bulbs burst into full bloom. Starting in late March and lasting through April, the hills are covered with the blossoms of more than three hundred varieties of bulbs, including daffodils, narcissus, tulips, hyacinths, crocuses, and more. The flowers were planted by the McLaughlin family, who have lived here since the Gold Rush days. More than twenty thousand people make the trek here each spring, so be prepared for large weekend crowds. Admission is free, although donations are requested. There's a picnic area near the front, but you might have to share your sandwich with one of the family peacocks that strut about the property. Public viewing depends on the whims of Mother Nature, so call before you go: 209/296-7048.

To get to Sutter Creek from Daffodil Hill, you can take a thirteen-mile scenic route via Shake Ridge Road, or you can return to Volcano and take Sutter Creek-Volcano Road, also a scenic drive. West of Jackson are Camanche Lake, Pardee Reservoir, and Lake Amador, all offering a complete range of water activities.

Sutter Creek

Snuggled in a little valley, Sutter Creek (pop. 1,705) is one of those charming gold country towns where you can easily spend an entire day just nosing around cozy antique stores, art galleries, and historic buildings. You can also eat your way through the town, since it has lots of cafes and several fine restaurants. The area between Jackson and Amador City is known for its antiques, and Sutter Creek lies right in the middle. The town has more than fifteen antique shops, each with its own colorful ambience. The well-preserved main street is lined with old buildings, many balconied, and a number of New England–style houses can be found in the residential areas. Much of the Gold Rush character of the town has been preserved, so you won't find a mishmash of old and new as in some other towns. The local merchants' association publishes a nicely illustrated walking tour of the town.

Sutter Creek was named for John Sutter, who tried his luck here at placer mining using Indian miners. He was not too successful, however, and returned to Sutter's Fort in Sacramento to try to protect his wheatfields. Thanks to the Lincoln and Eureka mines, the town later became firmly established as an important quartz mining center as well as a supply center for the entire county. It was with the Lincoln (also called the Union) Mine that Leland Stanford made his fortune, enabling him to join with Huntington, Crocker, and Hopkins in building the transcontinental railroad. The mine site is at the north end of town.

Once owned by Wall Street wizard Hetty Green (formerly the world's richest woman), the Eureka Mine was one of the longest-producing mines in the gold country. Between 1852 and World War II, when the mine was closed, some $36 million in gold was extracted. The remains of the mine are on a hill just south of town. Another interesting relic is Knight's Foundry on Eureka Street. It is the only hydraulic-powered foundry in the country, in continuous operation since 1873. It first made stamp mill machinery and now manufactures drill presses, metal wheels, and machine parts. Visitors are welcome during weekday working hours.

Other old structures to look for are the Masonic and I.O.O.F. Halls (1858), the Methodist Church (1862), and the Malatesta (1860) and Brignole (1859) buildings. On Spanish Street west of the business district is the Robert Downs

House, built for the foreman of the Lincoln Mine, and the Immaculate Conception Catholic Church (1861), rebuilt in 1972 after a fire.

Surrounded by lush gardens and redwoods in a serene setting, the Sutter Creek Inn remains one of the most popular bed and breakfast inns in the area. The main house was built in 1859 and was originally the home of State Senator E. C. Voorhies. The green-shuttered, New England–style white wooden inn is reputedly one of the first inns of its kind in the West. Although it's right on Main Street, it's set back far enough to provide a quiet retreat. Each of the seventeen comfortable rooms has a full private bath, and many have fireplaces. Some even have beds swinging by chains. Guests can socialize in a gracefully decorated living room and enjoy breakfast in front of the fireplace in the brick-walled country kitchen. The inn is geared for romantics, so children are not allowed. It's advisable to book reservations well in advance, especially during the summer: Sutter Creek Inn, P.O. Box 385, 75 Main Street, Sutter Creek, CA 95685, 209/267-5606.

Next door at 77 Main is the Foxes of Sutter Creek, an inn with three elegant suites (209/267-5882). Children are not allowed. Children are welcome at the Bellotti Inn, located in a three-story building that has a modernized façade. The restaurant is open daily, serving lunch and huge Italian-style dinners in grandly decorated surroundings (53 Main Street, Sutter Creek, CA 95685, 209/267-5211).

For a unique and delicious snack, try an authenic Cornish pasty at the Pasty Place, 35 Main. Pronounced "PAST-ee," they're not to be confused with the tasseled kind Gypsy Rose Lee swung around. Pasties are crescent-shaped meat and vegetable pies, and they're delicious. The Pasty Place also sells frozen pasties to take home and offers tastings of Amador County wines for a small charge. Next door is the Chatterbox Cafe, serving homemade biscuits, pies, and other specialties daily since 1939. The Sutter Creek Palace, decorated like an old Western saloon, serves gourmet lunches and dinners. For a light morning snack or lunch, visit the tearoom at Motherlode Tea and Spice Company, which offers such delectables as croissants, quiches, bagels, and pastries.

The people of Sutter Creek like to have a good time at festivals and fairs. Some of these include the Kit Carson Mountain Men Auction in February, the Italian Picnic and Parade in June, and the Sourdough Days Craft Fair during the Labor Day weekend in September.

AMADOR CITY

Just a couple of miles down the road from Sutter Creek is Amador City (pop. 165), the smallest incorporated city in California. Its block-long business district has several charming old buildings and numerous quaint antique shops. The Amador County Chamber of Commerce publishes a walking tour. Built in 1873, the two-story brick Imperial Hotel (1873) now houses four antique shops. You can see the rusty headframe of the Keystone Mine on a hill at the south end of town. Founded in 1853, the mine produced $24 million in gold until it was shut down by government edict in 1942. The two-story brick building that was built in 1881 as the headquarters of the mine has been refurbished as an eight-room inn. Each room is named for the purpose it served when the mine was in operation, and all rooms have distinctive antique furnishings and private baths. In the morning, push a buzzer and your coffee will be delivered right to your door. Children are welcome; there's even a pool. For reservations, contact the Mine House, P.O. Box 245, Amador City, CA 95601, 209/267-5900.

The Buffalo Chips Emporium serves breakfast and lunch and is also an old-fashioned ice cream parlor in a late-1800s building. The Cellar specializes in fondues, crepes, and sandwiches made with homemade sourdough bread; it also has a salad bar. Every year during the first week of December, Amador City celebrates an old-fashioned Calico Christmas.

From here it's another twenty-six miles to Placerville. Just outside of Amador City you'll pass Drytown, where you can enjoy raucous melodrama at the Piper Playhouse during the summer (209/245-3812). Next is Plymouth with the Amador County Fairgrounds, where the county fair is held the first weekend of August. This is also the site of the annual Fiddletown Fiddlers Contest on the last weekend of May and the Wine Festival on the fourth weekend of October.

For a real gastronomic treat, stop at Poor Red's in El Dorado, about five miles south of Placerville (622-2901). Located in the 1858 Wells Fargo Building, it's one of the most popular spots in the area. You'll want to bring a big appetite for their famous Western barbecued ribs, chicken, ham, and steaks cooked over an open oakwood charcoal pit. Be warned that Red's is quite small, and weekend dinner waits can be as long as one to two hours; you can get a take-out order instead, or you can kill time in the colorful bar frequented by locals and by cowboys at rodeo time in August. Belly up to the old-fashioned, two-level bar and try a Golden Cadillac. Red's claims to have been the originator of this drink, which is made from Galliano, white creme de cacao, and fresh cream.

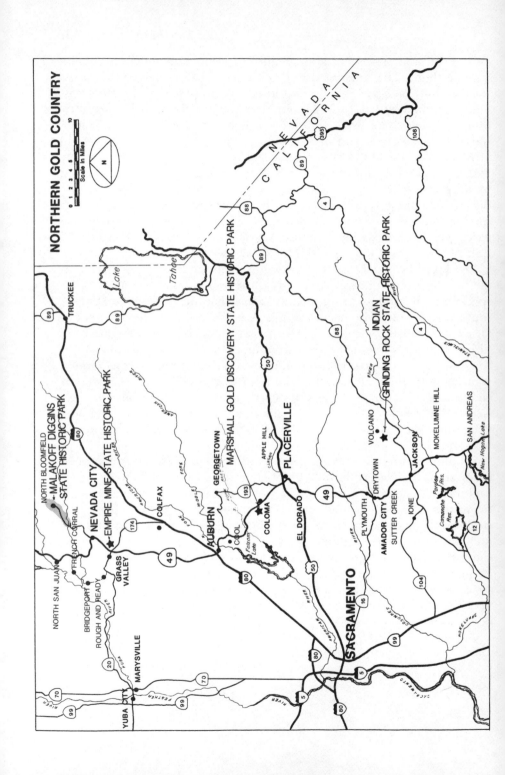

NORTHERN GOLD COUNTRY

9

The Northern Mines:
Placerville to Nevada City

In contrast to the many sleepy little villages of the southern region, the northern mines area has many larger cities such as Placerville and Auburn. The countryside differs markedly as well; the rolling, oak-dotted hills of the south are gradually replaced by steep, heavily forested slopes in the north, especially at higher elevations. The seasons are more distinct here, including falls with beautiful displays of colorful foliage and snowy winters. The region is historically significant as well. Gold was first discovered here at Coloma, and this was also the birthplace of deep-quartz mining and the highly destructive hydraulic mining.

Placerville

Located forty-five miles east of Sacramento via U.S. Highway 50, Placerville (pop. 7,200) serves as a trade center and the El Dorado County seat. The El Dorado County Chamber of Commerce distributes many maps and publications, including a county map, a Placerville map and tourist guide, and an El Dorado Ranch Marketing Guide, listing outlets for farm-fresh products. For a list of publications, contact the chamber of commerce at 542 Main Street, Placerville, CA 95667, 626-2344.

The original site of Sutter's Mill in Coloma, where gold was first discovered

Nestled in a pine-clad fold of the Sierra foothills, Placerville first strikes the visitor as not much more than a bustling county seat bisected by a major transcontinental highway. Most of its historic buildings have been modernized and are camouflaged with plaster, paint, and advertising signs. But there's plenty of history here; you only need to scratch the surface a bit to discover it. The hub of the city is still on or near Main Street in the historic downtown area, where the streets follow trails marked off by miners' pack mules. To get a feel for the town's past, try viewing the stores from the rear, or explore the narrow, winding residential streets north and south of downtown, where you'll see many beautiful old homes. El Dorado County also has a number of fine wineries that you can visit (see chapter 10).

Initially called Dry Diggings, Placerville was the first major camp to spring up after the discovery at Coloma, and it soon became the great rendezvous for all of the argonauts. News of the first large gold strike spread quickly, and by 1849 the area was teeming with some four thousand miners. The town attracted its share of unscrupulous characters, and the crime rate rose alarmingly. Dry Diggings soon became the first Gold Rush community known to dispense justice at the end of a rope; it even changed its name to Hangtown. By 1854 Hangtown had become the third largest town in California (behind Sacramento and San Francisco), and the more genteel society that had taken root there changed the name to Placerville.

Although Placerville was rich in gold, producing $25 million in placer gold alone, it owes its real success to its geographic location. It played a key role as a strategic communication and transportation crossroads, serving as a station on the routes of the overland mail and Pony Express, an important stop on the route between the northern and southern mines, and a key relay point for the stagecoach lines. This was also the site of the West's first telegraph (1853). With the discovery of the Comstock Lode in Nevada, Placerville became the chief outfitting point for the stampede back across the Sierra. From 1859 to 1866, the Placerville-Carson Road (now U.S. Highway 50) saw the greatest era of freighting and staging by horse-drawn vehicles ever known.

More than one famous entrepreneur got his start in Placerville. Mark Hopkins of railroad and hotel fame was a grocer here. Philip Armour of meatpacking fame ran a butcher shop. John Studebaker of automobile fame made wheelbarrows. Other well-known citizens included Snowshoe Thompson, who for twenty years ran a mail route across the Sierra during the winter; C. P. Huntington, a store owner who later became a railroad magnate along with Hopkins; poet Edwin Markham ("The Man With the Hoe"), then a teacher and superintendent of schools; and Ulysses S. Grant, who was stationed here as a young army officer and is said to have frequented a good many of the city's numerous saloons.

Although a disastrous fire destroyed most of old Hangtown in 1856, a number of old buildings and historic sites still exist along Main Street, many marked with plaques. The Placerville City Hall was built in 1857 and housed the Confidence Fire Department. The balconied building next door was built in 1862 by "Immigrant Jane" Stuart with funds received for driving a herd of horses across the plains and then selling them. Next to the chamber of commerce is the Pearson Soda Works Building (1852), a greenstone rock and brick building that is one of the few to have survived the 1856 fire. The Nuss Building, also of greenstone and brick, at one time housed John Fountain's soda bottling plant and also survived the fire.

The Placerville Hardware Store was built just after the fire. The brick structure is one of the oldest continuing hardware businesses in California. Go in and look at the traveling hardware ladders that reach up from the old floors to the thirteen-foot ceilings. The site of the original Hangman's Tree now bears a historical marker and a saloon called Hangman Tree. The tall monument at the intersection of Main and Cedar Ravine is the Druid Monument, honoring the founding of the first Grove of the United Ancient Order of Druids (a fraternal organization) in California in 1859. The Cary House at 300 Main was a popular inn built in 1857 that served as the town's stage stop and center of activity for many years. It was razed in 1915 and rebuilt as the Placerville Hotel, then renamed the Raffles Hotel in 1926. It since has been remodeled, converted to a residential hotel, and given its present name. While you're in the neighborhood, if you get a hankering for an omelette, try the Placer Station Omelette House, a popular spot for locals.

Located at the fairgrounds west of town, the El Dorado County Historical Museum (626-2250) houses a large collection of historical relics and antiques emphasizing local history. You can see an old Wells Fargo stagecoach, a wheelbarrow made in 1853 by John Studebaker, period furniture from a well-to-do Victorian household, a replica of a country store, and a restored Concord coach. Other sights include the Jewish cemetery on Myrtle Street, with at least eighteen graves dating as early as 1856, and the Methodist Episcopal Church on Cedar Ravine, built in 1851. The stone and wood structure was moved to this site and restored in 1961; it is the oldest church in the county. Also on Cedar Ravine is the Combellack-Blair House, a bed and breakfast inn housed in an elaborate late Victorian Queen Anne home (1895) that is a fine example of Victorian architecture (3059 Cedar Ravine, Placerville, CA 95667, 622-3764).

For a more rural experience, you may want to try the Fleming Jones Homestead, an 1883 farmhouse and the county's first bed and breakfast inn. You can explore eleven acres of woods, meadows, and wildflowers or participate in farm activities, complete with barnyard animals. For relaxing, there's a porch swing overlooking rose gardens and an old red barn. The rooms are colorfully decorated with country antiques; upstairs rooms open onto a balcony. Children, pets, and smoking are not allowed. For reservations, contact the Fleming Jones Homestead, 3170 Newtown Road, Placerville, CA 95667, 626-5840. The Placerville area has many other charming inns. For a brochure, write Historic Country Inns, P.O. Box 1849, Placerville, CA 95667, or call 626-5840.

For fine, romantic dining in a historic setting, a popular Placerville place is the Smith Flat House (626-9003), a restaurant and saloon located about a mile east of Placerville on Smith Flat Road in a historic 1852 building that used to be a stagecoach stop. Be sure to visit the Gold Bug Mine a mile north of town in Gold Bug Park, once the site of rich mining activity. The sixty-one-acre site, with more than 250 inactive mines and a running stream, is the city's largest municipal park. There are picnic areas, barbecues, and hiking trails. You can walk through the lighted Gold Bug Mine shaft on your own daily or arrange a guided tour through the parks department. You'll get a good idea of what underground mine conditions were really like. Future development plans include a new museum with historical exhibits. For more information, call 622-0832.

Placerville hosts a number of festivals every year to celebrate its historic and colorful past. Each June, the Highway 50 Wagon Train (designated an official California State Historical Event) makes the two-week trek from Carson City, Nevada, to Placerville and Sutter's Fort in Sacramento. Organized to commemorate the original Sierra crossings of pioneer wagon trains, the event is staged by the Highway 50 Association. As many as 34 wagons and 250 outriders form the caravan, which stops at various historic points along the way for overnight camps. Anyone can participate; you don't even have to have a horse or wagon. All you need to do to ride along in a wagon is wear authentic frontier clothing. Costumed riders on their own horses can join the outriders. The Hangtown Rodeo is held in May, the El Dorado County Fair and Mother Lode Antique Show in August, and the annual House and Heritage Tour in September. For more information on the wagon train and other events, contact the El Dorado County Chamber of Commerce at 626-2344.

APPLE HILL

If you plan to visit Apple Hill in the fall, you can buy freshly picked apples, taste local wines, and cut a fresh Christmas tree—all in the same area. Located on a mountain ridge east of Placerville, the Apple Hill tour follows an historic 1857 path originally blazed by Pony Express riders. Along this pleasant route are some forty-three apple ranches offering a delectable array of apples and apple products, including homemade apple pies, freshly squeezed apple juice, apple wine, apple doughnuts, apple butter, and apple jelly. Many of the farms also sell vegetables, other fruits, and nuts. Harvest season begins in mid-September and continues through December.

One of the most popular ranches in the area is High Hill Ranch on the Carson Road loop. Although it tends to have a circus-like ambience on weekends, especially in October (the ranch's busiest month), it's well worth a visit, especially if you have children along. Not only can you choose from a wide variety of apples at bargain prices, but you can also go trout fishing in a well-stocked pond, take a helicopter ride (on October weekends only), or explore an old mine shaft and enjoy a cup of cider at the end of the 150-foot path. Children love watching the large apple press as it squishes apples for apple juice. There's also a crafts barn selling handmade crafts and a snack bar. Picnic tables under a grove of redwoods make a nice spot for a picnic. You can also taste the dry apple wine produced by Harvest Cellars; it's really quite good. High Hill also sponsors the Apple Blossom Festival, held every weekend from mid-April to May 30, with hoedowns, hayrides, wine tasting, and a trout derby.

Most of the apple ranches are open from early morning to dusk seven days a week. If you don't like crowds, avoid going in October or on weekends. Apple Hill maps are available free from any grower or may be ordered by sending a large self-addressed, stamped envelope to Apple Hill Growers, P.O. Box 494, Camino, CA 95709.

The Apple Hill area is also the location of some nineteen Christmas tree farms where you can choose and cut your own tree. All the farms open on Thanksgiving weekend, and most are open daily from then until Christmas. Many sell refreshments and have picnic areas. For a map, send a large self-addressed, stamped envelope to the El Dorado County Christmas Tree Growers, P.O. Box 423, Placerville, CA 95667.

BRIDAL VEIL PICNIC AREA

For a lazy day of sunshine and beautiful scenery, pack a picnic lunch and head for the Bridal Veil Picnic Area on the South Fork of the American River. The turnoff is about seventeen miles east of Placerville on Highway 50; watch for the Bridal Veil sign past Pollock Pines. A short road winds down to the river. There are picnic tables and barbecue grills under the trees, and paths follow the river for easy hiking. Rock dams in the river create a small area where kids can splash and wade. Restrooms and drinking water are available. The picnic area is part of the El Dorado National Forest, which has numerous picnic areas and campgrounds. The forest information center is at 3070 Camino Heights Drive, Camino, CA 95709, 644-6048. Call the forest's recreational information service phone at 626-1551 for a recorded message with information on campgrounds.

Coloma and the Marshall Gold Discovery State Historic Park

A winding and scenic eight-mile drive on Highway 49 from Placerville through hilly countryside drops you into Coloma on the South Fork of the American River. Lying in a beautiful, broad valley that looks much as it must have to John Sutter and James Marshall some 140 years ago, the little town that once echoed with the shouts of ten thousand miners now dozes in the foothill sun. Soon after Marshall discovered gold, Coloma became the destination for a thundering rush of humanity with gold dust in their eyes and dreams in their hearts. As Coloma became the center for the thousands of miners who flocked here, Sutter's sawmill was soon forgotten, and the first Gold Rush town was born. By 1849, only a year after the discovery, the town swelled to ten thousand; thirteen hotels, two banks, and a variety of other businesses catered to the miners' needs. It was at Coloma that the practice of inflated prices got its start—for example, a $50 wool shirt cost $1 to be laundered.

Although Coloma was the birthplace of the Gold Rush, its placer gold gave out fairly early, and by 1851 the miners had begun spreading up the river canyons and into the mountains as news of other rich strikes spread. By 1857 only a handful of Chinese miners remained. The town became a peaceful agricultural hamlet specializing in grape growing. In fact, the first of El Dorado County's vines are believed to have been planted near Coloma.

Today Marshall Gold Discovery State Historic Park encompasses about 70 percent of the town of Coloma and attracts about 400,000 visitors annually. Except in the summer, when it gets crowded, the park has a serene atmosphere ideally suited for a leisurely stroll. On hot days, you can relax under the shade of oak, locust, persimmon, and mimosa trees, many of which were planted by the miners. In the spring, the grounds are covered with the blooms of poppies, sweet peas, and wild blackberries.

Among the Gold Rush buildings that still remain are a Chinese store, a blacksmith's shop, a jailhouse, and an old miner's cabin. The park features exhibits of Gold Rush–era items, including household implements, mining equipment, and horse-drawn vehicles. The best place to start your tour is at the Gold Discovery Museum, where you can get a detailed guide to the park. Many of the park's facilities are wheelchair accessible. Exhibits describe the miners' way of life, and movies recreate the gold discovery and explain mining techniques.

The most impressive structure in the park is the full-size replica of Sutter's Mill, which lies a short distance from the original mill site. The original sawmill, built in 1847, was powered by water from the American River, but this replica is electrically powered. You can watch it operate daily during the summer and on weekends during the winter. The site of the original mill is marked with a stone monument. Just downriver is the original gold discovery site.

Located on a hill on the outskirts of Coloma is an impressive bronze statue of James Marshall, pointing to the site of the gold discovery. Marshall, who never reaped the benefits of his historic discovery, died penniless and lies buried under its base. Down the hill from the monument is the simple clapboard cabin where Marshall lived. Every January, hundreds of visitors fill Coloma's streets to celebrate the anniversary of the gold discovery with parades, bands, and melodramas. On summer weekends, the Coloma Crescent Players present evening drama and melodrama at the Old Coloma Theatre.

Marshall Gold Discovery State Historic Park is open daily from 10–5. The buildings are closed on Thanksgiving, Christmas, and New Year's Day. There is a small admission fee. For more information, write P.O. Box 265, Coloma, CA 95613, or call 622-3470.

Several campgrounds and resorts are located in the Coloma-Lotus area, offering a variety of amenities and services. Camp Lotus (P.O. Box 578,

James Marshall Monument, Coloma

Lotus, CA 95651, 622-8672) is situated two miles downstream from Coloma on eighteen acres. The camp includes thirty campsites, restrooms, showers, a general store, volleyball, horseshoes, and a gently sloped beach with slow-moving water. Camp Coloma (P.O. Box 11, Highway 49, Coloma, CA 95613, 622-6700) is more commercial, with tent and RV campsites, cottages, cabins, showers, restrooms, a swimming pool, fish pond, general store, gift shop, restaurant, and bar.

Two lovely old churches on the grounds of the state park are becoming increasingly popular for weddings. The Emmanuel Episcopal Church (1856) seats 150, and St. John's Catholic Church (1859) seats 65. Both are available for weddings of any denomination. Outdoor areas may also be reserved for weddings. Only one wedding per church per day is scheduled, so it's a good idea to book well in advance. For more information, contact the park supervisor (622-3470).

For a real country touch, you might consider having your wedding reception at the historic Vineyard House in Coloma. You can even be transported there by a horse-drawn surrey with fringe on top and red velvet seats. Grant Hill Ranch of Placerville has an authentic replica of a four-passenger surrey available for rent for special occasions. For information contact the ranch at P.O. Box 1465, Placerville, CA 95667, 622-8954. The three-story, white frame Vineyard House was built in 1878 by Robert Chalmers, who also planted vineyards and built a winery behind the house. Now a family restaurant and Victorian-style seven-room inn, it is rumored to be haunted by the friendly ghost of Mrs. Chalmers. The downstairs dining room serving fine food seats 250 in former parlors, libraries, and sitting rooms. The saloon is located in a cool, stone-walled cellar. For reservations, contact the Vineyard House, Cold Springs Road, P.O. Box 176, Coloma, CA 95613, 622-2217.

You can even have your wedding invitations produced locally, featuring gold country scenes by the late George Mathis, a California artist who worked in pencil and in pen and ink. His daughter Carol Mathis, also an artist, will design your invitation using hand lettering and one of Mathis's lithographs depicting historic sites such as St. John's, Emmanuel Episcopal, and the Vineyard House. You can contact her at Friday House, the family's art gallery, formerly located in Coloma and now in Placerville (2936 Mosquito, Placerville, CA 95667, 621-1661).

Auburn

From Coloma it's an eighteen-mile drive to Auburn. Just past Cool, you descend steeply into the canyon of the North Fork of the American River. This area will be inundated if the nearby Auburn Dam is completed. After crossing the river, you enter Placer County and the town of Auburn (pop. 8,200), county seat and the metropolis of the gold country. Auburn, like Placerville, is a busy, thriving city that has survived because it's a busy transportation center; it is situated on the transcontinental railroad and bisected by a major interstate highway (I-80). Auburn is about thirty-five miles northeast of Sacramento via I-80. Agriculture and lumbering are the two economic mainstays, with tourism playing only a secondary role.

Auburn is a good base for exploring some of the mining camps and ghost towns in the area. There's Ophir to the west; Michigan Bluff, Yankee Jims, and Iowa Hill to the east; and Gold Run and Dutch Flat to the northeast. About eighteen miles east via Highway 193 is the quiet mountain hamlet of Georgetown. It's worth a visit for its many well-preserved 19th-century buildings and extra-wide streets, designed to thwart the spread of the destructive fires that were so common in gold country towns. The Georgetown Hotel, a restored Victorian hotel, is a well-known lodging and dining spot (P.O. Box 187, Georgetown, CA 95634, 333-4373).

One of the first things you'll notice about Auburn is the way it creeps up the hillside in a lovely mountain setting. It's really a three-level town; the oldest section initially sat in the bottom of the ravine where the first gold strikes were made. Nothing remains of the original tent city, which was destroyed by fire and abandoned for a more favorable site a little farther up the hill. This second level is known as Old Town and is the historic heart of Auburn. Along its narrow and winding streets are many old-time, false-fronted buildings, some dating from the 1850s. The modern part of the city occupies the upper slopes of the hills, providing a panoramic view of the American River valley.

The town got its start in May 1848 when Claude Chana, a friend of James Marshall's, and his party stopped for the night along the American River in the Auburn Ravine on their way to Coloma. Chana tried his luck at panning and found three nuggets; the trip to Coloma was quickly forgotten. The rich placer diggings in the area eventually yielded $75 million. After going through several name changes, the town was given the name of Auburn in 1849 by a group of miners from Auburn, New York.

Auburn's Old Town is similar in many ways to Old Sacramento. Many of its historic buildings were destroyed when the freeway was built, but it has undergone a historic revival, with many of its old buildings restored. It's now a national historic landmark. There are numerous restaurants and shops catering largely to tourists, as well as a sprinkling of professional offices. Unlike Old Sacramento, however, Old Town's streets angle off in every direction, following the original miners' trails; there is hardly a square block to be found.

As you head into town from the south, Highway 49 follows High Street for several blocks. Your first stop should be the Auburn Chamber of Commerce (1101 High Street, Auburn, CA 95603, 885-5616), where you can pick up a walking tour of Old Town.

Located on the old public square where "noose justice" was meted out, the stately domed courthouse (1894) stands out as a fine architectural gem. Nearby is the Pioneer Methodist Church, an attractive 1858 frame building. Old Town's most interesting—and most photographed—structure is the four-story red-and-white firehouse. Dating from 1893, its steeply pitched tower culminating in a cupola is a real eye-catcher. This is a good spot to begin your walking tour. You'll find many noteworthy buildings along Commercial Street, Lincoln Way, and Court Street. The U.S. Post Office at 1583 Lincoln Way is believed to be California's oldest, in operation since 1851. Along the steep slope of Sacramento Street are the remnants of what once was a substantial Chinese community.

Lots of antique shops, galleries, and specialty shops in Old Town sell everything from spinning wheels to gold panning equipment. You'll find a number of restaurants and cafes as well, including Awful Annie's, a patio cafe serving soups, sandwiches, quiches, etc., and the Blue Heron Gallery and Cafe, serving breakfast and lunch in rooms decorated with artwork for sale by local artists. A popular watering hole for locals is the Shanghai, housed in an 1855 building. Chinese fare and spirits are served up in surroundings that include elk antlers on the walls, miners' lamps, peanut shells on the floor, and

Old Town Auburn

a player piano with a repertoire of three thousand melodies. Butterworth's is a fine restaurant serving English and Continental cuisine in a former Victorian residence, the historic 1887 Brye Mansion on Lincoln Way. Butterworth's is well known for its prime rib and Yorkshire pudding, as well as the delicious Sunday brunch and daily English high tea it serves. The Old Auburn Hotel, in the newer section of town, offers lodgings, and its restaurant serves outstanding six-course, family style Basque/Italian meals at reasonable prices.

A variety of accommodations are available here, from a KOA campground (on Highway 49 north of Bell Road; 885-0990) to motels (many of which are located on "Motel Row" on Lincoln Way) and bed and breakfast inns. Power's Mansion Inn (164 Cleveland Avenue, Auburn, CA 95603, 885-1166) is an elegant 1883 restored mansion furnished with antiques. The Victorian (P.O. Box 9097, Auburn, CA 95603, 885-5879) is an 1850s restored Victorian on seven acres with a view of Auburn; there's a hot tub, sauna, gazebo, and garden, and the inn is available for weddings and receptions.

The Placer County Museum (885-9570), located at the fairgrounds, is one of the finest museums in the gold country, with several interesting exhibits. You'll find displays of Gold Rush–era Chinese and Indian objects, as well as old photographs, kitchen utensils, mineral displays, and a variety of weapons. To get an authentic picture of life in the foothills in the late 1800s, visit the Bernhard House, on Maidu Drive near the fairgrounds. It's located in the old Travelers Rest Hotel—Auburn's oldest hotel, built in 1851. It was purchased as a residence in 1864 by Benjamin Bernhard, a foothills winemaker, who used the land around it to become one of the county's most successful wine producers. The Greek Revival house was recently restored and furnished with Victorian antiques. It is now open to the public for tours and small luncheon parties (885-9570 or 885-0264). Also located here is the Bernhard Winery, built in 1873 and housing exhibits of wine-making tools and equipment.

Special events in Auburn include the Mardi Gras in February, Western Week and Rodeo in April, the Historic Old Town Flea Market in May, and the Gold Country Fair in September.

'49ER FRUIT TRAIL

The Placer County Visitors Information Center, off I-80 in Newcastle (661 Newcastle Road, Newcastle, CA 95658, 663-2061), has a free map of 100 farms and ranches in the area between Roseville and Nevada City where you can buy fresh produce. You'll find everything from boysenberries to honey to mushrooms. Several of these farms offer eggs, herbs, and catfish and trout fishing. If you need a sheep, a horse, or a Christmas tree, you'll find them, too. The area east of Auburn has the largest concentration of farms in the area, and the peak season is May through October. For a free map, send a large self-addressed, stamped envelope to '49er Fruit Trail, P.O. Box 749, Newcastle, CA 95658.

Grass Valley

From Auburn you can make good time on the twenty-four-mile stretch of Highway 49 to Grass Valley, which marks the beginning of the northern mines region. From Sacramento it's about fifty-nine miles via I-80 to Auburn and then Highway 49 to Grass Valley, about an hour away. Here the picturesque gold towns are nestled on the slopes of densely wooded mountains, in the bottom of deep canyons, or alongside swiftly moving rivers. You'll find four distinct seasons here, but this region stands out from the rest of the gold country for another important reason. It was here that hardrock mining of gold-laden quartz became an industry. Deep-quartz mining required sophisticated equipment and technological know-how, so it was up to the mining engineers and large mining companies like Empire and North Star to wrest the gold from the earth. This region was also the birthplace of the highly destructive, land-ravaging hydraulic mining.

Of all the northern mining towns, Grass Valley was the richest and most important, producing $415 million over the years. Although placer gold was taken early on, in 1850 George Knight made a discovery that brought Grass

Valley its fame. As the story goes, he was out chasing his cow one night when he stubbed his toe on a rocky outcropping. The rock turned out to be gold-bearing quartz, and soon thousands of miners flocked to the area. The ground beneath Grass Valley and nearby Nevada City was honeycombed with hundreds of miles of tunnels and shafts. Unlike most other gold mining towns, Grass Valley maintained a stable gold mining economy well into the 1950s, when the mines were closed because of high operating costs.

Grass Valley today (pop. 8,112) is a bustling, progressive city where the old and the new exist side by side. It's one of the fastest-growing foothill communities in the state, with a projected population of thirty-five thousand by the year 2000. After a disastrous fire struck Grass Valley in 1855, the town was rebuilt using heavy masonry walls, and many of these structures remain in the downtown area. Grass Valley is also known for its lovely Victorians, including the Glasson home at 515 Main, the Tremoreaux home at 403 Neal, and the Watt home at 506 Linden. Although it's not as quaint as Nevada City, its sister city five miles away, Grass Valley is still one of the most historic towns in the Mother Lode. For a walking tour of Grass Valley and other helpful information, including books on the history of the area, contact the Nevada County/Grass Valley Chamber of Commerce, 248 Mill Street (the Lola Montez House), Grass Valley, CA 95945, 273-4667.

The Empire Mine State Historic Park (273-8522), located a mile and a half east of Highway 49 on Empire Street, is recognized as the oldest, largest, and richest mine in California mining history. Preserved as a lush 784-acre state historic park, it is a living piece of history that tells the story of hardrock gold mining. An estimated 5.8 million ounces of gold were unearthed while the mine was in operation, from 1850 to 1956. Experienced miners from the tin mines of Cornwall, England, dug 367 miles of tunnels, some of which stretch beneath the streets of downtown Grass Valley. The deepest shaft drops to more than a mile below the surface.

Most of the mine's equipment has been sold, and many of the buildings have been torn down, including the mine's impressive headframe. The mine is flooded 180 feet below the surface, but the gold is still there, waiting for the time when hardrock mining again becomes profitable. You can pick up a self-guided map that points out the remaining buildings and foundations. A fascinating guided park tour helps you imagine a typical day in the life of a 19th-century Cornish miner. A highlight of the tour is the stately Bourn Cottage, former residence of the mine owner, William Bourn, Jr. The home is surrounded by formal English rose gardens, fountains, and ponds.

The park's biggest annual event is the Cornish Miners' Picnic, held in early June. The one-day event features colorful characters dressed in period clothing to recreate the atmosphere of the 1800s. Activities include gold panning and mucking contests, concerts, puppet shows, and children's races. Food and drink, including Cornish pasties, are available. This is also the only

Bourn Cottage, Empire Mine State Historic Park, Grass Valley

time during the year that visitors may bring picnic lunches onto the park grounds.

If you have even a passing interest in the technology of hardrock mining, you'll want to visit the North Star Powerhouse Mining Museum just south of town off Mill Street and McCourtney Road in Boston Ravine. The power station, built in 1895, was the first complete plant of its kind; power for the entire North Star Mine operation was provided by compressed air generated by Pelton water wheels in the powerhouse. The museum, considered to be the Mother Lode's finest mining museum, houses a large display of mining equipment and artifacts from the 1800s. There's a grassy picnic area across Wolf Creek. Park hours vary, so call to check (273-9853). About a half a mile further down Allison Ranch Road are the photogenic remains of the North Star sixty-stamp mill, where compressed air from the powerhouse was converted to power to crush the quartz so the gold could be extracted.

Some of the gold country's most colorful characters were attracted to Grass Valley, the most famous of whom was Lola Montez. She was the scandalous and glamorous femme fatale who was the mistress of mad Emperor Ludwig of Bavaria and whose circle of friends included Franz Liszt, Victor Hugo, George Sand, and Alexander Dumas. Born Eliza Gilbert in Ireland in 1818, she became a sensation in Europe as an exotic Spanish dancer and actress under the stage name Lola Montez. Lola came to California in 1853. After a brief stint in San Francisco, she moved on to the mining camps, where she met with mixed reviews. Lola was famous for her Spider Dance, in which spiders made of cork, whalebone, and rubber were shaken out of her skirt at the dance's climactic moment. She then would pantomime the actions of a frantic woman bent on crushing them.

Lola settled in Grass Valley in 1853, purchasing the house on Mill Street that today is the town's most famous residence. Here she gardened, kept a bear cub as a pet, and threw lavish parties for visiting theatrical people. During this time, Lola befriended a seven-year-old neighbor named Lotta Crabtree. Lola began teaching her young protegée songs and dance routines and had Lotta perform in her home for visiting actors. The red-haired, black-eyed Lotta went on to become an internationally famous entertainer and the first American performer to become a millionaire. Lotta died in 1924 at the age of seventy-seven, leaving an estate valued at $4 million.

Lola's career didn't fare as well. After a couple of years in Grass Valley, she got bored and toured in Australia. She wasn't well received, so she returned to the U.S., where her career continued its downward spiral. She spent her last few years in quiet seclusion in New York and died in poverty at the age of forty-two. Lola's home at 248 Mill Street is now a state historical landmark, housing the chamber of commerce and a gold mining museum. The original structure was condemned, and this replica was built in 1975. A few doors down at 238 Mill is Lotta Crabtree's home, also a state historical landmark.

Grass Valley has a growing number of fine restaurants and historic inns to visit. The Holbrooke Hotel was built in 1862 around the Golden Gate Saloon, originally built in 1852 and the oldest continuously operating saloon in the Mother Lode. Notable guests have included Mark Twain, Bret Harte, and Presidents Grant, Harrison, and Cleveland. The fieldstone and brick building, a state historical landmark, houses a basement cabaret, an elegant Victorian dining room serving breakfast, lunch, and dinner, and the original saloon, including the ornate bar that was shipped around the Horn. The second floor was recently converted from offices to lavish Victorian hotel rooms featuring private baths with clawfoot tubs, brass and canopied beds, antiques, and modern conveniences such as telephones and color TVs. The bridal and presidential suites, which open onto the front veranda, contain the original marble fireplaces and have separate sitting rooms. For reservations, contact the Holbrooke Hotel and Restaurant, 212 West Main Street, Grass Valley, CA 95945, 273-1353.

Next door at 302 West Main is Tofanelli's, a popular breakfast spot. The restaurant also serves lunch, dinner, and Sunday brunch. For great Cornish pasties, try Mrs. Dubblebee's at 251 South Auburn Street or King Richard's Pasties at 215 South Auburn. For something with a more Continental flair, try the charming Scheidel's Old European Restaurant, serving European and

Swiss cuisine. Scheidel's is on Highway 49 at Alta Sierra Drive, about six miles south of town. Reservations are recommended (273-5553).

Just behind and operated by the Holbrooke Hotel is the Purcell House, an 1874 Victorian that has been restored as a seven-room bed and breakfast inn with private baths, antique furnishings, brass beds, and plump comforters (119 North Church Street, Grass Valley, CA 95945, 272-5525). Nearby is Murphy's Inn (1866), with seven rooms decorated with antiques, lace curtains, and brass beds. You can summon a full breakfast in your room with a unique bell system or join other guests in the cheery breakfast room (318 Neal Street, Grass Valley, CA 95945, 273-6873).

Mount Saint Mary's Convent, Chapel, Cemetery, and Grass Valley Museum is located on the corner of Church and Chapel streets. The museum exhibits include an original classroom, parlor, music room, doctor's office, and memorabilia from Grass Valley's early days. The Pacific Library is also housed here, with a fine collection of old science, history, and other reference books.

Several annual Grass Valley events celebrate the city's Cornish past. In addition to the Cornish Miners' Picnic at the Empire Mine, a Cornish Christmas festival is held on weekend evenings during December. Mill Street is transformed into an old-fashioned country lane with Cornish treats, street vendors, musicians, jugglers, and carolers. Grass Valley has a full calendar of fairs and festivals, including the Bluegrass Festival in June, the Fourth of July Celebration (held in Grass Valley in odd-numbered years, Nevada City in even-numbered years), and the Nevada County Fair in August.

BRIDGEPORT LOOP

If the weather is nice, try a leisurely drive along the scenic Bridgeport loop, which will take you past Rough and Ready, Bridgeport, and French Corral. Rough and Ready is about five miles west of Grass Valley on Highway 20. The town was founded by Mexican War veterans and named after their ex-commander, General Zachary "Rough and Ready" Taylor. Although it's a sleepy little village today with just a few buildings reflecting its mining history, it was once a wild and colorful town. Rough and Ready's primary claim to fame is its secession from the Union in 1850 in protest over a miners' tax. The republic lasted only a few months—until residents wanted to celebrate the Fourth of July. For a long time Highway 20 was the only road to Sacramento from this region, and a toll was levied for its use. The Old Toll House, which charged from 25¢ to $3 to pass through, is now an antique store.

Five miles farther on Highway 20 is the junction with Pleasant Valley Road, which goes north through quiet pastoral countryside. After the road drops down into the canyon of the South Yuba River, you'll come to the Bridgeport Covered Bridge, the longest single-span wood-covered bridge in the United

States (230 feet). Now a state historical landmark and closed to vehicular traffic, it was built in 1862 by the Virginia Turnpike Company as part of the company's fourteen-mile toll road serving the northern mines and the busy Nevada Comstock Lode. The bridge was used as a public crossing from 1901 to 1971, when it was declared unsafe. A new bridge now crosses the river nearby and provides a fine vantage point for viewing this beautiful bridge.

Two miles up the steep winding road is the town of French Corral, the site of the world's first long-distance telephone line. Built in 1877 by the Ridge Telephone Company, it connected French Corral with French Lake, fifty-eight miles away. The line was operated by the Milton Mining Company primarily to keep track of the water level in the Sierra reservoirs to regulate flows for mining operations. You can continue on Pleasant Valley Road for a couple of miles where it meets Highway 49 just south of North San Juan.

Nevada City

During the Gold Rush, the four-mile stretch of road between Grass Valley and Nevada City was heavily traveled and notorious for bandits. The bandits are gone, but it's still a busy highway; in fact, it's a freeway now. Sitting prettily in the heart of the northern mines district is Nevada City (pop. 2,538), the Nevada County seat. It's a storybook town, considered by many to be the most charming of all the Gold Rush cities.

Like Rome and San Francisco, Nevada City was built on seven hills (Prospect, Piety, Cement, Wet, Aristocracy, American, and Lost Hill). Winding around the pine-clad hills are tree-shaded streets that zigzag across the uneven terrain along old miners' trails. In the fall, the sugar maples burst into brilliant autumn colors, giving the town a decidedly New England flavor. Nevada City is known for its elegant Victorians, many of which are an eclectic mixture of different architectural styles reflecting the tastes of the times. You'll find verandas and picket-fenced gardens, roof turrets and garden gazebos, broad balconies and mullioned windows. Daily bus service between Grass Valley and Nevada City is provided by Gold Country Stage (265-1411).

Located on Deer Creek, a tributary of the Yuba River's South Fork, the town dates to 1849. Centered in an area of rich placer and gravel diggings, it grew rapidly; about five thousand people were living in the area by July 1850. For a while, the town was called Coyoteville because of the dozens of "coyote holes" (short shafts and tunnels) dug by miners trying to reach the rich gravels. By March 1850 the name "Nevada" was chosen, only to be stolen in 1861 by the newly formed Nevada Territory. After Nevada was admitted into the Union, town residents begrudgingly added "City" to alleviate postal confusion. Nevada City had its share of devastating fires and floods, but residents steadfastly remained and rebuilt.

One of Nevada City's most colorful characters was the lady gambler, Elanor Dumont. Arriving in 1854, she shocked the local citizenry by opening a gambling parlor, where she dealt the game of blackjack. The charming and attractive Madame Dumont enjoyed success for a couple of years until the placer deposits wore out and business began slowing down. It was here that she acquired the unfortunate nickname of "Madame Moustache," prompted by the dark, downy growth on her upper lip. After leaving Nevada City, she traveled from camp to camp seeking wealth, but it always eluded her. Twenty-five years after her arrival in Nevada City, she was found dead in Bodie, an apparent suicide.

Nevada City today retains much of its early flavor, due in large part to residents who have worked to restore its historic face. A unique and fun way to see it is by horse-drawn carriage. Nevada City Carriage Company offers fifteen-minute and longer tours in a carriage pulled by a Percheron draft horse. You'll find the carriages in front of the National Hotel and Friar Tuck's daily or on weekends, depending on the season. Nevada City has plenty of interesting and historic buildings to see, and the best place to start a walking tour is at the South Yuba Canal Building at Main and Coyote streets. A state historical landmark, it was the headquarters for the South Yuba Canal Water Company, the first firm incorporated to supply water for hydraulic mining. The building now houses the Nevada City Bicentennial Museum and the chamber of commerce, where you may pick up a walking-tour map. The chamber of commerce also sells an informative walking-tour booklet written by longtime Nevada City resident Robert M. Wyckoff, titled *The Compleat Pedestrian's Partially Illustrated Guide to Greater Nevada City.* For information, contact the Nevada City Chamber of Commerce, 132 Main Street, Nevada City, CA 95959, 265-2692. Next door is Ott's Assay Office, where the rich find of the Comstock Lode was authenticated and formally announced to the world.

Nearby is the charming and photogenic Firehouse No. 1 (1861). Its Victorian bell tower and gingerbread trim were added later. The white frame building is the home of the Nevada County Historical Museum, which is open daily and includes interesting artifacts such as a Chinese altar, early Gold Rush attire, and relics from the Donner Party. The area in and around Nevada City is a haven for artists and craftspersons, and you'll find examples of their work in many shops and galleries here.

Lined with gas lamps, Broad Street is the main thoroughfare in town and has its share of historic buildings. Farther out on West Broad Street is the pioneer cemetery with many old headstones. The three-story brick and balconied National Hotel (1856) is one of many claiming to be the oldest continuously operating hotel in California. The large bar downstairs was shipped around the Horn, and the back bar, made of Honduras mahogany, was a buffet in the Spreckels Mansion on San Francisco's Nob Hill. The Victorian

Firehouse No. 1 with its Victorian bell tower, Nevada City

dining room serves Sunday brunch and is open daily for breakfast, lunch, and dinner. For information, contact the National Hotel, 211 Broad Street, Nevada City, CA 95959, 265-4551.

The historic Nevada Theatre (1865), at 401 Broad, is California's oldest existing structure erected as a theater and a state historical landmark. It was recently renovated and is now used as a community center for the performing arts and a residence for the Foothill Theater Company. For program information, write Nevada Theatre, 401 Broad Street, Nevada City, CA 95959, 265-6161. Across the street is the quaint New York Hotel (1857), housing small shops, and close by is the venerable brick Firehouse No. 2 (1861). A block away at 325 Spring Street is the American Victorian Museum (1856), located in the historic Miners Foundry, a group of brick and stone buildings where machine parts and architectural iron were once forged. It is the only museum in America devoted entirely to collecting, preserving, and exhibiting art, crafts, and artifacts from the Victorian period. Displays include a rotating display of Victoriana, an 1871 pipe organ, and—appropriately enough—a miners' foundry. The museum also serves as a cultural center for the community, hosting programs in music, dance, drama, and poetry in the huge Old Stone Hall (where weddings are also held). Dinners are served Friday and Saturday evenings with vegetarian dishes a specialty, and Sunday brunch offers more than thirty-five selections. Every Sunday at 4 P.M. is a concert followed by traditional English high tea.

Annual events at the museum include Robbie Burns Night in January, Queen Victoria's birthday celebration in May, and holiday meals. For an events calendar, call the museum at 265-5804. Also housed in the museum building is KVMR-FM, 89.5, a fine non-commercial educational radio station offering a variety of programming. Its signal is strong enough to be picked up in Sacramento.

Next door in what was formerly the foundry garage is Nevada City Winery, established in 1980. It's a low-tech winery that produces mountain white, zinfandel, and white Riesling using grapes grown in the Sierra foothills and other areas. The winemakers have plans to plant their own vineyards and eventually move to a ridge just outside of Nevada City. Until then, you can sample their wines daily at this location.

One of the primary activities in Nevada City is dining, and you'll find plenty of fine restaurants and cafes from which to choose. Friar Tuck's Restaurant and Wine Bar on North Pine Street features traditional fondue and fresh seafood, with live music nightly. Numerous restaurants can be found along Broad Street, including Selaya's, serving Continental cuisine in a Victorian atmosphere; Cafe Les Stace, with Continental and Mexican cuisine; and the Posh Nosh, featuring a complete deli menu with garden dining. Michael's Garden Restaurant on Main has a varied menu served in a Victorian dining room and an outdoor garden patio. The Burrito Factory on Commercial serves delicious Mexican food at reasonable prices in a friendly atmosphere.

Nevada City has two bed and breakfast inns worth investigating. Located on Prospect Hill across Deer Creek is the fire-engine-red-brick Red Castle Inn. The four-story, 1860 mansion features wraparound wooden porches, a balconied garret, and Gothic Revival icicles hung from the roof line. Rooms and suites are furnished with antiques, and private baths are available. Outside you can explore and relax in the beautiful gardens. A continental breakfast of fruits and homemade breads is included; children and pets are not allowed. Contact the Red Castle Inn, 109 Prospect Avenue, Nevada City, CA 95959, 265-5135. Another unique inn is the Piety Hill Inn, a refurbished 1934 auto court. Each of the seven private cottages is decorated with Victorian-style New England antiques, with homemade quilts on the beds and fresh flowers on the tables. Continental breakfast is served only on Sunday. Contact the Piety Hill Inn, 523 Sacramento Street, Nevada City, CA 95959, 265-2245.

A nice spot for a relaxed picnic is Pioneer Park, southeast of downtown on Solaro Drive off Park Avenue. Meandering through the wooded park is Little Deer Creek, where you and the kids can cool your feet on a hot summer day. There's also a wagon exhibit, a children's playground, and a municipal pool open in the summertime, complete with a lifeguard and a small concession stand.

Annual events in Nevada City include the House and Garden Tour in April, the Fathers' Day Bicycle Races and the Lola Montez Fair in June, the Fourth of July Celebration (every other year, shared with Grass Valley), the Constitution Day Celebration and Parade in September, the Artists' Christmas Fair on Thanksgiving weekend, and the Victorian Christmas in December.

If you are in the mood for an easy mountain hike and a picnic in a sylvan setting, visit the Independence Trail. It's a simple and scenic hike created especially for people in wheelchairs, parents pushing strollers, and senior citizens. The main trail is a mile long and follows the route of a canal built in 1856 to carry water for hydraulic mining. Beautiful wildflowers line the trail for much of the year, and wildlife is abundant. Along the trail are stunning views of the South Fork of the Yuba River below. You'll also see the old wooden flumes, which are trestles atop which wooden chutes carried water. Restroom facilities and benches are provided along the trail, and other trails are being developed. To get to Independence Trail, take Highway 49 north from Nevada City about six and a half miles to the broad turnoff with the blue disability sign on the right side of the highway. You go through a tunnel under the highway to get to the main trail.

Malakoff Diggins State Historic Park

Malakoff Diggins State Historic Park and the old mining town of North Bloomfield lie on remote San Juan Ridge between the South and Middle forks of the Yuba River. The shortest route to the park is via North Bloomfield Road, just north of Nevada City. This sixteen-mile road is graveled, steep, and winding, making it difficult in wet weather and not recommended for RVs and campers. An easier, though slightly longer, route (twenty-five miles) is via Tyler Foote Crossing Road, which is eleven miles north of Nevada City on Highway 49. The last six miles of this route are on a graded dirt road. Along the way you'll pass ravines filled with ferns, evergreens, and dogwood trees that flower in the spring. The park is on the site of what was the largest hydraulic mining operation in the world. Huge nozzles were used to direct powerful jets of water against entire mountainsides to dislodge gold-bearing gravels buried by hundreds of feet of topsoil. The muddy, gravel-laden water was then directed through large sluice boxes, where the gold was separated from the debris. Because tremendous amounts of water were needed for hydraulic mining, large reservoirs were built along with hundreds of miles of ditches and flumes to carry water to the diggings.

Although it was efficient and economical, hydraulic mining ravaged the countryside and caused serious environmental problems. The waste gravel and mud were initially dumped into Humbug Creek, then into the South Yuba River. The mucky tailings polluted streams, killed fish, and silted up the

Sacramento River and San Francisco Bay. This silt rendered the Yuba and Sacramento rivers unnavigable for ocean-going vessels for nearly one hundred years and resulted in destructive floods downstream in the rich agricultural valleys. After eighteen years, hydraulic mining was outlawed in 1884, and the Malakoff mine ceased operations.

This area has been referred to as a man-made miniature Bryce Canyon or Grand Canyon. Surrealistic, sheer gravel cliffs, minarets, and pinnacles tinted pastel shades by oxidized minerals stand in mute testament to the lengths to which men would go for gold.

Included in the twenty-six-hundred-acre park are the remains of the former mining town of North Bloomfield, now virtually a ghost town with no commercial businesses. Several restored buildings remain along its single main street, as well as a museum that portrays the lifestyle of a hydraulic miner. There is camping (some wheelchair-accessible) in thirty primitive campsites with drinking water and restroom facilities, as well as two rustic cabins. Trailers and RVs can be accommodated, but no hookups are available. Activities include swimming, hiking, picnicking in two small picnic areas, fishing, horseback trails, and guided tours in the summer. Because of its relative inaccessibility, the park is seldom disrupted by large crowds, except in June when it hosts its annual Homecoming Celebration. For more information, call 265-2740.

ANANDA COOPERATIVE VILLAGE

Ananda Cooperative Village is a spiritual community in a tranquil forest setting about sixteen miles north of Nevada City on the North San Juan Ridge. Its residents follow the teachings of the Indian yogi Paramahansa Yogananda with yoga and meditation. Through Ananda's guest program, you may visit the village on a daily, weekly, or monthly basis. You can participate in any of the numerous programs and seminars or just spend some time in self-renewal. Vegetarian food is served, and available activities include meditation, yoga, nature hikes, volleyball, and massages.

Accommodations are simple: dormitories or private cabins (the latter have no electricity or indoor plumbing). You can also stay in your own RV or tent. There is also a seven-room inn in a restored farmhouse. Advance reservations are required, so don't just show up. For a copy of the community's biannual newspaper, which describes the guest programs, write Ananda Guest Programs, 14618 Tyler Foote Road, Nevada City, CA 95959, 292-3494.

OREGON CREEK SWIMMING HOLE
AND PICNIC AREA

About eighteen miles north of Nevada City (three miles north of North San Juan) on Highway 49 is the Oregon Creek Swimming Hole, located on the Middle Fork of the Yuba River. It's a lovely spot with sandy beaches, swimming, and wading. A Tahoe National Forest day-use picnic area is also located here, with picnic tables, fireplaces, restrooms, and drinking water. For a map and information on this and other Tahoe National Forest facilities, contact the Tahoe National Forest Headquarters, SR 49 and Coyote Street, Nevada City, CA 95959, 265-4531.

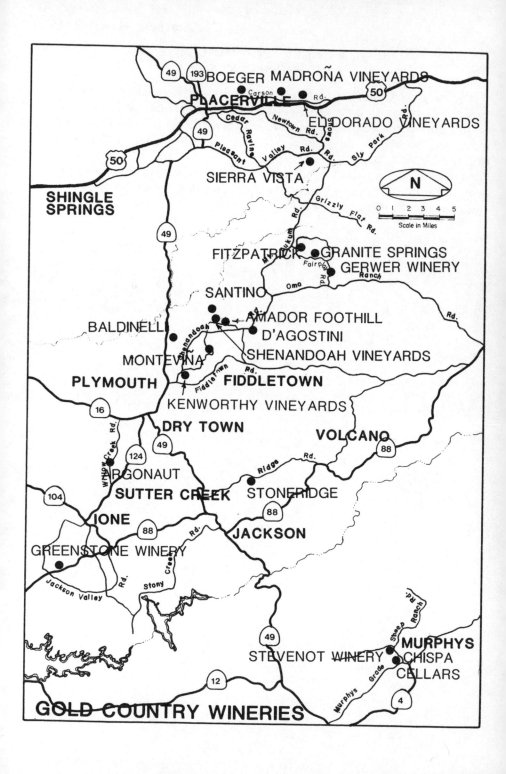

GOLD COUNTRY WINERIES

10

Off the Beaten Path

So now you think you've seen it all and done it all in the gold country, right? You've explored the antique shops, tried a Cornish pasty, picnicked by an abandoned mine, and spent a night at a cozy Victorian inn. Think it's time to leave? Don't go yet; there's plenty more to do and see—if you have the time and a yen for adventure. How about a hot-air balloon ride? Or a gold panning excursion? Or perhaps a trek through the foothills to taste some of the finest California wines? White-water rafting, llama pack trips, and bicycle adventures are also available for those willing to stray off the beaten path.

Winetasting in the Foothills

Until recently, the mention of California's wine country conjured up visions of the lush valleys of Napa and Sonoma. But there's a new kid on the block who's giving these well-established regions a run for their money. With vineyards planted from Calaveras County to Nevada County, the Sierra Foothills region is making a name for itself both for its award-winning premium varietal wines and as a touring and tasting destination for wine lovers.

Actually, the history of grape growing and wine producing in this region is a long and important one. Winemaking first came to the gold country during the Gold Rush to quench the miners' insatiable thirst for spirits. Some ten thousand acres were planted with vines, many by European miners who had

233

experience in grape production and winemaking. In 1870, fifty thousand gallons of brandy were produced in Nevada County. At the peak of the early winemaking days, in the 1890s, there were more than one hundred wineries in the area.

A number of elements combined to cause the decline and eventual ruin of the wine industry in the gold country. One of the most serious was the phylloxera vine disease, which destroyed the entire California grape industry for a time. Other factors included population loss, a series of economic depressions, insect invasions, large supplies of grapes that drove down prices, and Prohibition—the final blow.

With the exception of the historic D'Agostini Winery (established in 1856), winemaking in the foothills didn't return until the 1970s. In 1972 D'Agostini was joined by the first new winemakers of the 1970s, Boeger and Monteviña, with others hot on their heels. There are now approximately thirty wineries in the gold country; more pop up every year, and more land is being cleared all the time for vineyards. Unlike other California wine regions where some wineries are owned by huge multinational corporations and housed in grand old European-style structures, most of the Sierra Foothills wineries are small and family owned. Some are simple, located in rustic old barns and stone buildings. Others are complex and sophisticated, with modern, energy-efficient structures.

Except for the busy season (during the fall harvest and crush), the at-mosphere around the wineries is usually relaxed and informal. The winery tour guides are often the winemakers themselves, happy to take the time to talk about their art. Many are professionals who have traded the high pressures of city living for a calmer rural existence. You'll find many former aerospace engineers among them, with a sprinkling of attorneys, doctors, college professors, and homemakers. One reason they're drawn to the foothills is that arable land is much more affordable here than it is in other wine regions.

Most of the wine produced here is made from locally grown grapes, with zinfandel the most extensively planted wine grape. In fact, more than half of all the wine grapes grown in the foothills are zinfandel, and most of these are grown in Amador County. A few vines from just after the Gold Rush still survive, including the Downing planting in Amador County, which is more than a century old and the oldest zinfandel planting in the state. Mountain wines tend to be more intensely flavored than their valley counterparts, and the Sierra Foothills zinfandels are perhaps the best example. Ranging in color from salmon to dark purple and in taste from fruity to cinnamony, they're commonly referred to as "big and bold."

Vineyard owners in the gold country do experiment a great deal with their plantings, however, to see what will adapt to the region. More than twenty-five thousand acres, 87 percent of which are in Amador and El Dorado counties, are now planted in twenty-five varieties of grapes. One reason for the success of so many varieties of grapes is the region's different microclimates, caused by the range of topographies on the western slopes of the Sierra foothills. After zinfandel, the most popular grapes are sauvignon blanc and cabernet sauvignon. Other varieties include merlot, Chardonnay, Riesling, French Colombard, and Gewürztraminer. Most of the plantings are generally small, from five to ten or twenty acres.

Although there are a few wineries in Calaveras, Tuolumne, and Nevada counties, most of the wine in the region is produced in Amador and El Dorado counties, where vineyards range in elevation from twelve hundred to three thousand feet. Amador County is well known for its Shenandoah Valley, the oldest and now largest of the Sierra Foothills wine districts. The largest and best-known wineries are located here, with 75 percent of the vineyard acres planted in zinfandel grapes. The region is also known for its lighter white zinfandels and sauvignon blanc.

The eight wineries in El Dorado County produce a lighter zinfandel as well as cabernet sauvignon, chenin blanc, Chardonnay, and Johannisburg Riesling. Only about 35 percent of the acreage here is planted in zinfandel; El Dorado plantings are at higher elevations than Amador plantings, and El Dorado growers use irrigation, which produces more grapes and lighter wines.

This tour will focus on the Shenandoah Valley and El Dorado County wine regions, which have the largest concentration of wineries and can be easily toured in a day or two. The Sierra Foothills wine region is an ideal place to visit, because it is still off the beaten California-wine-tour track. The backroads are relatively untraveled, and you generally won't have the kinds of crowds you do in areas like the Napa Valley. A suggested loop trip from Sacramento: follow Highway 16 east from Sacramento thirty-seven miles to Highway 49. From there it's a short drive north on 49 to Plymouth, where you head east on Amador County Road E16. You can follow this road nearly all the way to Placerville and U.S. Highway 50, which will return you to Sacramento. Most of the wineries in the Shenandoah Valley and El Dorado County are located on or near this tour. Pack a picnic lunch with fruit, cheese, and french bread, as many of the wineries have picnic tables in pleasant surroundings. Nearly all offer tasting, informal or guided tours, and retail sales of their reasonably priced wines.

Spring is a good time to visit, as wildflowers are in abundance, new leaf is in the vineyards, and the rivers are high with snowmelt. It's exciting to visit in the fall during the harvest and the crush, but the winemakers won't have much time to chat. Most of the wineries are open on the weekends only from 10 A.M. or noon to 4 or 5 P.M., since many of the winemakers work at other jobs during the week to support their businesses. Some wineries are open by appointment only, so call first to arrange a visit. This section will focus on the wineries where no appointments are necessary for tours. For a detailed brochure and a map on winetasting in the Sierra foothills, send a self-addressed, stamped envelope to Sierra Foothills Winery Association, P.O. Box 425, Somerset, CA 95684.

SHENANDOAH VALLEY WINERIES

The Shenandoah Valley is the center of Amador County's wine production; eleven of the county's fifteen wineries are located here. About forty miles east of Sacramento, it's a serene, fertile valley characterized by oak-studded rolling hills and meadows. The actual valley lies at the bottom edge of the tree line and ranges from 1,400 to 1,800 feet in elevation. Some of the wineries are located atop rounded knolls that afford scenic views of the valley and the Sierra Nevada range in the distance. Most are open weekends and by appointment unless otherwise noted.

Kenworthy Vineyards, located on Shenandoah Road a half-mile north of the Fiddletown Road junction, has a modern winery inside the old white barn illustrated on its labels. John and Patricia Kenworthy got their start as home winemakers and produced their first commercial wine in 1980. They produce limited quantities of zinfandel, cabernet sauvignon, and Chardonnay. Kenworthy is open weekends by appointment; call 209/245-3198.

Baldinelli Vineyards lies on Shenandoah Road three and a half miles north of Plymouth (209/245-3398). Sitting on a knoll overlooking Shenandoah Road, it is a modern, small winery producing zinfandel, cabernet sauvignon, and sauvignon blanc made from grapes grown in the adjoining vineyard. Some of the zinfandel vines date to 1923. Ed Baldinelli began his career as a winemaker after thirty years as a design and construction engineer, producing his first vintage in 1979. Tasting is offered weekends and by appointment, and wheelchair access is provided.

Monteviña, three miles northeast of Plymouth on Shenandoah School Road, is the Shenandoah Valley's best-known and largest winery. Founded in 1973 and located on a 450-acre ranch, the winery produces fifty thousand cases of premium varietals annually. Its emphasis is on a variety of zinfandels, along with sauvignon blanc, a white cabernet, and cabernet sauvignon. All of the wines are produced from the 160 acres of vines surrounding the winery. Monteviña has an attractive tasting room open daily, and picnicking is available at shaded picnic tables. Large groups should make an appointment; call 209/245-6942.

The following three wineries are located on Steiner Road within close proximity of each other. Santino Winery (12225 Steiner Road, 209/245-6979) is a compact, modern winery specializing in French oak-aged zinfandel. The twelve-thousand-cases-a-year winery also produces sauvignon blanc and cabernet sauvignon from local vineyards. It is the only foothills winery built in the California Spanish style, with adobe blocks and a red tile roof. Tasting is offered Monday through Friday by appointment and generally on weekends, but phone first. Wheelchair access and shaded picnic tables are provided.

Across the road is Leon Sobon's seven-thousand-case, fifty-four-acre Shenandoah Vineyards. Shenandoah, perched on a knoll overlooking the valley, was founded in 1977 by Sobon (a former Lockheed scientist), his wife, and their six children. The winery produces ten varieties of award-winning wines, including zinfandel and cabernet sauvignon aged in American and French oak barrels. The tasting room is decorated with posters of the winery's colorful labels, which feature butterflies and flowers. The winery is open daily (209/245-3698). The Sobons also operate a tasting room at Columbia State Historic Park.

Amador Foothill Winery, next door, is also located on a hillock commanding a sweeping view of the valley. The passive solar structure was designed and built in 1980 by former NASA chemist Ben Zeitman and his wife, psychology professor Joan Sieber. The energy-efficient building provides a scientifically precise environment for producing fine zinfandel, white zinfandel, chenin blanc, and sauvignon blanc. Some of the zinfandel grapes come from the adjoining historic Downing Vineyard. The winery is usually open on weekends, but phone to be sure; 209/245-6307. If he has the time, Zeitman will be happy to show you how his winery functions. Be sure to try the delightful white zinfandel with its delicate salmon color. It's a fruity but not too sweet wine that goes well with seafood. Zeitman is collecting recipes to accompany the wines he produces.

D'Agostini Winery lies on Shenandoah Road about a mile east of Amador Foothill Winery (209/245-6612). The oldest of the foothill wineries, it was founded in 1856 by Adam Uhlinger and was run by the D'Agostini family from 1911 to 1984. Now a state historical landmark, the winery rests at the foot of a gentle, vine-clad slope. You can visit the original wine cellar with its hand-hewn beams, oak casks, and walls of locally quarried rock. Some of the original zinfandel vines are still in production. In the small tasting room (open daily except on major holidays), you can sample table wines, including Burgundy and zinfandel. The winery also now produces premium varietals, including Chardonnay, sauvignon blanc, and cabernet sauvignon. If you stop by in late September or early October, you can even watch the crush. Picnic tables are provided in a shaded lawn area.

Several fine wineries are located in Amador County outside of the Shenandoah Valley. Call for addresses and hours. The following are located near Ione: Argonaut Winery, 209/274-4106; Greenstone Winery (oak-shaded picnic area, RVs welcome), 209/274-2238; and Winterbrook Vineyards (in an 1860s barn), 209/274-4627. Stoneridge Winery (picnic area) is in Sutter Creek; 209/223-1761.

EL DORADO COUNTY WINERIES

Most of El Dorado County's eight wineries are small, family owned operations tucked in the nooks and crannies of the foothills between Placerville and the Amador County line. Because of special growing conditions, a section of El Dorado County between the elevations of 1,200 and 3,500 feet was designated a premium wine-grape growing region in 1983 by the U.S. Bureau of Alcohol, Tobacco and Firearms. Vintners in this new appellation area may now label their wines·"estate bottled," and any wine made predominantly from grapes in the new viticultural area may be identified with the words "El Dorado" on the label.

The route to take to visit the El Dorado County wineries is about twenty-five miles long, along scenic, winding backcountry roads. To begin the tour from D'Agostini Winery, continue on E16 for about three miles to Omo Ranch Road. Turn right and continue four miles to Fairplay Road (there's a fire station at the corner), then turn left.

Gerwer Winery (209/245-3467), a mile down Fairplay Road, is the first of three neighboring wineries on that road—all small and new operations. Formerly called Stoney Creek Vineyards, Gerwer Winery was founded in 1979 by Vernon and Marcia Gerwer. Vern comes from a family of Swiss immigrants who farmed extensively in the Sacramento region. The winery and vineyards are located on forty acres that used to be a mountain sheep ranch. At 2,600 feet, the Gerwer land is at one of the highest elevations used for grape growing in the state. The Gerwers are growing grapes to make ruby cabernet, sauvignon blanc, Semillon, and petite sirah. It's a real family operation; their children and grandchildren spend weekends and vacations helping in the vineyards. Tasting is on the weekends, and there's a picnic area.

Granite Springs Winery, off Fairplay Road at 6060 Granite Springs Road, is another small, family owned winery founded in 1981 by Les and Lynn Russell. The Russells had to blast into the granite hillside before laying the foundation for their 2,000-square-foot winery. Raised near Placerville, Les spent six years as a parks and recreation director before returning to the foothills as a winemaker. The hillside vineyards on the 40-acre site are planted in sauvignon blanc, zinfandel, chenin blanc, cabernet sauvignon, and petite sirah. Visitors are invited to feed the ducks and geese and to picnic by one of the tree-lined ponds. Open weekends for tasting and by appointment; 209/245-6395.

Fitzpatrick Winery has only been making wine since 1980, but its wines have already garnered gold, silver, and bronze medals. Brian Fitzpatrick, a former El Dorado County farm advisor, and his brother Michael, a former Wall Street banker, produce limited amounts of varietal wines from their own grapes combined with those grown in Amador County and elsewhere in El

Dorado County. Their vineyard includes plantings in cabernet, Chardonnay, and zinfandel. The winery has scenic picnic areas and is open for tastings on the weekends; 209/245-3248.

Continue on Fairplay Road to its terminus at Mt. Aukum Road (E16), then turn right. On the way to Sierra Vista Winery, the road crosses both the North and Middle forks of the scenic Cosumnes River.

Follow Mt. Aukum Road north to its terminus at Sly Park Road and turn left after a short distance onto Pleasant Valley Road. Turn left again onto Leisure Lane, and signs will show you the way to the winery, two miles up the hill. Located at 4560 Cabernet Way, Sierra Vista is named for its spectacular view of the Crystal Range of the Sierra Nevada, which is snowcapped most of the year. Founded in 1977 by John and Barbara MacCready, the vineyards and winery are located on a ridge at the 2,800-foot elevation. Varietals planted include cabernet sauvignon, Chardonnay, sauvignon blanc, and zinfandel. John has a Ph.D. in engineering and teaches at California State University at Sacramento. The MacCreadys do much of the winemaking process by hand and produce two thousand cases a year. Wine is fermented in stainless-steel tanks once used for milk as well as in barrels of American or French oak. Sierra Vista is open weekends or by appointment; 622-7221.

The following three vineyards are located in the Apple Hill region, on or near Carson Road. To get there, go north on Pleasant Valley Road for a mile to the intersection of Snows Road. Continue on Snows Road, which is a pleasant and scenic drive past small pastures and through madrone and pine forests. Dipping under Highway 50, Snows Road ends at Carson Road in Camino. Turn left on Carson Road.

Eldorado Vineyards, 3551 Carson Road, is housed in an unpretentious old wooden barn. The winery—the smallest in the county—is built on an old apple orchard that is still in production, so you can sample and buy apples as well as wine. Eldorado's cabernet sauvignon, chenin blanc, and zinfandel are produced from grapes purchased from local growers. The winery also makes apple wine and hard cider. Open daily from September through December and by appointment (call first; 644-3773). Wheelchair access is provided, and visitors are welcome to picnic.

Continue west on Carson Road a short distance to Gatlin Road and High Hill Ranch. Gatlin Road leads to Madroña Vineyards, nestled between apple orchards and wooded hills on a ridge near the town of Camino. Owners Dick and Leslie Bush had no previous experience in the wine business when they bought fifty-two acres in 1972. They planted thirty-five acres of grapes, sold them to other wineries, and used the profits to build their own winery in 1980. Later they added a tasting room finished in natural wood with a view of the vineyards and the main cellar. The large madrone tree standing in the center of the vineyard inspired the winery's name. At 3,000 feet above sea level, Madroña is the highest vineyard in California. The winery and tasting room are housed in a modern 7,700-square-foot building shaded by a picturesque grove of conifers and oaks. The winery currently produces about ten thousand cases of estate-bottled wine annually, including Chardonnay, white Riesling, Gewürztraminer, cabernet sauvignon, merlot, and zinfandel. Open weekends or by appointment; 644-5948.

Boeger Winery, 1709 Carson Road (622-8094), is a few miles down from Madroña. It's a scenic drive—especially in the fall, when you can also stop at the apple farms along the road. Tucked between gently rolling hills covered with vines, the winery is built on the site of the historic Fossati-Lombardo Winery founded in 1857. Winemaker and owner Greg Boeger is the grandson of Anton Nichelini, a Swiss-Italian who founded a winery and vineyard in Napa County in 1883. The Boegers built the current winery in 1973 after purchasing a seventy-acre pear orchard (they still grow pears). The twenty acres of vines provide about half the grapes for the winery's seven varietals; the rest of the grapes come from other El Dorado County vineyards. Tasting is available Wednesday through Sunday in the historic 1872 stone wine cellar. In good weather, you can picnic in a lovely setting shaded by immense fig trees alongside a little stream.

OTHER FOOTHILL WINERIES

Three wineries are located near the Calaveras-Tuolumne county line, two in the Murphys area, and one near Columbia State Historic Park. Stevenot Winery (209/728-3436) is located in a picturesque narrow valley about three miles north of Murphys on San Domingo Road. Owner Barden E. Stevenot, a fifth-generation member of a Calaveras County family, has twenty-six acres planted in cabernet sauvignon, Chardonnay, and zinfandel and produces twenty-six thousand cases annually. Tasting is offered daily in a historic wood-frame house. The winery itself is located in the original buildings of the historic Shaw Ranch, built in the 1870s on the former site of a Miwok Indian village. Tours and picnic areas are provided. Stevenot's wife, Debbie Collins, began producing premium dry apple wine in 1982 under the Harvest Cellars label. Harvest Cellars apple wine may be tasted at the winery and at High Hill Ranch at Apple Hill.

Chispa Cellars is a small winery housed in a former feed store at the end of Main Street in Murphys. Winemaker Robert Bliss produces three hundred to five hundred cases annually of zinfandel made from Amador County grapes. Informal tours are available by appointment or by chance; 209/728-2106. Yankee Hill Winery (209/532-3015) is a mile east of Columbia State Historic Park on Yankee Hill Road. The Erickson family produces a different varietal

White-water rafting on the South Fork of the American River (courtesy Sierra Shutterbug Photography/Paul Ratcliffe)

each year, as well as a large selection of fruit wines and vinegar. Tasting is by appointment only.

White-Water Rafting

Since the early 1960s, the Sierra foothills have been the destination of a new breed of adventurer. These new explorers are seeking not gold, but the thrill and adventure of white-water rafting. Highway 49 crosses some of the finest rafting rivers in the state, and since the Stanislaus has been dammed, the South Fork of the American River is second only to the Colorado in popularity nationwide; more than 100,000 people annually shoot its rapids. Coloma lies right in the middle of the most popular run, making it the rafting center of the gold country.

Several other gold country rivers are popular with rafters. The Cosumnes and Mokelumne rivers have sections that are good for rafting and kayaking, although commercial trips are not available. In addition to the South Fork of the American, commercial trips are available on the Tuolumne River, which has an eighteen-mile stretch of some of the wildest white-water rapids in the West. There were plans to build a dam on the Tuolumne, but that river's recent designation as a Wild and Scenic River has saved it from the same fate as the Stanislaus. The North and Middle forks of the American have also gained popularity, but if the Auburn Dam is completed, it will flood both rivers about twenty-four miles upstream.

About 80 percent of the commercial rafting in the area is done on the South Fork of the American. One reason for its popularity is that its water has everything from calm flat stretches to challenging rapids. Most of the trips on the South Fork are guided, either by commercial outfits or nonprofit groups. All of the guides are trained and give a full safety talk before the trip. Rivers are classified according to level of difficulty on an international scale of I (the easiest) to V (experienced rafters only); most of the South Fork is rated Class III.

The most popular run is the twenty-one-mile trip between Chili Bar and Folsom Lake. To stretch it to a two-day run, you can stop overnight at a campground in Coloma, the halfway point. The stretch between Coloma and Lotus is Class II and is also popular for canoeing and kayaking. About 90 percent of the land along the river is private property, so you should stop only at designated public areas, and under no circumstances should you camp or build fires. If you bring your own boat, there are put-in points along the run, all requiring a small fee. They include Chili Bar, Marshall Gold Discovery State Historic Park, and Camp Lotus. Private boaters are required to carry a registration tag issued by the county; tags are available from El Dorado County and at resorts along the river. The county also publishes a useful river information brochure, available with a self-addressed, stamped legal-size envelope sent to El Dorado County, 360 Fair Lane, Placerville, CA 95667. Experienced rafters rely heavily on the State Flood Operations Center's "Flow Fone," which provides a recorded message on current river conditions: call 322-3327.

To prevent—or at least discourage—inexperienced rafters from going out on their own, there are no boats for rent at the river. A few more tips: don't bring children under eight on a raft trip; wearing life jackets is required by law; and keep a plastic trash bag with you. During the height of the season, Memorial Day to Labor Day, some stretches of the river become uncomfortably crowded on weekends. Schedule your trip for another time of year or during the week to avoid the masses. Several useful books on white-water rafting are available at bookstores and outdoor shops. A good one is *A Guide to the Best White Water in California* by Lars Holbek and Chuck Stanley, published by Friends of the River Books.

Buying your own equipment can cost you hundreds of dollars. The most economical way to enjoy river rafting is with an organized group. It's also a good idea if you're a beginner, since many of the nonprofit groups also conduct classes in safety, paddling techniques, water reading, and equipment. Groups such as Friends of the River and the Sierra Club are actively engaged in preserving the rivers and conserving water and energy supplies. The following organizations offer raft trips:

Friends of the River
909 12th Street, #207
Sacramento, CA 95814
442-3155

Sierra Club—River Touring Section
P.O. Box 1335
Sacramento, CA 95806
444-2180

River City Whitewater Co-op
5441 Tenth Avenue
Sacramento, CA 95820
451-5720
(A nonprofit membership club)

Environmental Traveling
   Companions
Fort Mason Center
Building C, Room 360
San Francisco, CA 94123
415/474-7662
(White-water tours for the physically handicapped, developmentally disabled, etc.)

A number of commercial outfitters conduct tours on the South Fork of the American as well as on other gold country rivers. The American River Recreation Association (P.O. Box 221, Coloma, CA 95613), a nonprofit educational association that works to preserve the American River, publishes a brochure listing commercial outfitters who are ARRA members. Here are just a few of the many commercial outfitters located in the gold country and in Sacramento:

California River Trips
P.O. Box C
Lotus, CA 95651
626-8006

Chili Bar White-Water Tours
1669 Chili Bar Court
Placerville, CA 95667
622-6104
(No reservations required)

American River Recreation
11257 South Bridge Street
Rancho Cordova, CA 95670
635-4479 or 635-4516

O.A.R.S. Inc.
P. O. Box 67
Angels Camp, CA 95222
209/736-2924

Bicycling in the Gold Country

Although much of the gold country terrain is hilly, the area does offer many opportunities for pleasant bike rides, even if you're not an Olympic athlete. Still, it's probably best if you have a ten-speed bike and are in reasonable shape. Next to walking, bicycling is the best way to get to know the terrain and the countryside; you see things you would miss if you were speeding by in a car, and you can take the time to explore an interesting ruin or a field of wildflowers. It's a good idea to do some advance scouting of a potential route, because steep canyons and mountain slopes don't show on road maps. Nor do dead ends or flooded roads. Because Highway 49 is the main route through the gold country, it's best to avoid it as much as possible when you're on a bicycle. This is true of some of the other heavily traveled roads as well. If you must use these roads, use extreme caution and ride defensively.

The state parks and recreation department publishes a fine guide called *Bicycling Through the Mother Lode*. The fifty-six-page illustrated pamphlet describes more than twenty tours with degrees of difficulty ranging from Class 1, the easiest, to Class 4, the most difficult. The guide costs only a few dollars and is available at state parks or by contacting the Publication Section, Department of Parks and Recreation, P.O. Box 2390, Sacramento, CA 95811, 322-7000. Caltrans also publishes bike route guides for the gold country, though they're not as detailed.

One pleasant route runs twenty-five miles from Folsom along Green Valley Road to Placerville. It's a scenic country road that has less traffic and several possibilities for pleasant side trips. You might want to ride it from Placerville to Folsom to take advantage of the downhill slope. A good day trip is the twelve-mile run from Volcano to Sutter Creek via the Sutter Creek-Volcano Road. It's a gentle downhill run through forests and fields with a creek running all along the route and a number of nice picnic spots. For group excursions, you may want to contact a group like the Sierra Club, which also leads hiking tours through the Mother Lode, or a bicycle club like Sacramento's Golden Wheelmen. Bicycle repair shops are located in Sonora, Jackson, Placerville, Auburn, Grass Valley, and Nevada City.

From the Air

For a bird's-eye view of the countryside, there's nothing like an early morning ride in a hot-air balloon. Champagne Sunrise, one of several hot-air balloon companies in the gold country, is located in Placerville and usually flies out of Cameron Park in the spring and fall. Owner and pilot Annemiek Storm says you never know where you'll end up because you go where the winds take you, although the trip generally goes south. Storm's flights stay at an average altitude of about one thousand feet and provide spectacular views of the valley and foothills; she recommends that you bring your camera. A chase car meets the balloon after it sets down and takes you back to the lift-off point. The cost averages around $200 per couple for a trip that lasts one to one and a half hours, and reservations are recommended. Champagne Sunrise, P.O. Box 2115, Placerville, CA 95667, 626-3202.

Airplane pilots will be interested in the sixty-six-page *Mother Lode Sky Trail,* also published by the state parks and recreation department. It's an aerial guidebook describing historic mining towns along Highway 49 as they appear from the air. Also listed are landing strips and airports. You can make the tour in six hours or expand it to a couple of days. If you prefer to have someone else do the flying for you, contact Carlen Flying Services, located in Columbia. Pilot Leo Koponen runs chartered sightseeing flights over Yosemite Park and the gold country for one to three passengers for a flat rate of about $100 an hour. Contact Carlen Flying Services at 10749 Airport Road, Columbia, CA 95310, 209/533-4645.

Llama Pack Trips

Backpackers know that schlepping a thirty-pound pack around can be hard work. Wouldn't it be great to let a nice, fuzzy llama carry all that stuff for you? It's true—llamas are now available for guided pack trips in the gold country. Don't let their cuddly looks fool you; they've served as pack animals in the Andes for more than two thousand years. Since 1976 Mama's Llamas has been organizing llama pack trips at various Northern California locations, including the gold country. Natural history buffs and nature lovers may want to try one of two three-day trips offered in the early summer. The Yuba River trip follows the South Yuba River, with a stopover at Malakoff Diggins State Historic Park. The Rubicon River trip covers the area near Georgetown. Both are short treks of moderate intensity, averaging three to five hiking miles per day (the llama will carry your gear, not you).

Naturalist and photographer guides join the experienced guides, and the itinerary allows plenty of time for nature study, photography, fishing, swimming, and exploring. Meals? Throw away your freeze-dried stroganoff; you'll enjoy gourmet backcountry meals prepared from fresh ingredients, such as eggs benedict, teriyaki, and chicken paprikash. You can even combine a river rafting trip along the South Fork of the American River with a pack trip. If you prefer, the guides will pack you into a base camp and come back for you on a prearranged day. For information, contact Mama's Llamas, P.O. Box 655, El Dorado, CA 95623, 622-2566.

Gold Prospecting

One great way to get into the spirit of the Gold Rush is to try your hand at gold prospecting, and lots of folks are ready to help you. There's still plenty of gold left in "them thar hills," and most of the prospecting tour companies guarantee that you won't leave empty-handed. (Some geologists estimate that only about 10 percent of the gold in the gold country was found during the Gold Rush.) With the price of gold up again, large mining corporations are starting up operations throughout the Mother Lode.

Located in the Old Livery Stable in Jamestown, Gold Prospecting Expeditions offers a variety of tours and programs, including a popular gold prospecting day trip. You don't have to know anything about prospecting, and the company supplies all the equipment. The company also conducts tours lasting from one to three hours, as well as river raft tours, five-day campouts, and weekend helicopter drop-in trips. The tours are led by experienced prospectors who will teach you all the basics. Group rates and family discount packages are available, and the company's offices are open every day of the year except Christmas; contact Gold Prospecting Expeditions, P.O. Box 974, 18172 Main Street, Jamestown, CA 95327, 209/984-4162; toll-free in California, 800/822-2267.

Sports Unlimited Prospecting and Mining Supply in Placerville offers day-long gold tours that include equipment and instruction. The firm will also rent you any prospecting equipment you need, including a dredge, if you'd rather set out on your own; experts will be glad to steer you in the right direction. For information and reservations, contact Sports Unlimited, 1271 Broadway, Placerville, CA 95667, 622-2484.

Four-hour guided tours to Roaring Camp, an old gold camp with a working mine on the Mokelumne River east of Jackson, are available from Roaring Camp Mining Company. You'll have a chance to swim in the river, fish, pan for gold, collect rocks, and visit a wildlife museum. The company offers a special dinner trip on Wednesdays; you can pan for gold and then enjoy a barbecued steak dinner served under the stars on the riverbank. If you'd like to stay a week or longer, you can rent a prospector's cabin, but you must bring all your own gear. However, there is a modern bathhouse, trading post, saloon, and snack bar. For information and reservations, contact the Roaring Camp Mining Company, P.O. Box 278, Pine Grove, CA 95665, 209/296-4100.

Every year on a weekend in early April, the town of Jackson sponsors Gold Dust Days. Activities include gold panning lessons, field trips, a visit to a small working mine, and a gem and mineral display. Also, many gold country resorts offer gold panning; check with the resorts for more information.

Appendix

The following selective listings are intended as a guide for visitors and a convenient reference for residents. It is obviously not possible to list every restaurant, shop, organization, or service for each heading—the phone book does a much better job. These listings are intended to give you a sampling of what's available to help you get started. The local newspapers are the best source for up-to-date information on what's going on around town (see the section on Publications). Wherever possible, resources that will help you find the service or product you need (e.g., directories and referral services) have been included.

Most of the listings are for the city of Sacramento and vicinity. For restaurants, lodging, recreation, etc., outside this area, see the index and individual chapters. All telephone numbers have a 916 prefix unless otherwise noted.

Sacramento Restaurants

What follows is a sampling of the large variety of restaurants in and around the city of Sacramento, divided according to location and type of food served. These are representative of what Sacramento has to offer, but they are not necessarily the most popular or the best. Criteria used for listings include atmosphere and setting, ethnic variety, price, and unique entertainment. Except as noted, restaurants are moderately priced (dinner without drinks priced mostly under $12). For more specific information on prices, reservations, hours, and credit cards accepted, call ahead.

Restaurants outside the city of Sacramento and vicinity are listed in the chapters on the regions in which they are located. Codes used are as follows: B—Breakfast; L—Lunch; D—Dinner; SB—Sunday brunch; and FB—full bar.

DOWNTOWN

American/Mixed

Alhambra Fuel and Transportation
1310 Alhambra Blvd.
452-4624
L/D/SB/FB
Bistro atmosphere; shaded patio; piano.

Firehouse
1112 2nd St. (Old Sacramento)
442-4772
L/D/FB
Popular Sacramento restaurant with elegant Victorian atmosphere; romantic; courtyard with fountains and gas lamps; expensive.

Harry's Bar & Grill
400 L St.
448-8223
L/D/FB
Old Chicago financial district style; steak sandwiches, burgers, crepes; entertainment.

Limelight
1014 Alhambra Blvd.
446-2236
B/L
Patio dining.

Melarkey's Place
1517 Broadway
448-2797
B/L/D/SB/FB
Political hang-out; California cuisine; entertainment.

Metro Bar & Grill
1225 K St.
447-3837
L/FB
Pasta, steak sandwiches, fish, burgers, desserts; entertainment.

Pearson's Natural Eatery
2019 I St.
447-1616
B/L/D
Specializes in vegetarian dishes.

Rosemount Grill
3145 Folsom Blvd.
455-5387
L/D/FB
Since 1920; wide variety of food served.

Schooner's
2730 N St.
452-7427
D
Warm, woodsy; specializes in seafood and ribs.

Sturgeon II
1704 Broadway
441-4650
L/D/FB
Political hang-out owned by former legislative staffers; seafood, burgers.

Chinese

Hong Kong Cafe
5th St. at Broadway
442-7963
L/D
Simple atmosphere; good food at low prices.

The Mandarin
1827 Broadway
443-5052
L/D/FB
Specializes in Mandarin, Szechuan, Shanghai, Hunan; full bar next door, On Broadway, with live entertainment.

Coffee/Dessert

La Boulangerie
1400 J St.
448-5233
Croissants, coffee.

de Ville's Desserts
2416 16th St.
443-0656

Gelato, cheesecakes, chocolate desserts, espresso, Italian sodas; good after-movie spot.

Continental

The Broiler
1013 J St.
444-3444
L/D/FB
Steaks, prime rib, lobster are specialties; expensive.

Bull Market
815 11th St.
446-6757
B/L/D/FB
Continental cuisine, specializing in flambéed entrees and desserts; romantic atmosphere; live jazz.

Crêpe Daniel
2326 J St.
446-6644
B/L/D
Crêpes.

Gourmet to Go
1331 O St.
446-8646
L/D
Continental cuisine; outdoor dining.

Harlow's Bar & Cafe
2712 J St.
441-4693
L/D/FB
Art Deco decor; dark and cozy; Italian entrees, seafood.

Joan Leineke Cafe
800 Alhambra Blvd.
448-2761
L/D/FB
Classy atmosphere; terrace dining; expensive.

John Q's
16th Floor, Capitol Plaza Holiday Inn
300 J St.
446-0100
L/D/FB

Classy, elegant atmosphere; great view of Sacramento River and capitol; expensive; cocktail lounge with entertainment.

Nicole's
2815 J St.
441-7815
B/L/D/SB
Specializes in omelettes; long lines on Sunday mornings.

Pava's
2330 K St.
443-2397
B/L/D/SB
Victorian atmosphere; cozy, often crowded; seafood, quiche, salads.

French

Cafe La Salle
1020 2nd St. (Old Sacramento)
442-9000
L/D/SB/FB
Elegant surroundings; terrace dining; expensive.

Italian

Americo's
2000 Capitol Ave.
442-8119
L/D
Northern Italian; fresh pasta; long waits.

Old Spaghetti Factory
1910 J St.
443-2862
L/D/FB
Good family restaurant.

Paragary's Bar & Oven
28th at N St.
457-5737
L/D/FB
Gourmet pizza, Italian specialties; unique wood-burning brick oven; espresso; live entertainment on weekends.

River City Ravioli
1331 O St.
442-8516
L/D
Fresh pasta made daily; cozy; everything on menu can be taken out.

Zelda's Gourmet Pizza
1415 21st St.
447-1400
L/D/FB
Chicago-style thin-crust pizza; call ahead to order (25-minute wait); take-out available.

Japanese

Aoba
1108 T St.
443-4041
L/D
Good Japanese fare in casual environment.

Fuji Sukiyaki
2422 13th St.
446-4135
L/D/FB
Sushi bar; large dining room.

Kagetsu
1628 Broadway
446-0984
L/D
Friendly, small cafe.

Sakura
1111 2nd St. (Old Sacramento)
448-8334
L/D/FB
Teppan-style food prepared at your table; tempura; lovely Japanese decor.

Mexican

El Charro
2019 Q St.
446-7276
L/D

A true Mexican cafe; special green chili burritos, Mexican beers; popular hang-out for *Sacramento Bee* employees.

524 Restaurant
524 12th St.
446-6147
L/D
Carnitas a specialty; open late.

La Fiesta Mexican Foods
910 X St.
444-7761
L/D
Cafeteria-style service; tortillas and *pan dulce* made at adjoining bakery; menudo on weekends; carnitas; all food can be taken out.

Middle Eastern

Juliana's Kitchen
1800 L St.
444-0187
L
Salads, sandwiches, falafel; other Middle Eastern specialties.

Thai

Amarin
900 12th St.
447-9063
L/D
Cuisine of Thailand; curry, Thai barbecued chicken; comfortable atmosphere.

Vietnamese

Andy Nguyen's
2007 Broadway
736-1157
L/D
Excellent Vietnamese and French cuisine.

Miscellaneous

Célestin's French Caribbean Restaurant
2516 J St.
444-2423
L/D
Shrimp Creole, seafood, lamb; relaxed atmosphere.

Fox & Goose
1001 R St.
443-8825
B/L/D/SB
English pub; British draught beers, pasties, Welsh rarebit, bangers; live entertainment; dart boards.

Franke's Pharmacy
3839 J St.
452-3333
L
Not a restaurant, but the last pharmacy in Sacramento with an old-fashioned soda fountain that also serves lunch.

Le Grand Confectionary
1402 J St.
448-7764
Also not a restaurant, but a delightful candy store specializing in handmade truffles and Italian ices.

Luna's Cafe & Juice Bar
1414 16th St.
441-3931
L
Fresh juices, light lunch, espresso, beer and wine; art by local artists.

Shanley's Bar & Grill
427 Broadway
442-4044
L/FB
True Irish pub with 19th-century back bar and memorabilia; oak and mahogany interior; great burgers with thick fries.

OUTSIDE DOWNTOWN

American/Mixed

Chart Room Marina
County Rd. 136, Broderick (quarter mile north of I St. Bridge, west bank of Sacramento River)
371-0471
B/L/D
On a floating barge; casual, friendly atmosphere; large breakfasts including omelettes, fried catfish, and chunky fried potatoes; sandwiches, burgers.

L. W. Calder's
8999 Greenback Ln., Orangevale
989-5050
L/D/SB/FB
Beef, seafood, pasta served in historic 1907 mansion with walls decorated with historical photos; bar has more than 1,000 bottles on 20-foot glass/mirrored shelves; garden deck.

Mace's
Pavilions Shopping Center
Fair Oaks Blvd. at Howe Ave.
922-0222
L/D/SB/FB
American cuisine in a quietly stylish environment; greenery, marble tiled floors, multi-level dining areas; fresh seafood, chicken, lamb, steaks, pasta.

Red Baron Steak House
6151 Freeport Blvd.
391-1007
L/D/SB/FB
At Executive Airport; steaks and seafood; watch planes as you dine.

River Galley
County Rd. 136, Broderick (across I St. bridge from downtown; turn right at 4th St. and follow levee road)
372-0300
L/D/SB/FB
Floating restaurant with great river view; seafood.

Virgin Sturgeon
1577 Garden Hwy. (on Sacramento River)
921-2694
L/D/SB/FB
Floating restaurant; light seafood meals served in a casual atmosphere.

Chinese

Great Wall Mongolian BBQ
Century Plaza
1537 Howe Ave., Suite 100
925-5347
L/D
Cafeteria-style Mongolian barbecue with thinly sliced meat, vegetables, sauces; chef cooks in front of you on 1,000-degree grill; all you can eat.

Hoi Sing
7007 S. Land Park Dr.
392-9630
L/D/SB
Live lobster, crab, catfish; Chinese *dim sum* on Saturday and Sunday.

Wong's Islander
5675 Freeport Blvd.
392-3340
L/D
Large *dim sum* brunch on weekends.

Continental

Aldo's Restaurant
Town & Country Village
Marconi at Fulton Ave.
483-5031
L/D/FB

Expensive French, Italian, and American cuisine; entertainment; monthly Opera Night banquets.

El Condor
Hotel El Rancho
1029 W. Capitol Ave., West Sacramento
371-6731
B/L/D/SB/FB
Lush outdoor patio with fountain and aviary; lavish Friday seafood buffet and Sunday brunch; located in refurbished 1930s hotel; expensive.

Movable Feast
601 Munroe St.
971-1677
L/D/FB
French Continental; patio dining; light meals available.

Rancho Murieta
14813 Jackson Rd. (24 miles from downtown)
985-7200
B/L/D/SB/FB
Expensive French, Italian, and American cuisine; reservations required for lavish Sunday brunch with 44 entrees.

Slocum House
7992 California Ave., Fair Oaks
961-7211
L/D/SB/FB
A 1925 house with homey atmosphere; lush patio for drinks, lunch, and Sunday brunch.

French

Bon Appétit
11773 Fair Oaks Blvd., Fair Oaks
966-9666
L/D/SB/FB
Elegant atmosphere; fireplace, crystal chandeliers; expensive.

Flambard's
9634 Fair Oaks Blvd., Fair Oaks

965-1071
L/D/FB
Country French cuisine; elegant decor; 12 entrees, including sautéed fresh fish, shrimp, steak, and poultry; expensive.

Wuff's French Restaurant
2333 Fair Oaks Blvd.
922-8575
L/D/FB
French country inn atmosphere.

Greek

Cafe Europa
Arden Fair Mall
1607-E Arden Way
922-0419
L/D
Cozy taverna; gyro, shishkabob, stuffed grape leaves, lemon soup, baklava; beer, wine.

Mykonos
6628 Fair Oaks Blvd., Carmichael
485-8810
D/FB
Strolling musicians.

Indian

Taj Mahal
2355 Arden Way
924-8378
L/D
North Indian; curry; great atmosphere; belly dancers.

Italian

Club Pheasant
8022 Jefferson Blvd., West Sacramento
371-9530
L/D/FB
Great steak sandwiches; homemade ravioli.

Pasta Fresca

1407 Howe Ave. (also at Birdcage Walk in Citrus Heights)
921-2797
L/D
Popular; reasonably priced fresh pasta made daily on premises and served 32 ways.

Japanese

Aomi Teppan
2623 Fulton Ave.
481-1850
D/FB
Teppan-style; sushi bar. Tatami Room (by reservation) with floor seating, traditional service, no shoes allowed; expensive.

Mexican

El Novillero
4216 Franklin Blvd.
456-4287
L/D
Cozy family atmosphere; patio dining.

Emma's Taco House
1617 Sacramento Ave., Bryte
371-1151
L/D
Since 1953; large Mexican menu; great tacos; casual.

Russian

Nina's Deli
316 6th St., Broderick
371-7080
A mom-and-pop deli with a few tables; piroshki, cabbage rolls.

Turkish

Istanbul
6020A Fair Oaks Blvd., Carmichael
486-0149
L/D
Shishkabob, Turkish coffee, baklava.

Miscellaneous

Brothers Delicatessen
Town & Country Village
2918 Fulton Ave.
482-4524
B/L/D
One of Sacramento's only kosher delis.

Chuck E. Cheese's Pizza Time Theater
1690 Arden Way
920-9181
Florin Mall
7020 Stockton Blvd.
393-3456
L/D
A popular spot for children's birthday parties; restaurant supplies pizza, party hats, balloons, drinks; 82 video games, circus of rides, mechanical singing animals.

Top Bar-B-Que & Soul Food
3408 3rd Ave.
456-7085
B/L/D
Smothered chicken, Louisiana-style gumbo, black-eyed peas, sweet potato pie, chitterlings, BBQ ribs.

Vic's Ice Cream
3199 Riverside Blvd.
448-0892
Authentic old-fashioned soda fountain; a neighborhood institution since the 1940s; homemade ice cream.

Sacramento Lodging

HOTELS/MOTELS

Clarion Hotel
700 16th St.
(across from Governor's Mansion)
444-8000

Days Inn
200 Jibboom St.
(off Richards Blvd. near downtown)
448-8100

Capitol Plaza Holiday Inn
300 J St.
446-0100

Hilton Inn
2200 Harvard
922-4700

Holiday Inn—Holidome Northeast
5321 Date Ave.
338-5800

Host International Hotel
Sacramento Metro Airport
922-8071

Rancho Murieta Country Club
14813 Jackson Rd.
Rancho Murieta
985-7200

Red Lion Motor Inn
2001 Point West Way
(near Cal Expo)
929-8855

Sacramento Inn
1401 Arden Way
(near Arden Fair Mall)
922-8041

Vagabond Inn
909 3rd St.
(near Downtown Plaza)
446-1481

Woodlake Inn
500 Leisure Ln.
(Hwy. 160 at Canterbury Rd.)
922-6251

BED AND BREAKFAST INNS

Amber House
1315 22nd St.
444-8085
1905 California bungalow with stained
  glass, antiques. Breakfast (pastry and
  fruits) on Limoges china with crystal
  and silver. Four rooms decorated with
  English antiques, two with private
  bath.

Aunt Abigail's
2120 G St.
441-5007
White, 1909 Colonial Revival house. Five
  rooms, each with special features.
  Warm and hospitable atmosphere.
  Children, smoking, TV watching
  allowed. Continental breakfast.

Bear Flag Inn
2814 I St.
448-5417
1910 California bungalow with two-
  tiered deck shaded by fruit trees. Two
  blocks from Sutter's Fort. Two
  bedrooms with private baths.
  Continental breakfast. Children,
  smokers welcome.

Briggs House
2209 Capitol Ave.
441-3214
1901 Colonial house. Sacramento's first
  bed and breakfast (est. 1981). Elegant
  surroundings with dark wood
  paneling, hardwood floors, antiques.
  Six rooms, two with private bath. Spa,
  sauna. Light gourmet breakfast.
  Separate carriage house room for
  privacy.

Driver Mansion Inn
2019 21st St.
455-5243
1899 Colonial two-story. Four
  bedrooms, three with private bath.
  Walnut and mahogany decor.
  Continental breakfast. Spa.

Morning Glory Inn
700 22nd St.
447-7829
1906 Colonial Revival home decorated
  with turn-of-the-century oak furniture, antique lace, memorabilia. Four
  rooms. Large gourmet breakfast
  indoors or in colorful garden.

CAMPGROUNDS AND RV PARKS

Bamboo Tree Rec-Vehicle Park
8545 Folsom Blvd.
(near Sac State)
383-5303

KOA
4851 Lake Rd.
(I-80 at W. Capitol Ave.)
West Sacramento
371-6771

Oakhaven Mobile and RV Park
2150 Auburn Blvd.
(Bus. 80 at Howe Ave. near Del Paso
  Park)
922-0814

Transportation

AIR

Sacramento Metropolitan Airport
12 miles north of Sacramento via I-5
929-5411 for a schedule listing flights, destinations, and times
920-4700 for a recorded listing of current fare discounts
Nearly 100 daily flights via seven major carriers and four commuter lines. Direct service to major cities. Host International Hotel, restaurant, coffee shop, snack bars, cocktail lounge, gift shop. Airport transportation via Yellow Cab airporter van every half-hour between airport and downtown Sacramento; call 444-2222. Taxis and hotel courtesy vans available. For airport service for the disabled, call Paratransit at 454-4131.

Sacramento Executive Airport
6151 Freeport Blvd. (at 43rd Ave.)
428-8429
South of downtown. General aviation airport serving rental and charter aircraft.

BUS

Amador Stage Lines
444-7880
Buses to Reno and South Lake Tahoe.
  Call for pick-up locations.

Greyhound Bus Lines
Downtown terminal, 715 L St.
444-6800
North area substation, 2426 Marconi
  Ave.
482-4993
Rancho Cordova substation, 10167
  Folsom Blvd.
363-1036

Sacramento Regional Transit
1400 29th St.
321-BUSS
Serving Sacramento and neighboring
  cities. Call for schedules.

Trailways
1129 I St.
443-2044

TRAIN

Amtrak
4th St. at I
485-8506 for information and reservations
444-9131 or 444-8739 for station
Daily service to Portland, Seattle, the Bay Area, Los Angeles, Reno, Salt Lake City, Denver, and Chicago. No restaurant or gift shop at terminal.

BICYCLE

Caltrans Office of Bicycle Facilities
445-4616
Information on routes, statewide programs, bicycle parking, and showers for cyclists.

Sacramento City Bicycle Coordinator
Traffic Engineering Division
449-5307
Bicycle route maps.

TOURS AND EXCURSIONS

Cal-Events
924-8661
Narrated historical tours for groups to Sacramento, gold country, wine country, and San Francisco.

Capital City Cruises
1207 Front St.
Old Sacramento
448-7447
Pleasure cruises on the Sacramento River on the riverboat *River City Queen.* Cocktails, snacks.

Sacramento Sightseeing Service
442-7564
Variety of daily tours in 15-passenger vans. Depart from your hotel or other location by arrangement. Tours of capitol, Folsom, night life.

Services and Resources

MAPS AND INFORMATION

Sacramento Convention and Visitors Bureau
1311 I St.
442-5542
Free brochure with downtown map, main attractions, restaurants, and hotels.

California Office of Tourism
1121 L St., Suite 103
322-1396
Numerous free publications and maps, including state visitors' map, state calendar of events, bed and breakfast inns, golf courses, visitor information sources. Although listings are for the entire state, many are in or near Sacramento and the gold country. A great information resource.

Sacramento Chamber of Commerce
917 7th St.
443-3771
Information on Sacramento's business community. Ask about their newcomers' package.

Sacramento Public Library
Central Library
828 I St.
449-5203
Great resource for visitors and residents. Newspapers, maps, phone books, local histories, reference librarians. Houses Community Information Center (resource for senior citizens); call 442-4995.

PUBLICATIONS

Sacramento Media Guide
Walsmith Productions, publisher
Updated annually; a useful guide to Sacramento area newspapers, magazines, and TV and radio stations. Available at bookstores.

Sacramento Bee
21st at Q St.
321-1000
Daily. Publishes a weekly entertainment/recreation guide.

Sacramento Union
301 Capitol Mall
442-7811
Daily. Publishes a weekly entertainment/recreation guide.

Aardvark
2322 J St.
448-2235
Weekly. Geared to college audience; focuses on entertainment. Distributed free on campuses and around town.

Mom . . . Guess What!
1400 S St.
441-6397
Monthly. Focuses on Sacramento's gay and lesbian community. Calendar of events.

On the Wing
1725 I St.
443-3395
Monthly arts publication. Published by Sacramento Regional Arts Council. Calendar of arts events.

Senior Citizen Weekly
1744 36th St.
454-2105
Weekly. Calendar of events.

Suttertown News
2424 Castro Wy.
451-2823

Weekly. Alternative newspaper distributed primarily in downtown area. Extensive calendar of activities.

Sacramento Observer
3540 4th Ave.
452-4781
Weekly. Focuses on issues in the black community. Calendar of events.

Sacramento Magazine
1021 2nd St.
446-7548
A slick monthly focusing on the Sacramento lifestyle. Calendar of events, dining guide.

HUMAN SERVICES

Community Services Directory
Community Services Planning Council
909 12th St.
447-7063
Updated annually, a valuable resource listing hundreds of agencies and organizations providing human services. Includes nursing homes, day care centers, recreation, law enforcement, libraries, disabled services. Available at bookstores.

Sacramento Religious Community for Peace
P.O. Box 163078
Sac., CA 95816
456-2616
Educational programs and activities working for peace and justice. Monthly meetings and newsletter.

Emergency Phone Numbers
Police, fire, ambulance, Calif. Highway Patrol (Sacramento County): 911
Battered women: WEAVE shelter: 944-4011
Burn Center (University Medical Center): 453-3636
Poison control (UCD Medical Center): 453-3692
Psychiatric emergency/crisis intervention:
—UCD Medical Center: 453-3696
—Sacramento County: 732-3637
Rape Crisis Hotline: 447-7273
Suicide prevention: 441-1135
Travelers and emergency assistance: 443-1719

Other Useful Phone Numbers
Professional referrals:
Dental Society: 446-1226
Lawyer Referral Service: 444-2333
Medical Society: 456-1017
Optometric Society: 447-0270
Psychologist Referral Service: 334-3888
Road conditions (Caltrans): 445-7623
Seniors (Community Information Center): 442-4995
Time: 767-2676
Flood forecast: 445-7571

Handicapped Resources
Resources for Independent Living
1230 H St.

446-3074 (voice or TTY)
Information, resources and referral for adult disabled persons.

Seniors' Resources

Community Information Center
Located at Central Branch of Sacramento Public Library, 828 I St.
442-4995
Nonprofit information and referral service for senior citizens. Information on housing, transportation,

medical assistance, income taxes, 600 agencies and programs.

Women's Resources

YWCA
1122 17th St.
442-4741
Programs for women. Workshops, classes, seminars, swimming pool in summer. Senior activities, quarterly newsletter. Houses several women's organizations.

Culture and Entertainment

GENERAL INFORMATION

Ticketron ticket sales
Available at Tower Video stores throughout Sacramento
489-7469 for information, charge by phone
Tower Video also serves as an independent ticket agency for entertainment events.

BASS ticket sales
Available at Record Factory stores and Weinstock's throughout Sacramento
395-2277 for information, charge by phone

Arco Arena
922-7362, ticket information

Sacramento Metropolitan Arts Commission
800 10th St., Suite 2
449-5558
A city/county arts agency offering arts information services, an art in public places program, the *Cultural Resources Directory,* and an annual cultural awards program. The directory lists artists and organizations in dance, music, theater, visual arts, and literature. The Discover Sacramento Hotline is a 24-hour service providing information on cultural and arts events in Sacramento (449-5566; Touch-Tone phones only). Use with the commission's *Discover Sacramento Hotline Directory.*

California State University, Sacramento
6000 J St.
278-6011
University Theater: 278-6604
Numerous programs in art, music, dance, theater.

Sacramento Community Center Theater
1100 14th St.
Box office: 449-5181
Taped message of upcoming events: 449-5324

Sacramento's largest performing arts center, with concerts, ballet, opera, and touring Broadway productions.

Sierra 2 Center
2791 24th St.
452-3005
Houses a diverse collection of arts-related groups. The 24th Street Theater hosts musical, dance, and theatrical performances. Monthly newsletter.

University of California, Davis
1-752-1011
Information on arts programs at the Main Theater: 1-752-0889
Information on programs sponsored by the Committee for Arts and Lectures: 1-752-2523

MUSIC

Camellia Symphony Orchestra
451-9466
Volunteer orchestra; concert series, free pops concerts. Usually plays at Hiram Johnson High School Auditorium.

Sacramento Opera Association
920-4587
Local productions of opera on professional basis; performs in Community Center Theater. Hosts "Brown Bag Opera" year-round (informal noontime performances).

Sacramento Symphony Association
973-0300
Tickets: 973-0200
Some 200 performances per year at the Community Center Theater. Full orchestra, chamber orchestra, pops orchestra, Sacramento Youth Symphony, Sacramento Symphony Chorus.

BALLET

Capitol City Ballet
Sierra 2 Center
2791 24th St.
451-7437
Two major performances per year of original, contemporary works. Cabaret-style performances in the studio throughout the year.

Sacramento Ballet
4052 Manzanita Ave.
487-9875
Annual production of *The Nutcracker* in Community Center Theater. Fall and spring performances of classical and story ballet.

Theater Ballet of Sacramento
4430 Marconi Ave. .
485-7244
Spring and fall productions, usually at Community Center Theater.

THEATER

Chautauqua Playhouse
5325 Engle Road, Carmichael
489-7529
Contemporary dramas and comedies, children's shows, acting classes.

Garbeau's Dinner Theater
1970 Nimbus Winery
(U.S. Highway 50 and Hazel Ave.)
985-6361
Plays and musicals in 300-seat dinner theater.

New Theater of Sacramento
2130 L St.
447-1935
In the basement of an old Victorian; bohemian atmosphere.

Sacramento City Actor's Theater
Art Court Theatre
Sacramento City College
3835 Freeport Blvd.
449-7228
Classics and older 20th-century dramas and comedies throughout the year.
  Shakespeare in summer.

Sacramento Repertory Theater
3116 Stockton Blvd.
457-8827
Specializes in black theater; original material by local and national black writers.

Sacramento Theater Company
(formerly Eleanor McClatchy Performing Arts Center)
1419 H St.
443-6722
Founded in 1942 by the McClatchys, publishers of the Sacramento Bee. Operates the
  Mainstage Theater October–May, a smaller Stage Two theater, and the Music
  Circus, offering summer stock in an air-conditioned tent (441-3163). Children's
  theater presented some seasons.

Stagedoor Comedy Playhouse
Sacramento Inn Plaza
927-0942
Comfortable 220-seat theater presenting comedy productions year-round.

ART

Guide to Art Galleries and Art Museums in the Sacramento Area, a free brochure published by the Jerome Evans Gallery (1826 Capitol Ave., 448-3759), lists more than 30 galleries in the Sacramento, Folsom, and Davis areas.
The following is a greatly abbreviated list of Sacramento galleries. Check newspapers and the Yellow Pages for more complete listings.

Artists' Collaborative Gallery
1007 2nd St.
(Old Sacramento)
444-3764
Pottery, paintings, woodwork, graphics, photos, jewelry, glass, weavings, and sculpture.

Artists Contemporary Gallery
542 Downtown Plaza
446-3694
Established 1958. Paintings, drawings, prints, and sculpture by prominent area artists and promising newcomers.

Crocker Art Museum
216 O St.
449-5423
Major exhibitions and art events, plus a permanent collection of contemporary and traditional art. The oldest art museum in the West. Contemporary Northern California artists.

Djurovich Gallery
727½ J St.
446-3806
Paintings, prints, sculpture, and photographs by West Coast artists.

Himovitz/Salomon Gallery
1020 10th St.

448-8723
Contemporary paintings, watercolors, drawings, prints, photos, and sculpture by California artists.

I Street Gallery
1725 I St.
447-7014
Contemporary paintings, crafts, sculpture, fiberworks, and drawings by Californians. Traditional art from Africa and Oceania.

IDEA (Institute for Design and Experimental Art)
824½ J St.
448-9382
Contemporary, improvisational art by Sacramento artists, including sculpture, installations, painting, poetry readings, dance companies, musical groups, and video art.

Jerome Evans Gallery
1826 Capitol Ave.
448-3759
Masks, sculpture, textiles, basketry, and ceramics from Africa, Oceania, and the Americas. Housed in a downtown Victorian.

MOVIES

See local newspapers for complete listings of Sacramento's theaters.

Tower Theater
16th St. at Broadway
443-1982

Old theater divided into three screening rooms. Revival films, current foreign films, and new releases. Fresh coffee, herb tea, popcorn with real butter. Discount passes and bargain matinees. Two wheelchair-accessible theaters.

CLUBS

Many clubs have a "repertory" approach to booking acts. Depending on the night, they may offer jazz, rock, blues, or oldies. The best thing to do is check the weekly entertainment listings in local newspapers to see who's playing where.

Brooks' Zombie Hut
5635 Freeport Blvd.
421-7333
Nightly Polynesian floor shows.

Club Can't Tell
1227 K Street Mall
447-3888
Located in a remodeled vintage 1940s theater. Live music, food, dancing, feature films, other entertainment. Reggae, funk, rock, new wave.

Confetti
1696 Arden Way
922-6446
High-tech, glittery environs with neon. Dancing, dress code.

Danseparc
2400 W. Capitol Ave., West Sacramento
371-6232
For hard-core dancing. Not a pick-up joint. Casual dress; mostly recorded music.

D. O. Mills & Co.
111 K St. (Old Sacramento)
442-1866
Pianist and vocalist.

El Dorado Saloon
6309 Fair Oaks Blvd., Carmichael
486-1666
Large mainstream rock club.

Fox & Goose
1001 R St.
443-8825
English pub and restaurant with nightly live music—folk, jazz, country, blues.

Harry's Bar & Grill
4th St. at L
448-8223
Live jazz, rock, new wave, dancing. Chicago-style saloon serving lunch and dinner.

Laughs Unlimited
1124 2nd St. (Old Sacramento)
446-5905
(Also at Birdcage Walk, 5957 Sunrise Blvd., Citrus Heights, 962-1559)
Comedy and magic acts. Drinks and hors d'oeuvres available. Usually sold out weekends.

Masonic Ballroom
12th St. at J
443-1478
Live orchestra plays for ballroom dancing on Saturday nights.

Melarkey's
1517 Broadway
448-2797
New annex makes this the largest music club downtown. Live jazz, blues, rock and roll, dancing.

Murph's Lounge
2730 Stockton Blvd.
454-2344
Live jazz and jam sessions.

On Broadway Bar & Cafe
1827 Broadway
443-8492
Live jazz nightly. Special concerts by big-name performers. Hors d'oeuvres, desserts, and coffees available.

Shire Road Pub
525 Auburn Blvd.
334-7900
Popular dance spot. Live music nightly.

Recreation

Sacramento City Department of Parks and Community Services
1231 I St., Suite 400
449-5200
Publishes the useful *Facility Guide* (fee) listing city parks and maps, recreation, museums, golf courses, and arts programs. Special programs for children, seniors, disabled. Operates a costume bank at Coloma Community Center; Camp Sacramento, a seasonal mountain retreat; and a talent bank of entertainers. City Safari Tours, local and international sightseeing tours available. Publishes seasonal recreation guides listing classes, events, programs; available at libraries or from the department.

Sacramento County Department of Parks and Recreation
3711 Branch Center Rd.
366-2061
Free brochure and map listing all county parks and facilities. Maps of American River Parkway and Jedediah Smith National Recreation Trail. Recreation program for the disabled. Brochure on Sacramento Delta fishing.

California State Parks and Recreation Dept.
Publications Section
P.O. Box 2390
Sacramento, CA 95811
322-7000
Publishes a handy brochure and map (small fee) listing all California state parks and their facilities, including those in the Sacramento area and gold country. Write or phone to order. Reservations advised for state campgrounds during summer; call the state park reservation information number at 445-8828.

Shopping

Arden Fair Shopping Center
Arden Way at Bus. 80
920-4808
Some 80 shops and restaurants; movie theaters; Weinstock's, Sears; indoor mall.

Birdcage Walk
6185 Sunrise Blvd. at Greenback Ln., Citrus Heights
969-1717
Sixty-five shops and restaurants; Macy's, Montgomery Ward & Co.; theaters, bowling alley; park-like setting with two outdoor aviaries.

Country Club Centre
Watt Ave. at El Camino Ave.
481-4044
Cheerful indoor mall with 61 shops and restaurants.

Country Club Plaza
Watt Ave. at El Camino Ave.
481-6716
Weinstock's, JC Penney; 56 stores and restaurants.

Downtown Plaza
K Street Mall between 3rd and 7th
442-4000
Fifty shops and restaurants, many open Sundays; I. Magnin, Macy's, Weinstock's, and
   Livingston's.

Florin Mall
Florin Road off Hwy. 99 at 65th St.
421-0881
Indoor mall with 100 shops and restaurants; Weinstock's, Sears, JC Penney.

Fountain Square
7115 Greenback Ln., Citrus Heights
969-6666
Exclusive specialty shops surrounding a large and unique nursery. The Trellis Cafe
   (969-1580), in the middle of the nursery, offers gourmet lunch and Sunday brunch.

Pavilions
Fair Oaks Blvd. east of Howe Ave.
925-4463
Open-air mall with 6 red brick and glass buildings and large outdoor areas under roof
   or glass canopies; cosmopolitan shopping at more than 20 specialty shops in an
   upscale European village atmosphere; Julius, Canfield's, Benetton, Polo/Ralph
   Lauren, Franco Ferrini, Wm. Parrish, Ltd.

Sunrise Mall
6041 Sunrise Blvd. at Greenback Ln., Citrus Heights
961-7150
Large indoor mall with more than 100 shops and restaurants. Weinstock's, Sears, JC
   Penney.

Town and Country Village
Fulton Ave. at Marconi Ave.
489-3614
Spanish-style architecture with specialty shops.

University Village Courtyard
Fair Oaks Blvd. at Howe Ave.
A charming brick courtyard flanked by 30 specialty shops featuring women's designer
   fashions and gifts.

Bibliography

Sacramento

American Association of University Women, Sacramento Branch. *Vanishing Victorians*. Sacramento: Historic Homes Committee, 1973.

Blenkle, Joe. *Gold, Blood, Water: Folsom-Auburn and the Mother Lode*. Sacramento: Western Wonder Publications, 1976.

California Department of Parks and Recreation. *California Historical Landmarks*. 2d rev. ed. Sacramento: California Department of Parks and Recreation, 1982.

Dana, Julian. *The Sacramento: River of Gold*. New York: Farrar & Rinehart, 1939.

Donnelly, Loraine B., and Cray, Evelyn T. *California's Historic Capitol*. Davis: Craydon Publishing Co., 1983.

Kroeber, A. L. *Handbook of the Indians of California*. Berkeley: California Book Co., Ltd., 1970.

McGowan, Joseph A., and Willis, Terry R. *Sacramento: Heart of the Golden State*. Woodland Hills, Calif.: Windsor Publications, Inc., 1983.

Miller, Robert. *Guide to Old Sacramento*. Sacramento: River City Press, 1977.

Mims, Julie, and Mims, Kevin. *Sacramento: A Pictorial History of California's Capital*. Virginia Beach, Va.: Donning Co., 1981.

Mitchell, Richard L., and Henriksen, F. M. *The Best of Sacramento and the Gold Country*. Sacramento: Phoenix Publications, 1978.

Munizich, Joseph M. "The Governor's Mansion." *Golden Notes* 19(1) (February 1973).

Muro, Diane P. *A Complete Guide to Sacramento and Surrounding Areas*. Sacramento: Camellia Press, 1981.

Neasham, V. Aubrey. *Old Sacramento: A Reference Point in Time*. Sacramento: Sacramento Historic Landmarks Commission, 1972.

Neasham, V. Aubrey; Henley, James E.; and Woodruff, Janice A. *The City of the Plain: Sacramento in the Nineteenth Century.* Sacramento: The Sacramento Pioneer Foundation, 1969.

Oliver, Raymond. *Rancho Del Paso: A History of the Land Surrounding McClellan Air Force Base.* Sacramento Air Logistics Center Historical Study No. 82 (1983).

Reed, G. Walter, ed. *History of Sacramento County, California.* Los Angeles: Historic Record Company, 1923.

Sacramento Bee. *Sacramento Guidebook.* Sacramento: *Sacramento Bee,* 1938.

Sacramento County Department of Agriculture. *Agriculture Crop & Livestock Report: 1984* (1985).

Severson, Thor. *Sacramento: An Illustrated History: 1839 to 1874.* Sacramento: California Historical Society, 1973.

Smith, Jesse M., ed. *Sketches of Old Sacramento.* Sacramento: Sacramento County Historical Society, 1976.

Winterstein, Herb. *Tales of Old Folsom.* Folsom, Calif.: Folsom Historical Society, 1981.

Sacramento Delta

Dillon, Richard, and Simmons, Steve. *Delta Country.* Novato, Calif.: Presidio Press, 1982.

Graham, Kathleen. *Historic Walnut Grove.* Walnut Grove, Calif.: Sacramento River Delta Historical Society, 1982.

_____. *The Sacramento River Delta.* Walnut Grove, Calif.: Sacramento River Delta Historical Society, 1982.

Harvie, Jean. *An Account of Locke, Its Chinese and the Dai Loy Gambling Hall.* Walnut Grove, Calif.: Sacramento River Delta Historical Society, 1980.

Hayden, Mike. *Guidebook to the Sacramento Delta Country.* Los Angeles: Ward Ritchie Press, 1973.

Miller, Ron, and Miller, Peggy. *Delta Country.* Glendale, Calif.: La Siesta Press, 1971.

Minick, Roger, and Bohn, Dave. *Delta West.* Berkeley: Scrimshaw Press, 1969.

Schell, Hal. *Cruising and Houseboating the Delta.* Stockton, Calif.: Schell Books, 1982.

_____. *Dawdling on the Delta.* Stockton, Calif.: Schell Books, 1979.

Walters, Bob E. *Delta: The Cruising Wonderland of California's Sloughs and Rivers.* Fullerton, Calif.: Cordrey & Walters Publishing, 1983.

Gold Country

Automobile Club of Southern California. *The Mother Lode.* Los Angeles: Automobile Club of Southern California, 1982.

Brockman, C. Frank. *A Guide to the Mother Lode Country.* Mariposa, Calif.: Mariposa County Historical Society, 1948.

Cassidy, John. *A Guide to Three Rivers: The Stanislaus, Tuolumne and South Fork of the American*. San Francisco: Friends of the River Books, 1981.

Dillon, Richard. *Exploring the Mother Lode Country*. Pasadena, Calif.: Ward Ritchie Press, 1974.

Golden Chain Council of the Mother Lode. *California's Golden Chain, Vol. 1*. Sutter Creek, Calif.: Golden Chain Council of the Mother Lode, 1983.

Gudde, Erwin G. *California Gold Camps*. Berkeley, Calif.: University of California Press, 1975.

Jackson, Donald Dale. *Gold Dust*. Lincoln, Neb.: University of Nebraska Press, 1980.

Jackson, Joseph Henry. *Anybody's Gold: The Story of California's Mining Towns*. San Francisco: Chronicle Books, 1970.

Jones, Paul, and Flora, Dan. *California Gold Country: A Great Escapes Guide for the Mother Lode*. San Francisco: Great Escapes Publications, 1973.

Levinson, Robert E. *The Jews in the California Gold Rush*. New York: Ktav Publishing House, 1978.

Nadeau, Remi. *Ghost Towns and Mining Camps of California*. Los Angeles: Ward Ritchie Press, 1970.

Poss, John R. *Stones of Destiny: A Story of Man's Quest for Earth's Riches*. Houghton, Mich.: Michigan Technological University, 1975.

Robins, Winifred. *Gold Country Renaissance: A Guide to the Artists and Artisans of California's Historic Mother Lode Country*. San Francisco: Chronicle Books, 1982.

Sunset Books. *Gold Rush Country*. Menlo Park, Calif.: Lane Publishing Co., 1979.

Time-Life Books. *The Forty-Niners*. New York: Time-Life Books, 1974.

Index